Antitrust in Emerging and Developing Countries: *Featuring China, India, Mexico, Brazil, South Africa*

2014 CONFERENCE PAPERS

Editors

Eleanor M. Fox

Harry First

Nicolas Charbit

Elisa Ramundo

Assistant Editors

Matilda Sarpong; M. Luisa Di Lauro

Concurrences Review, 2015

60 Broad Street, Suite 3502, NY 10004
www.concurrences.com
contact@concurrences.com

Printed in the United States of America
First Printing, 2015

Publisher's Cataloging-in-Publication
(Provided by Quality Books, Inc.)

Antitrust in Emerging and Developing Countries (Conference)
(2014 : New York University. School of Law)
Antitrust in emerging and developing countries :
featuring China, India, Mexico, Brazil, South Africa /
editors, Eleanor M. Fox, Harry First, Nicolas Charbit, Elisa Ramundo.
pages cm
Includes bibliographical references.
LCCN 2015951156
ISBN 9781939007469
ISBN 9781939007476

1. Antitrust law—New democracies—Congresses. 2. Antitrust law—Developing countries—Congresses. 3. Conference papers and proceedings. I. Fox, Eleanor M., editor. II. New York University. School of Law. III. Institute of Competition Law (New York, N.Y.) IV. Title.

K3850.A974 2014 *343.07'21*

Cover and book design: Yves Buliard, www.yvesbuliard.fr
Layout implementation: Darlene Swanson, www.van-garde.com

Concurrences Books

Ian S. Forrester QC LL.D. A Scot without Borders – Liber Amicorum (Vol. I)
Sir. David Edward, Jacquelyn MacLennon, Assimakis Komninos • 2015

Ian S. Forrester QC LL.D. A Scot without Borders – Liber Amicorum (Vol. II)
Sir. David Edward, Jacquelyn MacLennon, Assimakis Komninos • 2015

Competition Digest – A Synthesis of EU and National Leading Cases — 2nd Edition
Nicholas Charbit – Elisa Ramundo • 2015

Consumer's Choice: The Emergence of a Powerful Concept in Competition Law
Paul Nihoul • 2015

Google, la presse et les journalistes – Analyse interdisciplinaire d'une situation de coopétition
Guillaume Sire • 2015

Les grands arrêts du droit de la concurrence
Laurence Idot • 2015

Les pratiques restrictives – L'application de l'article L. 442-6 du code de commerce à travers la jurisprudence
Erwann Kerguelen • 2015

William E. Kovacic: An Antitrust Tribute – Liber Amicorum (Vol. II)
Nicolas Charbit – Elisa Ramundo • September 2014

Competition Law on the Global Stage: David Gerber's Global Competition Law in Perspective
Nicolas Charbit - Elisa Ramundo • January 2014

Day to Day Competition Law: A practical Guide for Businesses
Patrick Hubert, Olivier Lecroart, Marie Leppard • March 2014

A quoi sert la concurrence ?
Martine Behar-Touchais, Nicolas Charbit, Rafael Amaro • October 2014

William E. Kovacic: An Antitrust Tribute – Liber Amicorum (Vol. I)
Nicolas Charbit – Elisa Ramundo • January 2013

All books are published in print and electronic format.

Editors' Note

Eleanor M. Fox
Harry First
Nicolas Charbit
Elisa Ramundo

On October 24, 2014, Concurrences Journal in partnership with New York University School of Law presented the inaugural conference, "Antitrust in Emerging and Developing Countries." The conference was a tremendous success. Five panels of 24 prominent speakers representing 10 jurisdictions, and two eminent keynote speakers explored the economic context and addressed the challenges and developments in competition law and policy in emerging and developing jurisdictions. Recognizing the coming of age of developing countries' competition law systems, the panelists (academics, enforcers and practicing lawyers) engaged in passionate debates about what this means in law, policy and on-the ground reality for business, consumers, and the world.

The conference underscores the reality that, in this globalized business landscape, firms must have regard to the competition laws of emerging economies, including in particular China, India, Mexico, Brazil and South Africa, whether they are merging, collaborating with competitors, or designing distribution systems. Business is facing dedicated enforcers who are trying to make their markets work in the face of challenges posed by public and private power; and the conference revealed that the challenges and therefore the responses are not always the same in the developed and developing world.

This book collects the papers of the conference participants on unique and pressing competition issues in developing countries presented and debated at this one-day event. Our deepest thanks go to the authors of the papers and to all panelists who made the conference a success.

Table of Contents

Editors' Note v

Part I: Brazil

Competition Law Enforcement in Brazil: How CADE Is Overcoming Deep Structural Problems to Become an Internationally Recognized Agency 11

André M. Gilberto

Mergers (and Similar Arrangements) in Brazil: Reflections of an Experience as a Commissioner 23

Alessandro Octaviani

Brazil's Antitrust Law: Status Quo 41

Mariana Tavares de Araujo

Part II: China

Dawn Raids in the EU and China: Fact and Fantasy 57

Frank Fine

Merger Remedies of China's Ministry of Commerce 67

Elizabeth Xiao-Ru Wang, Yong Huang

Part III: India & South East Asia

Competition Commission of India: Market Activism, Competition and Development of Markets in India 77

Geeta Gouri

Making Markets Work in Developing and Emerging Economies: Has Competition Law and Policy Played Any Role? Some Notes and Observations on the Case of India 99
R. SHYAM KHEMANI

Making Markets Work in Southeast Asia: A Background Note 111
R. IAN MCEWIN

Part IV: Kenya & South Africa

Competition in Kenya and Its Impact on Income and Poverty: The Case of Sugar and Maize 123
JONATHAN ARGENT, TANIA BEGAZO

The South African Competition Experience: A Review of Fifteen Years into a New Regime 159
DENNIS M. DAVIS

Part V: International Cooperation

International Antitrust Cooperation: Expanding the Circle 169
MOLLY ASKIN, RANDOLPH W. TRITELL

International Cooperation on Competition Matters: An Emerging Enforcer's Perspective 186
KIRAN NANDINEE MEETARBHAN

Antitrust in Emerging Economies 191
BLANCA RODRIGUEZ GALINDO

Editors' Bios 207

Contributors' Bios 209

Contributors

Jonathan Argent
World Bank

Molly Askin
US Federal Trade Commission

Tania Begazo
World Bank

Dennis M. Davis
High Court of Cape Town

Frank Fine
DeHeng Law Offices

André M. Gilberto
Chaves, Gelman, Machado, Gilberto e Barboza

Geeta Gouri
Formerly Competition Commission of India

Yong Huang
University of International Business and Economics (UIBE)

R. Shyam Khemani
SKP

R. Ian McEwin
University of Malaya
Malaysian Centre of Regulatory Studies

Kiran Nandinee Meetarbhan
Formerly Competition Commission of Mauritius

Alessandro Octaviani
University of São Paulo Law School

Blanca Rodriguez Galindo
European Commission

Mariana Tavares de Araujo
Levy & Salomão Advogados

Randolph W. Tritell
US Federal Trade Commission

Elizabeth Xiao-Ru Wang
Charles River Associates

Competition Law Enforcement in Brazil: How CADE Is Overcoming Deep Structural Problems to Become an Internationally Recognized Agency

André M. Gilberto

andre.gilberto@cgmlaw.com.br

Partner, Chaves, Gelman, Machado, Gilberto de Barboza Advogados–CGM

Abstract

The Brazilian antitrust regime changed drastically when Law No. 12529/2012 ("Antitrust Law") came into force, in May 2012. After more than two years, it is possible to assess the impact of the new law and how the local competition agency (the Administrative Council for Economic Defense—"CADE") has dealt with the many challenges it has faced, such as a complete modification of the merger control system. On the other hand, important promises made by the Federal Government by the time the Antitrust Law was passed have not been fulfilled so far; consequently, CADE remains understaffed—this causes conduct investigations to take an unreasonable amount of time to be concluded. Yet, CADE has been lauded over recent years by respected international publications for its efforts in coping with its structural problems, and it continues to launch important conduct investigations and to clear merger review filings within an adequate timeframe. This paper analyzes the most important changes brought by the Antitrust Law *vis-à-vis* CADE's efforts to cope with its long-standing staffing issues.

I. Antitrust Enforcement in Brazil: From 1934 to 2014 in Twenty Paragraphs

"But my surprise was considerable when I reached the small corridor at the second floor of Annex 2 of the Ministry of Justice. CADE was tiny. A confusion of doors, where it was enough to knock three times for the doors to be opened by the commissioners themselves. The tribunal in which the big cases were decided had two sections of tied seats with four or five places each. There were some plastic chairs at the end of the room and an old sofa, which probably was acquired by means of a public tender bid years ago, below a power box that eventually exploded one day, causing (former CADE President) Gesner Oliveira to rise up and help the people who were attending the public hearing. It was in that small tribunal, in the most precarious conditions, that the seven commissioners seated—most of the scholars and researchers in their 30s or 40s—to rule on the largest business in Brazil."[1]

The Federal Constitution of 1934 was the first one to include rules related to the protection of the "popular economy,"[2] stating that a specific law should promote the enforcement of the popular economy. The Federal Constitution of 1937, on the other hand, made the so-called "crimes against the popular economy" illegal and punishable by means of a proper legal procedure; this was the pioneer piece of legislation in Brazil when it came to this type of conduct.

Indeed, in 1938 the Decree-Law No. 869 came into force to define the many practices that could result in violations of free competition, such as entering into agreements to obtain excessive profits and participation in consortiums with the purpose of limiting competition and predatory pricing. However, only in 1945, by means of Decree-Law No. 7666, did the Federal Government create an administrative body to be in charge of punishing crimes against the popular economy—the Administrative Commission for Economic Defense, which is clearly CADE's predecessor.[3]

The Federal Constitution of 1946 included the first rule which expressly referred to the abuse of dominant power, and soon after that the National Congress begun the discussion of a bill to regulate this constitutional disposition. The debates lasted for sixteen years, and in 1962 Law No. 4137 was finally enacted. Law No. 4137/1962 created CADE and established the different types of abuses of economic power.

CADE, however, remained relatively low profile for almost thirty years. Enforcement of Law No. 4137/62 was practically non-existent owing to the lack of a competition culture—the Brazilian economy was highly closed and regulated by the Federal Government, who controlled prices in many sectors, and owned or authorized private monopolies in most of the country's largest industrial, transportation and financial

1 Journalist, Juliano Basile, reporting the first time he attended a public hearing at CADE, in the mid 90s. See *Defesa da concorrência no Brasil - 50 anos*, 18, 2013. (Free translation: *50 years of Competition Defense in Brazil*). Document *available at* http://www.cade.gov.br/publicacoes/livro/CADE_DEFESA_DA_CONCORRENCIA_NO_BRASIL_50_ANOS.pdf.

2 The term employed by article 117 of the 1934 Federal Constitution.

3 Once this Decree was approved, there was a considerable reaction by international companies acting in Brazil: "*the regulation of the economy – inspired by the north-American antitrust legislation – caused justified commotion in international players, which did not want in Brazil and of the market controls that they are subject there* (in the United States)." (*Defesa da concorrência no Brasil - 50 anos*, 37, 2013").

enterprises.[4] At that time, it was common for the Federal Government to encourage competitors to reach agreements on prices, market conditions and volume of sales.

The scenario started to change with the enactment of the Federal Constitution of 1988, which stated that the economic order should respect principles such as free competition; to enforce those principles, Article 173 of the 1988 Federal Constitution set forth that a specific law should punish the abuse of economic power aiming to dominate markets, suppress competition and increase profits unreasonably.[5] This was accompanied by significant economic changes, including a better control of inflation, leading to the beginning of a process of stabilization of the Brazilian currency through the establishment of the Real Plan (in 1994) that introduced tighter fiscal and credit policies.[6]

Aiming to protect the principles of the Brazilian Federal Constitution, Law No. 8137 was passed on 27 December, 1990, defining: crimes pertaining to tax and economic orders and against consumer relationships; crimes perpetrated by individuals and public officials; and conduct that could be sanctioned with fines and/or imprisonment.

One year later, Law No. 8158/91 was enacted to adopt provisions concerning protection of free competition. Law No. 8158/91 established proceedings, sanctions, penalties for violation and the responsibility of the Secretariat of National Economic Law (*Secretaria Nacional de Direito Economico*)—to verify any individual or collective act or economic activity that attempts or may attempt to harm the economic order, free initiative, or free competition—in order to correct behavior that may interfere in the formation of prices and placement of goods and services in the market.

However, Law No. 8158/91 was deemed by Brazilian scholars as largely ineffective, since some of its dispositions overlapped with the ones provided by Law No. 4137/62.[7]

In 1994, Law No. 4137/62 was replaced by Law No. 8884. Law No. 8884 was later repealed by Law No. 8158/91. The new law was brought in to reflect all the changes taking place with the Brazilian market conditions that demanded a higher control of economic power. It was only upon the enactment of Law No. 8884 that CADE was transformed into a federal independent agency, reporting to the Ministry of Justice and bearing powers to monitor and curb potential abuses of economic power.

Under Law No. 8884, CADE exercised its competencies through a board composed of a president and six board members, selected from citizens who are older than thirty years of age, known for their legal or economic knowledge and unblemished reputation, duly appointed by the President of Brazil and

---

4 According to the OECD, "*Brazil's economic policies after World War II relied on pervasive government intervention in market operations. The State controlled prices in many sectors, and most of the country's largest industrial, transportation...*" Besides, CADE "*had marginal economic impact because its authority extended only to private firms.*" See The Organization for Economic Co-operation and Development ("OECD"), *Brazil – Peer Review of Competition Law and Policy*, 2005, at 13, available at http://www.oecd.org/daf/competition/38835344.pdf.

5 1988 Federal Constitution: "Article 170. The economic order, founded on the appreciation of the value of human work and on free enterprise is intended to ensure everyone a file with dignity, in accordance with the dictates of social justice, with due regard to the following principles: I–national sovereignty; II–private property; III–the social function of property; IV–free competition; V– consumer protection; VI–environment protection, including by means of different treatments in accordance to the environmental impact of products and services and their respective production and rendering; VII–reduction of regional and social differences; VIII–pursuit of full employment; IX–preferential treatment for small enterprises organized under Brazilian laws and having their head office and management in Brazil. Sole Paragraph–Free exercise of economic activity is ensured to everyone, regardless of authorization from government agencies, except in the cases set forth by law." (free translation) "Article 173. With the exception of the cases set forth in this Constitution, the direct exploitation of an economic activity by the State shall only be allowed whenever needed to the imperative necessities of the national security or to a relevant collective interest, as defined by law. (...) Paragraph 4–The law shall repress the abuse of economic power that aims at the domination of markets, the elimination of competition and the arbitrary increase of profits." (free translation)

6 Source: Instituto Brasileiro de Geografia e Estatística–IBGE. Source: IBGE 2005.

7 According to Professor João Bosco Leopoldino da Fonseca (a former CADE commissioner), the "overlap" between certain rules provided by Laws No. 4137/62 and 8158/91 caused "*enormous confusion*" and prevented that CADE could enforcer any of them properly until 1994. (*Lei de Proteção da Concorrência*, Forense, Rio de Janeiro, 67, 2007).

approved by the Brazilian Senate. The president and the members of the board were elected for a two-year term mandate—re-election being permitted only once.

In addition to CADE (a decision-making body), two other government agencies had powers to enforce Law No 8884: the Secretariat for Economic Defense ("SDE") and the Secretariat for Economic Monitoring ("SEAE"), both had analytical and investigative functions. The SDE and SEAE were headed by secretaries appointed by the Minister of Justice and the Minister of Finance, respectively, and duly commissioned by the President of Brazil.[8]

Finally, Law No. 12529, the current Antitrust Law, came into effect on 30 May, 2012.[9] The new law has brought several material changes to Brazil's competition system. The first—and arguably the most important—was the consolidation of the investigative, prosecutorial and adjudicative functions into one agency. Based on the new system, CADE is the only agency with competition-related duties in Brazil. It is divided into three parts: (1) the Administrative Tribunal is the decision-making body responsible for enacting final decisions; (2) the Superintendent General is in charge of investigating anti-competitive practices, approving mergers that do not raise competitive concerns and providing non-binding opinions in mergers that cannot be cleared unconditionally; and (3) the Department of Economic Studies is responsible for issuing non-binding economic opinions and studies.

Another very important change was the introduction of a pre-merger notification system. As of 30 May 2012, transactions that are subject to a mandatory merger filing in Brazil can only be closed and "implemented" after receiving the respective clearance from CADE. Consequently, the parties are required to remain independent from each other until they have obtained CADE's approval.

Also, the new law has substantially modified the definition of "concentration acts" that are subject to mandatory merger filings. According to the new rules, a "concentration act" consists of: (a) the merger of two or more previously independent companies; (b) the acquisition of direct or indirect control of part(s) of one or more firms, whether by purchase of shares, quotas or securities in general, assets, contract or "any other means"; and (c) association agreements, consortia and joint ventures, except if created for the purposes of a tender process launched by a public authority.

If a given transaction amounts to any of the "concentration acts" listed above, the submission of a merger filing in Brazil is mandatory whenever one of the groups involved in the deal has achieved group-wide revenues of at least 750 million BRL in Brazil during the fiscal year immediately prior to the transaction, and another group has earned group-wide revenues in Brazil of 75 million BRL in the fiscal year prior to the transaction.[10]

Failure to notify reportable transactions and the practice of "gun-jumping"' (i.e., failure to comply with such standstill obligations) are subject to the imposition of fines by CADE of between BRL60,000 and BRL60 million. The Antitrust Law provides CADE with powers to seek the required administrative and/or court remedies to have the acts implemented in violation of the standstill obligations declared void or null.

---

8 SDE performed investigative functions in order to identify possible violations and some preliminary enforcement functions, and could initiate an investigation upon complaint or request of an interested party or *ex officio* whenever there is no evidence available to commence an administrative proceeding. The investigative functions of the SDE comprised the gathering of information for both preliminary investigations and administrative proceedings. The SEAE was responsible for performing investigative and advisory functions, providing economic analysis for economic regulatory programs and providing SDE with technical reports on transactions filed for merger review and monitoring market conditions.

9 Law No. 12529, November 30, 2011, *available at* http://www.cade.gov.br/upload/LAW%20N%C2%BA%2012529%202011%20%28English%20 version%20from%2018%2005%202012%29.pdf.

10 The original turnover thresholds set forth by the new law were increased by a joint administrative rule issued by the Ministries of Justice and Finance on May 2012.

There are two review procedures under the new regime: the fast track and the regular procedure. The "fast track procedure" applies to non-complex cases, including transactions resulting in only minor horizontal/vertical overlaps (involving market shares below 20%) and other transactions that do not require a more detailed review, as determined by CADE. Cases eligible for the fast track procedure shall be filed based on a short form. On the other hand, the "complete filing form" applies to transactions that are not eligible for the fast track procedure, and require a significant amount of information, internal documents and extensive market data. CADE may take up to 240 days to review a case. This review period may be extended for an additional 60 days at the request of the parties, or 90 days by means of a justified order issued by CADE's Tribunal. The current regulation does not set forth intermediary review periods for non-complex transactions.

On the conduct front, the changes have not been so drastic, but some of them are worth stressing. For instance, the Antitrust Law provides for an entirely different range of corporate fines for companies that are found guilty of anticompetitive behavior, ranging from 1 percent to 20 percent of a company's gross revenue earned in the area of business in which the conduct took place. Fines imposed on directors and other executives found responsible for anti-competitive behavior are now calculated based on the fine imposed on the respective undertaking, ranging from 1 to 20 percent.

Investigations resulting from leniency applications were also affected. The Antitrust Law has eliminated the former provision that prevented the "leader"' of a cartel from negotiating a leniency agreement with local authorities, and it has also extended the criminal immunity granted to a leniency applicant to include the crime of fraud relating to public bids (connected with the cartel). On the criminal side, the new law increases the maximum term of imprisonment for individuals found guilty of anti-competitive behavior from two to five years, while also being subject to fines.

II. The New Antitrust Law: Thirty Months On

This section assesses how CADE has been handling its duties in regards to merger control and conduct investigation, since the Antitrust Law came into effect in May 2012.

One of the main concerns of the business community is the statutory time period of 240 days. In spite of the statutory time period being unreasonably long, before the law came into force, CADE's officers repeatedly stated to the media that "non-complex transactions" would be reviewed within 30-40 days.

The analysis of the average timetable for review of merger cases by CADE within the first two years of the law shows that the efforts by the agency, to make sure that companies would not have to wait for an unreasonable period of time for transactions to be cleared, have paid off. According to official statistics regarding the first year after the law came into force (from May 2012 to May 2013),[11] 250 transactions were approved by CADE, in an average time of 21 days. Out of those 250 cases, 227 were cleared by means of the fast track procedure and were reviewed in an average of 20 days. There were 22 more complex cases, which were reviewed by CADE in an average of 74 days. In the second year after the

11 *CADE: balanço do biênio da Lei 12529/11 e perspectivas da defesa da concorrência no Brasil* (free translation: *CADE: an overview of the first two years of enforcement of Law No. 12,529/11 and the perspectives for the competition defense in Brazil.*) Document *available at* http://www.cade.gov.br/Default.aspx?44e427e936d457f3480b.

Antitrust Law was in force, 354 were cleared by CADE, in an average time of 25 days. The 38 more complex cases were reviewed by CADE in an average of 98 days.

Under the new Antitrust Law, transactions that do not result in the application of any remedies may be decided directly by CADE's General Superintendent, without any involvement of CADE's Board of Commissioners. Out of the 593 cases reviewed in the first two years after the Antitrust Law came into force, CADE's Board of Commissioners decided only 16.

On the conduct front, cartel prosecution has received most of CADE's attention. Many investigations have been launched since the Antitrust Law came into force and others have been resolved. For instance, on May 2012, CADE concluded the peroxide market (H2O2) cartel investigation with the imposition of a fine of about BRL134 million on Peróxidos do Brasil Ltda—in addition, a group of individuals received fines amounting to BRL16.3 million. The investigation began with a leniency agreement signed with Degussa Group, and a number of its employees who confessed to taking part in anti-competitive activities and cooperated with CADE in identifying co-authors and providing data and materials that proved the infractions. Degussa Group and its employees received full criminal and administrative immunity in exchange for their cooperation.

On November 2012, the General Superintendent of CADE proposed the punishment of three executives for cartel practices in the national market of refrigeration compressors (equipment used in the production of fridges, freezers and air conditioners). According to the General Superintendent, between 1996 and 2004 the supposed cartel was active mainly in Brazil, then it expanded worldwide, especially in Europe and North America. The administrative proceedings begun in July 2009 on the basis of evidence brought by a cartel leniency agreement. In 2009, dawn raids in offices of companies and in residences of executives were conducted to collect further evidence. These agreements resulted in the payment of voluntary contributions of more than $104 million.

On August 28, 2013, CADE issued its decision regarding an alleged cartel in the market for international air cargo. CADE punished ABSA Aerolinhas Brasileiras S.A., Varig Logistica S.A., American Airlines, Inc., Alitalia Linee Aeree Italiane S.p.A. and seven individuals for involvement in the formation of a cartel within the international air cargo sector, with fines amounting to more than BRL293 million. This investigation began in 2006 after the signing of a leniency agreement between CADE and airlines Deutsche Lufthansa AG, Lufthansa Cargo AG and Swiss International Air Lines AG.

In March 2014, CADE opened an investigation to verify alleged cartel practices in train and subway procurements carried out from 1998 to 2013, in the Federal District and in the states of São Paulo, Minas Gerais, Rio Grande do Sul and Rio de Janeiro. In total, 18 companies and 109 employees are being investigated by CADE. This case began in May 2013 following a leniency agreement signed between Siemens, who denounced the cartel, CADE's General Superintendent, the Federal Prosecutor's Office ("MPF") and the São Paulo State Prosecutor's Office ("MP/SP").

More recently, in September 2014, CADE launched an investigation into a possible cartel in the national and international market of spark plugs. According to CADE's preliminary findings, Bosch and NGK, agreed on prices offered to their clients, volume of sales, amounts to be charged and price adjustments offered to automakers, dealerships and car fixing offices. The case began in July 2014 with the signing of a leniency agreement between CADE's General Superintendent, the Federal Prosecutor's Office, the State Prosecutor's Office of São Paulo and the company Bosch.

Finally, in October 2014, CADE launched an investigation regarding possible cartel practices in the market of antifriction bearings. The target companies were, among others, AB SKF, INA-Holding Schaeffler

GmbH & Co. KG, JTEKT Automotiva Brasil Ltda., JTEKT Corporation, Koyo Rolamentos do Brasil Ltda., Nachi Brasil Ltda., Nachi Fujikoshi Corp., NSK Brasil Ltda., NSK Europe Ltd., NSK Ltd. and NTN-SNR Roulements SA.

Cases involving dominance and vertical issues have also received some attention from CADE in the first thirty months since the new Antitrust Law came into force, but to a lesser extent. For instance, in January 2013, CADE executed a Cease and Desist Agreement with Philip Morris, in the context of an investigation concerning vertical restrictive agreements in the tobacco industry. The target of this investigation were the exclusive merchandising agreements that cigarette companies, Souza Cruz and Philip Morris, entered into with their respective retailers, which resulted in the retailers not being allowed to exhibit posters or any other advertising that displayed the trademarks of their competitors.

Also in January 2013, CADE punished Brazilian SKF's subsidiary for fixing the retail prices of its products for seven months, between 2000 and 2001. Due to the lack of consistent decisions regarding practices of fixing retail prices in Brazil, this case represented a paradigmatic precedent.

In October 2013, CADE launched three administrative proceedings to investigate alleged anticompetitive practices carried out by Google Inc. and Google Brasil Internet Ltda. in the Brazilian market of online search. The investigation began after CADE received complaints from E-Commerce Media Group Informação e Tecnologia Ltda., owner of websites Buscapé and Bondfaro, and by Microsoft Corporation, owner of online search provider Bing.

In the first two years of applying the Antitrust Law, CADE has decided a total of 63 conduct cases, and imposed fines reaching over $200 million. During this period CADE's General Superintendent performed 7 dawn raids and signed 14 leniency agreements. Overall, those are certainly very impressive numbers, but, as it will be shown in the next section, CADE's structural problems certainly prevent the Brazilian competition agency from performing more efficiently.

III. CADE: A Long History of Structural Problems

It has been widely reported in reports produced by the Organization for Economic Co-operation and Development ("OECD"), over the past 15 years, that one of the most serious problems confronting the Brazilian competition system has been lack of resources and that the agencies—especially CADE—were critically understaffed.

Back in 2000, the OECD stressed that CADE was afflicted with the "lack of a permanent, stable group of career officials whose presence preserves 'institutional memory' and enhances enforcement expertise over time," and urged that the "provision of such staff be made a top priority within the government and the Congress."[12] According to Marco Botta, "[a]lthough Article 3 of Law 8884/94 made CADE an independent agency (*autarquia federal*), for a number of years such independence was undermined by a lack of human and financial resources."[13]

12 See OECD, *Competition Policy and Regulatory Reform in Brazil: A Progress Report*, 2000 at para. 78, *available at* http://www.cade.gov.br/internacional/OECD_2000_Report.pdf.

13 See Marco Botta, Merger Control Regimes in Emerging Economies: A Case Study on Brazil and Argentina, at para. 2.2.2.1 (2011).

The scenario did not change materially five years on. In 2005, the OECD indicated "[t]he absence of a career position, coupled with the general problem of low government salaries in Brazil, confronts CADE with a chronic shortage of appropriately qualified staff personnel".[14] OECD's recommendations were extremely clear:

> "Adopt legislation creating CADE career positions and provide adequate resources to hire and retain a sufficient number of qualified professional staff [...]. No agency should be expected to operate for a decade using borrowed and temporary staff, especially where effective and efficient performance of the agency's mission depends so greatly on accumulated institutional knowledge. Without career and permanent positions, CADE cannot compete effectively against other agencies to hire qualified personnel." Finally: "The problems that CADE faces will not, however, be resolved simply by the creation of career staff positions. The number of, and the compensation associated with, those positions are also critically important. The present employee staff at CADE, even including the 28 temporary assistants, is not sufficient to permit expeditious completion of the agency's work, thus contributing to the delay that afflicts CADE's proceedings."[15]

Another five years, and the OECD continued to identify significant issues regarding the structure of CADE and the other Brazilian competition agencies:

> "[a]ll three of the BCPS agencies suffer from a shortage of qualified professional staff and high turnover. At CADE the turnover problem has been especially acute. The 1994 competition law provided for the creation of a permanent staff at CADE, but it was never done. Until 2006 CADE had no permanent positions assigned to it. All of its professionals were either DAS[16] contract employees or were permanently employed at other government agencies and assigned to work at CADE. Staff turnover was high. The turnover was exacerbated by the fact that many of the professionals were assigned to a specific commissioner. The commissioners' term of office was, and continues to be, short—only two years with the possibility for one re-appointment. When a commissioner left office his or her staff usually departed too. The average tenure of a CADE professional has been about three years. This has obvious detrimental effects on the "institutional memory" at the organization."[17]

According to the OECD, "[i]n 2006 CADE received authority for 27 permanent positions (in late 2009 25 of these positions were filled). While these positions accounted for less than half of CADE's total civil service employees, the situation there has improved. In years past, many of the professionals who worked there had no special interest in the field, and were ready to move on if an opportunity presented itself. Today, those who occupy CADE's permanent positions have affirmatively selected CADE. They say they enjoy the work, and the prestige that accompanies it."[18]

Still, "[o]ne result of this resource problem is the continuing backlog in conduct investigations [...], and the length of time that it takes for the average conduct case to be resolved."[19]

---

14 See OECD, *Competition Law and Policy in Brazil: A Peer Review*, 2005, at 78, *available at* http://www.oecd.org/daf/competition/38835344.

15 Id., at para. 6.25 2005.

16 An English translation of DAS would be "high level management and advising." DAS authority comes in seven grade levels and is a mechanism for hiring non-permanent contract employees.

17 See OECD, *Competition Law and Policy in Brazil: A Peer Review*, 2010, at 47, *available at* http://www.oecd.org/daf/competition/45154362.pdf.

18 Id,. at 47.

19 Id., at 73-74.

In conclusion, the 2010 OECD Peer Review recommended that the Brazilian Government should "[c]reate CADE career positions and provide adequate resources to hire and retain a sufficient number of qualified professional staff." There were already references to the 200 positions that were expected to be created when the new Antitrust Law passed: "The bill provides for 200 permanent career positions at CADE. It is understood that these positions would not be 'competition' career positions, that is, created for CADE, requiring qualifications specific to its mission, but rather they would be permanent positions assigned to the agency that would be filled by federal civil servants. The former is preferable, as likely to result in an even more qualified cadre of professionals as well as reducing turnover, but the creation of a permanent staff of this size is nevertheless highly important."[20]

Two years on, however, and the OECD concluded that understaffing was still a problem in Brazil: "[s]taffing is the greatest constraint faced by the two organizations in being able to select and prioritize their cases. The problem is particularly acute in the case of the CADE (20 staff reviewed 700 mergers in 2011)."[21]

The 2009 edition of "Rating Enforcement," annual research performed by Global Competition Review ("GCR") on the most important competition agencies,[22] summarizes CADE's structural problems accurately: "As CADE has limited resources, it has undertaken several initiatives to become more efficient while at the same time increasing the quality and excellence of its activities [...]. However, CADE is aware that it is necessary to overcome the limitations resulting from its current structure and restricted human and financial resources, in order to continue to meet the growing demand for the analysis of competition cases, as well as to make it possible for CADE to achieve the goal of further increasing the efficiency and excellence of its activities."

Indeed, to keep track with its list of tasks, several formal and informal arrangements have been made by CADE (and, while Law No. 8884/94 was still in force, by, and between, the SDE and the SEAE as well). One of those initiatives involved the SDE not playing a role in the analysis of merger control filings reviewed under the "fast track regime."

Another mitigatory initiative resulted in the launching, in October 2009, of a task force between several Brazilian authorities with focus on cartel prosecution; the ENACC ("The National Strategy for Cartel Prosecution") gathers representatives from the SDE, the SEAE, CADE, the States' Public Prosecutors, the Federal Prosecutors, the Federal Police Department, the Ministry of Justice's National Secretariat of Justice, Ministry of Justice's National Secretariat of Public Security, the States' Secretariats of Public Security, the National Group for Anti-Criminal Organizations Enforcement, the Criminal Public Prosecutors National Association, and, finally, the Offices of the Comptroller General Secretariat of Corruption Prevention and Strategic Information.

Ultimately, such a network is aimed at overcoming CADE and the SDE's limited resources by creating a considerable amount of synergy among the various institutions that creates the potential for the development of more solid mechanisms and tools that will enhance the authorities' capacity to conduct investigations. The second edition of the ENACC that took place in June of 2010 had "Cartel Prosecution in Public Bids" as its theme, and was attended by authorities from several bodies responsible for the antitrust law enforcement in the administrative and judicial areas.

---

20 Id., at 75.

21 OECD, *Follow-up to the Nine Peer Reviews of Competition Law and Policy of Latin American Countries: Argentina, Brazil, Chile, Colombia, El Salvador, Honduras, Mexico, Panama and Peru*, 2012, *available at* http://www.oecd.org/daf/competition/2012Follow-upNinePeer%20Review_en.pdf.

22 See *Rating Enforcement 2009*, Global Competition Review, *available at* http://globalcompetitionreview.com/surveys/survey/161/rating-enforcement-2009/.

When the SDE disappeared after the new Antitrust Law came into force, naturally, the ENACC went away as well, but it is certainly a very good example of how local competition authorities have learned, over the years, to be creative in order to cope with their structural issues and the lack of adequate human and financial resources.

The prevailing mindset at the agency is captured, in an interview with GCR in March 2014, CADE's former Superintendent General, Carlos Raggazo, admitted that the agency is still understaffed for the amount of work currently in its docket, but stated that "problems hiring trained workers have prompted CADE to find innovative ways to achieve enforcement goals."[23]

IV. International Recognition

It is remarkable how the Brazilian competition system as a whole (and CADE in particular) has established a solid reputation amongst its sister competition agencies despite the staffing problems described in Section III of this paper. In fact, in February 2011, GCR awarded CADE the 2010 "Antitrust Agency of the Americas." This recognition was due to both the impressive development of the agency and the fines imposed, in September 2010, on a number of industrial gas companies for price fixing and customer allocation.[24]

In the 2012 edition of "Rating Enforcement," the GCR continued to recognize CADE's efforts to cope with its institutional mission in Brazil, despite its well-known problems; GCR mentioned, for instance, that "more and more management positions have been filled by career civil servants, who usually have a longer tenure at the organization. As a result, we expect turnover to be largely reduced. CADE has been gradually recruiting new staff in an effort to allow more experienced employees to train newcomers. CADE has invested a considerable amount of time training and building a staff level settlement negotiation commissions and working group. The goal was to keep a record of previous negotiations, and to discuss international best practices and techniques."[25]

CADE's position in GCR's rankings has actually improved in the most recent years. Both the 2013 and the 2014 editions of "Rating Enforcement" give provided CADE four out of five stars; according to GCR's rankings, CADE currently only stood behind the agencies from the European Union, France, Germany, United States (DOJ and FTC), United Kingdom and Japan.

Despite focusing on CADE's efforts to continue to clear merger control filings efficiently, the 2014 "Rating Enforcement" did mention the agency's efforts to reduce the backlog of anticompetitive conducts cases, highlighting the condemnation of ten cartel cases in the fuel market and the air cargo cartel in 2013.[26]

---

23 See Harry Phillips, *Ragazzo: Staffing problems have made CADE stronger*, Global Competition Review, 2014, *available at* http://globalcompetitionreview.com/news/article/35612/ragazzo-staffing-problems-made-cade-stronger/.

24 See Administrative Proceeding No. 08012.009888/2003-70, final decision issued on Sept. 22, 2010; SDE x White Martins Gases Industriais Ltda., Air Liquide Brasil Ltda. and others, case no. 08012.009888/2003-70.

25 See *Rating Enforcement 2012*, Global Competition Review, at 34, *available at* http://www.cade.gov.br/upload/Brazil%20CADE_GCR.pdf.

26 See *Rating Enforcement 2014*, Global Competition Review, *available at* http://globalcompetitionreview.com/surveys/survey/161/rating-enforcement-2014/.

V. Conclusions

Thirty months into the enforcement of the new Antitrust Law, and it is evident that CADE has learned—by employing creative solutions—how to cope with its structural and staffing issues. As explained in Section II, relevant conduct investigations continue to be launched and merger filings are being cleared in a very reasonable timeframe. This has brought CADE some well-deserved recognition from the business community and other international competition agencies.

According to CADE,[27] on May 29, 2013, there were 333 conduct decisions investigations pending; on May 29, 2014, the backlog reduced only slightly, to 296 cases. Additional statistics provided by CADE show that the agency took an average of almost 1200 days to rule the 36 conduct cases decided in 2013; the 31 investigations concluded in 2014 were decided after an average time of 1000 days.

The numbers for both—the backlog of pendent conduct investigations and the average timeframe for CADE reach a final decision on cases finished in 2013 and 2014—show that despite the repeated warnings made by the OECD over the past fifteen years (described in Section III) and the impressive efforts put together by CADE during the past 30 months to put in place a completely new competition system, there is still much to do on the conduct front. The new Antitrust Law tried to resolve this problem by creating 200 permanent positions within CADE; however, those positions have not be filed so far and there is no indication whatsoever from the Federal Government that they will be filled in the near future.

The adoption of innovative techniques has brought CADE the respectability it has been looking for a very long time. Still, to reach new levels of excellence CADE will inevitably need to address the very significant backlog of conduct cases and it will need to reach a decision on anticompetitive investigations in a much more timely fashion. To achieve such a goal, without receiving the permanent positions that were promised by the Federal Government, may be one of the toughest challenges CADE has ever faced.

27 See, *supra* note 11.

Mergers (and Similar Arrangements) in Brazil: Reflections of an Experience as a Commissioner[1]

Alessandro Octaviani

aleoctaviani@gmail.com

Former Commissioner, Administrative Council for Economic Defense, Brasilia
Professor, Faculty of Law, São Paulo University

Abstract

The purpose of this work is to systematize aspects of my experience, which came to an end recently, as a member of the Tribunal of the Administrative Council for Economic Defense ("CADE")—the Brazilian Antitrust Authority. It is the narrative of an experience. Therefore, the work tries to present: (i) a specific narrative about Brazilian antitrust; (ii) a narrative about general aspects of my practical life as a commissioner; (iii) the typology of the mergers (and similar arrangements) with international links, that I experienced in detail and which point to four "models; and finally, (iv) suggestions for a more relevant practice of antitrust policy: (a) two comforting but false premises to distance ourselves from ("antitrust is technical not political" and "convergence along a single path"), (b) "does antitrust really have something to say about the two nuclei of the contemporary economy, technology and credit?", and (c) antitrust limits in the general ecosystem of the economic policies that are necessary for a good life in societies that are located on the periphery and semi-periphery of world capitalism.

---

1 Presented at the Antitrust in Emerging and Developing Countries Conference, at the New York University School of Law, on October 24, 2014.

I. Introduction

The purpose of this short work is to systematize, albeit in a minimal way, aspects of my experience, which came to an end recently, as a member of the Tribunal of the Administrative Council for Economic Defense ("CADE")—the Brazilian Antitrust Authority. The text is not theoretical neither does it seek to systematize empirical data. It is the narrative of an experience, in which theories might have been an existing element and only to this extent will they be mentioned. That is why (unlike the academic practice in which I was educated and from which I have been unable to rid myself, even when engaged in the exercise of judging) I made every effort to eliminate bibliographic citations and references. I only left what I understood to be absolutely indispensable for clarifying some point of view or, eventually, what seemed to me to summarize extremely well some aspect of the matter being dealt with.

The following reflections do not, under any circumstance, imply any manifestation by CADE itself or by the Brazilian authorities, except in the case of the decisions that are mentioned, which constitute official manifestations by the Brazilian State. I deal with this period in an exclusively personal manner, as a way of organizing a period of practical experience, by manipulating, in a specific political and economic force field, various decision technologies, namely Brazilian economic law and the economic instruments it authorizes.

Therefore, the work tries to present: (i) a specific narrative about Brazilian antitrust, indicating: (a) how the political economy of development (understood as both social conflicts and the instrumental theory that tries to describe them) created the Brazilian antitrust discipline, (b) how the current Federal Constitution, which is simultaneously democratic and dirigiste, reorganized the normative basis for this policy and is the backdrop against which disputes about the meaning of the Brazilian antitrust policy are being fought over, and (c) how the antitrust authority has been institutionally transformed, which can be summed up, even though in caricature-like fashion, in the expression that is much used by the Brazilian press, "from CADE to SUPERCADE"; (ii) a narrative about general aspects of my practical life as a commissioner, which involves: (a) the process by which I was chosen by the President of the Republic and approved by the Federal Senate, (b) my academic and professional background in Economic Law, (c) the routine construction of policy, which involves an internal, technical aspect (integration between the two bodies of knowledge, law and economics, reflected in the formation of the Tribunal), and an external aspect (interaction with company representatives—lawyers, economists or administrators); (iii) the typology of the mergers (and similar arrangements) with international links, that I experienced in detail and which point to four "models": (a) "cases abroad, with effects felt in Brazil," (b) "cases abroad and in Brazil, with effects both there and here," (c) "cases in Brazil and abroad, with effects both here and there," and (d) "cases in Brazil, with effects felt abroad," and finally, (iv) suggestions for a more relevant practice of antitrust policy.

The latter item regarding suggestions for a more relevant practice of antitrust policy points to three topics that I judge to be worthy of attention: (a) two comforting but false premises to distance ourselves from ("antitrust is technical not political" and "convergence along a single path"), (b) "does antitrust really have something to say about the two nuclei of the contemporary economy, technology and credit?," and (c) antitrust limits in the general ecosystem of the economic policies that are necessary for a good life in societies that are located on the periphery and semi-periphery of world capitalism.

II. A Narrative of the Brazilian Antitrust System

1. The Political Economy of Development Generates the Brazilian Antitrust System

Crane and Hovenkamp make an effort to reposition the historical narrative about the North American antitrust system.[2] Basically, today's winning forces seek to reinterpret the past by eliminating what is uncomfortable and emphasizing elective affinities, thus building, in short, an ideology. Something similar is happening in Brazil. The antitrust system came about as a response to the challenges of an economy that was engaged in a struggle against its peripheral, semi-peripheral or under-developed colonial condition (using the critical vocabulary that originated from and sustained a series of political decisions on which the country's economic policies were modeled and are still being modeled).

The scenario of the rise of antitrust in Brazil is connected to the difficult birth of a national economy, with its decision centers minimally managed on the basis of decisions taken internally. This same process had already occurred in other countries with different colors and adjustments, but basically it corresponds to the formulations of the various economic nationalisms that form an integral part of the deep structure of capitalism. The antitrust system in Brazil is one of the policies included in the "Great Transformation"[3] movement and an attempt to organize decision centers during what followed the political and economic changes of the 1930s. That is why it is far from being the main economic policy, but instead it is one that is subordinated to other economic policies.

2. The Current Narrative

The contemporary Brazilian interpretation of antitrust will incriminate this past period, by caricaturing it as a political (when we were not a civilized nation, to the point of not having "good institutions") or intellectual (when we did not know the "correct economic theory") anomaly. These two presuppositions hide the main point: the choices made by players led to another diagnosis. They chose to create a capitalist economy that would demand the creation of companies capable of competing with the oligopolistic capitalism of those countries that already had a consolidated industrialization.

Therefore, it is not for lack of access to a good manual of legal rules or the best economic theory that the antitrust system was not viewed as being central or even important, but because the forces that won the battles for conducting the Brazilian economy (which can be summed up by the "tripod" of private multinational capital, State-owned Brazilian capital and private Brazilian capital, which certainly left the workers in a subordinate role for most of the period) did not see this instrument as a central tool, but just

2 See The Making of Competition Policy (Daniel Crane and Herbert Hovenkamp ed., Oxford University Press 2013).

3 See Karl Polanyi, The Great Transformation: The Political and Economic Origins of Our Time (Beacon Press 1944).

as a rhetorical and instrumental one (and mainly against the economic powers that were really recognizable, multinational capital and international trusts).

The presence and influence of Roberto Campos and Octávio Bulhões during the period summarized makes it clear that what happened in the USA and in the orthodox centers of the economy was always known, but such interests were incapable of imposing themselves for decades. The narrative that criminalizes this period, in fact, is based on a great sympathy for the economic regime of "openness" that was installed in the 1990s, after the electoral victories of the neo-liberal governments of Fernando Henrique Cardoso.

In the final analysis, the past, the "Vargas era," the "import substitution policies," state-owned companies, public employees and the existence of the State itself, would be responsible for the low rates of growth starting in the 1980s, high inflation that harmed the economy in the 1980s and 1990s, crisis of violence that ravaged our cities and the despair of the people who lived in the major urban centers. That narrative states that exchanging "the State" for the "market" would guarantee a new civilizing level. Even though the "State" might appear to have a more sympathetic bias, as an "institution" that must be strong in order to guarantee legal security for contracts and property, its position is one of subservience to the "market," which would then allow it to exist.

So the Brazilian antitrust system gains new apparel. It is no longer the rhetorical and symbolic fight against the international cartels that are capable of blocking the rise of the fledgling industry of the first period, but "the rational science" that is capable of sending the appropriate signals to foreign investors who, calmed and comforted by the environment created by the only correct institutions, would deposit their money with us.

In fact, this brief narrative of discursive transformation about the Brazilian antitrust system merely reflects a much deeper change: the substitution of projects among the economic and political elite of the country, the passage from a strategy which aimed to build an industrialized country with some capacity for self-management to a strategy that localizes in the foreign investors and financial markets that are key to the new world order that will bring freedom, money and happiness.

This current narrative about the Brazilian antitrust system will be structured on the basis of empirical data about how economic players barely adhered to the Law of 1962 (Law 4137/62)[4] and the poor capacity of the competition authority to issue sentences during the 1960s through to the 1990s. This current narrative, however, will not value the formal creation of the system, its symbolic effectiveness in relation to some of its own objectives (like affirming the authority of the State economic police over private players, which is a premise without which any antitrust policy could simply not exist), the discovery that the antitrust policy was never, and is still not in any country in the world, the only existing economic policy for defining the size and structure of markets and the very objectives of the system that has been put together.

The current narrative will make a comparison of the criminalized and caricatured past with the present, which is praised and idealized. On the one hand, everything was very bad and only could have led to a general crisis in the country, while on the other hand rationality has arrived, which will be able to save the country from the monumental mistakes it made in an age that deserves to be forgotten.

But the past was not as bad as this narrative preaches-growth rates were high, higher than in the neoliberal period of Cardoso and the Lula-Dilma period, in fact; the degree of openness in the Brazilian economy was enormous, as Evans, among so many others, indicates when studying the move from "classic depen-

---

4 Law 4137/62, September 1962.

dence" to "dependent development," which was consolidated once and for all in the 1980s;[5] CADE operated at various times, as Navarrete shows.[6] Nor has the present been as auspicious as the heralds hoped (the growth of the economy as a whole has never been satisfactory; the comparison with East Asia has always left Brazil in an inferior position). It is difficult to safely correlate the action of the antitrust system with the main economic successes of the country. It is difficult to state the effectiveness of CADE and its capacity to impose itself, given the short period during which it has operated and the absence of more solid and conclusive research.

On this basis, I have reached two conclusions: (i) the current narrative is constructed on erroneous bases about the past and has not been confirmed in the present; and (ii) more and better quality research will be necessary so we can test, over time, the promises that have been fulfilled.

3. The Democratic and Dirigiste Federal Constitution Reorganizes the Brazilian Antitrust System

From 1946 to 1964 Brazil underwent an experience that until then had been unheard of: a reasonably long period during which political freedoms were linked to the construction of an economy that was not exclusively directed towards the production of raw materials. This period saw the election of Dutra, Getúlio Vargas, Juscelino Kubitschek and Jânio, and after the latter renounced, the government of João Goulart. The political base of these presidents (with the exception of Jânio Quadros) was the PSD and PTB parties; the Social Democratic and Labor parties, respectively. Their social base was comprised of land-owners and the holders of power within the state ("PSD") and urban, non-communist workers ("PTB"). The affinities and tensions between these bases and their representations help explain both the stability and instability of the period, and the possibilities that materialized and failed to materialize during this time.

In 1964, the PSD left this block[7] and the block of anti-Vargist radicals, who until then were not in a position to come to power through the vote, and managed to impose a military solution, which was widely supported by the USA. There followed a period of fierce political repression, and the suppression of democratic life. In 1974 there began to appear the first signs of weakness in the military-business regime, with its rout in regional elections. This period slowly extended for the next ten to fifteen years. In 1984 there was a great popular campaign ("Direct Elections Now!"), in 1986 the process for preparing a new Constitution started (it was concluded in 1988) and in 1989 the first direct election for president since the military coup was held.

The Constitution of 1988 is considered to be a "ruling Constitution" (dirigiste) because it establishes goals and objectives for the country's economy and determines the means by which such goals are pursued. So the economy or the market are not "free," but serve politically defined ends that are democratically chosen. Among others, Article 219 in particular states that the domestic market must serve the welfare of the population, its cultural development and the technological autonomy of the country.[8] From this

5 See Peter Evans, Dependent Development: The Alliance of Multinational, State, and Local Capital in Brazil (Princeton University Press 1979); Alessandro Octaviani, Recursos genéticos e desenvolvimento: os desafios furtadiano e gramsciano (Brasil, Saraiva 2013); Alessandro Octaviani, Estudos, Pareceres e Votos de Direito Econômico (Brasil, Singular 2014).

6 See Pedro Navarrete, As origens do Sistema Brasileiro de Defesa da Concorrência: o CADE (1962-1994) (Mestrado na UFRJ – IE, 2013).

7 Lucia Hippolito, De raposas e Reformistas: o PSD e a Experiência Democrática Brasileira (1945-64) (Brazil, Nova Fronteira 2012).

8 See Constitution of the Federal Republic of Brazil, 1988, Article 219.

finalistic perspective, which legally organizes the politicization of the market by way of a profoundly democratic process, relations between economic players are instruments for achieving ends. So relations between economic players, within the terms of the constitutional system of (a) non-competition, (b) competition, or (c) limited/regulated competition, can be politically determined and legally organized, depending on the ends sought. This is certainly nothing new or exclusive to the Brazilian economic system (there is no relevant economy in the world, even if the discourse about them may be liberal, that does not contain sectors in which competition is suspended because of strategic or political decisions).

Submitted to this constitutional substrate, in 1994 the Competition Defense Law[9] was enacted, the objective of which was to reorganize the Brazilian antitrust system. This law was the meeting point for the creation of the above narrative. As we can see, there is a contrast between the constitutional design and the current narrative. This contrast derives from the change in the political forces that modeled the Constitution: basically the Brazilian Social Democracy Party ("PSDB") adopted a neoliberal creed in the 1990s and created a series of new laws that included the antitrust law. The Cardoso governments tried to impose (and managed in a few cases) constitutional changes and implement laws that accentuated the liberal character of the Constitution, by blocking its nationalistic, dirigiste and pro-worker side. For many, approval of the Competition Law of 1994 was packaged up within this context.

4. From CADE to SUPERCADE

With respect to the current narrative, the 1994 law placed the Brazilian antitrust system in the center of the functioning of our institutions, thus leading to the promised growth stemming from the liberal reforms of the 1990s. In a movement that was different from the rise of the North American antitrust model, this was not a case of regulating the market by creating protection for society by way of the State, but of protecting society, which identified with the market, through the withdrawal of the State, in a movement that led to less regulation. As already mentioned, this narrative was certainly incapable of being pragmatically sustained for a series of reasons. One of them has to do with the very dynamic construction of institutions, which demands a considerable number of regulations and consequently brings the impetus needed for the bureaucracies that are responsible for such regulations to seek to increase their power in the constellation of bureaucracies established in the State.

Another impediment to the effectiveness of the current narrative has to do with the dynamics of political life and its usual contradictions. Merely by way of example: the period that gave rise to the current narrative, which is here taken as a caricature, pointed to the independence of the competition authority as a fundamental factor for the success of the model. A strong agency would be capable of disciplining the players in the market, who would understand that they must compete, thus issuing positive signs for the whole economy. However, in one of the first decisions that was contrary to the interest of players, who had weight in the economy (a case involving the steel market), the government, with its neoliberal court, decided to punish the agency by not renewing the mandates of the commissioners who were involved in this "independent, but disagreeable" decision.[10] On the other hand, in another situation, the government that was dominated by a party with origins in a socialist tradition (PT/Lula-Dilma), perceiving the political gain to be had by approving a new competition law, in 2011, did so and presented itself as being responsible for "transforming CADE into SUPERCADE."

---

9 Law 8884, June 1994 *available at* http://www.cade.gov.br/internacional/Law-8884-1994.pdf.

10 PEDRO DUTRA (ORG.), CONVERSANDO COM O CADE (Brasil: Singular, 2009).

Therefore, the development of the competition policy from 1994 to now can be summarized, not in accordance with the cannon that the current narrative intended to impute, but something simpler, more modest and more realistic, namely: (i) a public economic policy; (ii) in a more complex ecosystem, comprising various public economic policies; (iii) with constitutional and legal competences that are simultaneously stable and dynamic; (iv) with a young but vibrant bureaucracy; (v) a management body recruited, as a rule, from staff considered to be academically excellent, with professors from the most distinguished educational institutions in the country, like USP ("University of São Paulo"), UFMG ("Federal University of Minas Gerais"), UNB ("Federal University of Brasília"), FGV ("Getúlio Vargas Foundation") and others; (vi) relying on political sympathy in academic circles and the press; (vii) which has achieved reasonable success in imposing itself *vis-à-vis* companies and other bureaucracies in issues that are sensitive, but which has also suffered being blocked by other bureaucracies and the strategies of private players.

This process continued gradually until approval of the "new competition law" of 2011. Basically, the main points of change have to do with (i) prior analysis (eliminating "a posteriori analysis," by which the parties did the business and submitted it to the authority, which bore the political burden of having to point out some restriction possibly months or years after it was presented); (ii) the combining of investigatory and judging competences in a single organ (CADE), now organized to fulfill two functions, investigation (by way of its General Superintendent's office) and judgment (the CADE Tribunal) area; (iii) the official creation of the Department of Economic Studies of CADE ("DEE"); (iv) the legal provision for hiring public managers to structure the administrative activities; and (v) an increase in the threshold for mergers that have to be submitted for analysis by the competition authority.

As can be observed, although important and certainly having an impact on the daily experience of the companies that are the customers of the system and of the bureaucrats who manage it, there were no significant changes in the typification of illegal bids or any change that might substantially alter the analysis of mergers. The superlative "SUPER," which was added to the authority's name in various press manifestations, is due mainly to the legal disposition that determines the prior analysis, since this brings something reasonably new to large Brazilian companies that operate in markets that are not regulated by sector: the need for administrative authorization to undertake their main business and model the design of the very market in which they operate. Moreover, (i) a growing capacity to impose its decisions with structural remedies; (ii) to carry out investigations and make convictions in various markets; and (iii) a reduction in tolerance towards wrongly supplied information throughout the proceedings ensure that the superlative has some resonance in reality.

III. A Narrative about My Experience as a Commissioner

1. The Selection Process

The selection process for CADE commissioners is both formal and routine at the same time. I was chosen by the President of the Republic's office (President Dilma Rousseff) to be formally cross-examined for the post by members of the Federal Senate.

Prior to this, I had an academic career and had also worked as a lawyer. As an academic, I graduated from the oldest law school in the country (University of São Paulo), the university where I also did a Master's degree in political science, my PhD in Economic Law and where I became a tenured professor of Economic Law (antitrust is one of the compulsory topics you have to take before you become this type of professor). As a lawyer and consultant, I had practiced for several years dealing with issues that involved economic regulation, insurance and technological innovation. I was a member of CADE's training program.

The term of office under Law 8884/94 was two years,[11] with one reelection permitted, which is why I underwent this process twice.

The cross-examination is held by the Federal Senate's Economic Affairs Committee. This committee tends to consist of Senators who have an affinity with economic matters specifically or public spending generally. Furthermore, because this committee is considered to be "powerful," the parties tend to choose some of their most prominent people to serve on it.

The questioning tends to be general (the role of CADE in relation to other economic policies and agencies, like the Economic and Social National Development Bank ("BNDES"), concerns with the quality of those selected to check whether they will respond to political demands or be committed to taking technical decisions) or about specific markets that are affected by mergers, acquisitions or illicit practices (how to deal with the effects of unemployment caused by those mergers, or the potential outcome of investigations that have had repercussions in the press, like the so-called "orange cartel" or "subway cartel").

2. My Background: Economic Law

My background is in Economic Law. Brazilian Economic Law is based on the Constitution, which has set objectives for the national economy and organizes legal competences. So this area of law is very close to being the legal face of the "Great Transformation"[12] rather than being a field for applying the assumptions and normative conclusions of the law and economics movement.

In a nutshell: the purpose of the law is defined by the mass political democracy, which culminates in the Federal Constitution. Therefore, it is not based on the calculations of efficiency that a jurist, helped, as a rule, by economists with a neoclassical background can technocratically intend to impute to the law. These economists opt to stand far from the uncomfortable political arena, preferring to remain close to their own

11 See *supra* note 8, at Chapter II, Paragraph 1.

12 See *supra* note 2.

comfortable theorems. The most that this normative economic analysis of law can advocate is that of being a (suspicious) technical assistant, never the definer of what the law should be. Such a suspicion comes about because it is an instrument (a) in its most fanatical versions, which contains many premises that are unsustainable in the face of the minimally sophisticated scrutiny of the social or neurological sciences, and (b) in its more pondered versions, most of the time incapable of dealing with the required informational complexity, given the wealth of destabilizing information that a dynamic reality brings to static models (a fact that has so far not been exceeded by any available combination of software, as the crisis of 2008 painfully showed).

3. Internal Interaction: Jurists and Economists

The conversation between operators of the law and economics is one of the most complex aspects of the implementation of Brazilian competition policy, because it has obliged changes in a culture that is deep-rooted in both fields. The academic culture of the operator of the law in Brazil, as a rule, will not be open to other social technologies, except in a very superficial way. Economic Law, as presented above, can be considered to be an exception, and this is a valuable asset for implementing an antitrust policy.

On the side of Brazilian economists, despite all the pressure for academia to mimic the financial market and, therefore, to adopt neoclassical premises and all of their consequences, like an image of the real world, among Brazilian economists, derived from a series of reasons, there are suspicions about how the market really behaves (as may occur, among other hypotheses, because of the force of the heterodox schools, which refer back to Prebisch, Furtado and CEPAL—but also to Keynes and Schumpeter—or by observations of a politically complex reality, in which the world, free of distortions, is perceived as an unsustainable premise. This subjective experience, which is shared by various orthodoxically trained economists, seems to have an as yet unmeasured impact on their theoretical flexibilization). This capacity to understand that, between the neoclassical theorem and the real world (into which the policy will be introduced) there exists the phenomenon of power, is also an important asset for the effectiveness of the policy.

This meeting of the structured decision technologies—on the one hand economic law based on the Federal Constitution and a social value of a distributive nature and, on the other hand, economics based on investigating cognitive values that are sensitive to power—becomes an important amalgam that is capable of feeding the routine of complex decisions, mainly in the face of the high quality of the arguments presented by companies.

4. Application: Companies, Lawyers and Bureaucracy

Companies that have a case that is being reviewed by CADE are always represented by a body of top-level professionals, including lawyers and economists. If it is necessary to produce arguments in other areas of knowledge (engineering, marketing, etc.), they will experience no difficulty in finding the best professionals, either externally or from their own staff. From many points of view, in fact, such teams, when individually considered, can reach a figure similar to, or greater than, that of the authority as a whole. In the case of teams of economists, there is no doubt about this, since the Department of Economic Studies ("DEE"), with fewer than a dozen economists, is smaller than any of the companies that provide economic advice to large companies that have cases brought before CADE. Here the myth of the "great Leviathan" against the "defenseless entrepreneur" finds no support in reality. The capacity of companies to mobilize information, academic support and political and journalistic sympathies is unparalleled.

The way out for the Brazilian competition authority has been quite adequate: (i) to put together a base of directors consisting of people who are academically highly respectable; (ii) to carry out procedures that are open to contradictory arguments, in such a way that they are able to hear possible competitors of the companies involved in the case (which are always capable of reducing the current information asymmetry); (iii) to seek to communicate in a clear way in the public arena, by clarifying its objectives and, as a result, to have an impact (a) on market conditions as a whole (competition defense as a process), (b) on the life of competitor companies (competition defense as a defense against predatory practices), (c) on the life of consumers (competition defense as a defense of the wellbeing of the consumer), or (d) on the life of the population in general (competition defense as an objective added to the development goals contained in the Constitution), which are discursive hypotheses that are reasonably easily found in various important decisions by the authority over the last few years.

Meetings between various highly respected company economists (one who is interested in getting the case approved and the other interested in blocking it either totally or partially) defending completely opposing conclusions, based on the same pretensions of objectivity and scientificity, is an experience that, in the internal culture of the competition authority, reinforced the need for suspicion with regard to hyper-rationality models. In a few words: the arrangement of the economic theorem and hypothesis variables presented to the authority depends on the interest sought, which makes the scientificity of this practice highly questionable. Antitrust economics must be dealt with on the basis of the hermeneutics of suspicion.

IV. Dealing with Mergers in Brazil that Have International Connections: an Initial Typology

It is within this context, as summarized above, that the contemporary practice of merger (or agreements with similar effects) analysis in Brazil is based. Below I have chosen four examples that have connections with economies beyond the Brazilian economy. The examples can be taken as "ideal types" or caricatures, and allow us to emphasize some aspects of the reality. The cases are basically structured on the basis of two main questions: (i) Where are the mass of assets involved and the decision centers located? (ii) Is the stance of the Brazilian competition authority more prone to seek information that is comforting to it (therefore, more collaborative/passive) or to send out strong signals with regard to its points of view (therefore, more inquisitive/active)?

This typology can be expressed as: (a) "cases abroad, with effects in Brazil"; (b) "cases abroad and in Brazil, with effects there and here"; (c) "cases in Brazil and abroad, with effects here and there"; and (d) "cases in Brazil, with effects felt abroad."

The type "a" cases involve a mass of assets and decision centers mainly located abroad; their presence in Brazil is residual, at least in the present. There may be legal structures or business plans for the future and that is why these "cases abroad" cause "effects felt in Brazil". The tension level is reasonably low. The fact that a foreign competition authority is facing the issues brings a degree of comfort to the case (although it is necessary to check the criteria usually chosen by this authority and its degree of combativity or scrutiny). The stance adopted by the authority will tend to be collaborative/passive.

Type "b" cases involve a mass of assets that are simultaneously located abroad and in Brazil, but the most sensitive parts of the assets and the decision centers with the greatest power are located abroad. So the cases occur "abroad" and "in Brazil," and their effects are felt "there" and "here." The importance of the transaction is considerable for the Brazilian market and the authority will not only seek "to be informed," but will prepare studies and carry out diagnoses based on the information obtained. It will also seek out the information that is peculiar to Brazil. The stance adopted, therefore, will tend to be collaborative/active.

Type "c" cases involve a mass of assets located simultaneously in Brazil and abroad, but the most sensitive parts of the assets and the decision centers with the most power are in Brazil. So cases occur "in Brazil" and "abroad," and their effects are felt "here" and "there." The importance of the transaction is crucial to the Brazilian market and the authority will face a lot of tension, which is why it will seek all possible information, including that coming from abroad (but that will not be essential for the final decision, given the nature of the assets). Furthermore, it will provide information to the authorities affected by the operation, if so requested. The stance adopted, therefore, will tend to be inquisitive/passive.

Type "d" cases involve a mass of assets and decision centers located in Brazil and abroad, but for some reason the Brazilian authority shows a greater degree of concern than other authorities and, therefore, the companies will have to adapt in some way to a practice that is not routine for them. That is why these "cases in Brazil" result in "effects felt abroad." The tension level is reasonable and any dissonance has to be disclosed and clarified. The stance adopted by the authority, therefore, will tend to be inquisitive/active.

Below is a brief description of cases that exemplify such typology.

1. "Cases Abroad, with Effects Felt in Brazil" (MACH–Syniverse)

The case represented the merger of the two main players (MACH and Synnverse) in two extremely concentrated markets: the DC market (GSM data clearing service) and the NRTRDE ("Near Real-Time Roaming Data Exchange") market.

The solution was to formalize an agreement, involving the disinvestment (with the consequent sale to a third party) of certain assets related to the DC and NRTRDE markets of MACH, specifically in the European Economic Area ("EEA"), in order to make actual competition feasible between the buyer and Syniverse in the DC and NRTRDE markets immediately after the acquisition.

The nerve center of the operation was located outside Brazil. The most relevant assets existed and central economic decisions were made outside the country. Those involved had legal and economic representation in the country, but it was not considered significant. But there were effects in Brazil; Brazilian jurisprudence has been very careful about circumscribing such effects, mainly because they may become more relevant in the future. So the authority was faced with a mass of assets and decision centers that were located abroad, with just a residual presence in Brazil, which if not exactly eliminating the tension or concern, considerably reduced its intensity. The stance the authority adopted can be considered to be collaborative/passive.

2. "Cases Abroad and in Brazil, with Effects Both There and Here" (EMI–Universal)

The second case is more complex, because the mass of assets involved had decision centers abroad and in Brazil and the Brazilian regime was not yet that of prior analysis.

The case represented the merger of two major companies in the recorded music market, Universal Music and EMI. Brazil is probably the only place in the world in which most of the music consumed by way of the record companies is not of Anglo-Saxon origin, but "national". This cultural characteristic is also expressed in a market structure in which there is one Brazilian recording company, which behaves like a truly major company, and various independent and dynamic regional cultural companies that postulate the erosion of the very logic of the traditional recorded music industry.

In this case, far from concerning itself merely with collaborating with the foreign authorities in order not to cause undue damage to those involved, the Brazilian authority would be unable to carry out its legal obligation adequately without a very detailed set of information. Hence, another element played an important role in the composition of a proper informational framework for the case: the aggressive challenge to the merger led by Warner (one of the "majors").

In addition to (i) requesting information, and (ii) monitoring the result of the analysis carried out by the foreign authorities, the Brazilian authority (iii) had to organize its own data and take decisions in procedurally different times. The end result was approval of the merger (after a period in which it was "suspended" or "under suspicion"), but the tension of the economic players involved was very obvious, mainly because another negotiation with foreign authorities had already occurred. A new negotiation (which was a possibility and, in fact, an obligation of CADE, if the data had indicated a high concentration and entry difficulties) would have meant a cost that had apparently not been accounted for in the previous negotiation. The disparity of procedures was pointed out by various observers as something capable of clouding the information environment of the companies (which would become irrelevant, given the fact that the Law of 2011 came into effect).

The mass of assets were located simultaneously abroad and in Brazil, but the most sensitive parts of the assets and the decision centers with the greatest power were abroad. However, the importance of the transaction was considerable for the Brazilian market and the authority did not merely seek to "be informed," but carried out diagnoses based on the information it obtained; it also sought out its own information. The stance adopted by the authority can be considered to be collaborative/active.

3. "Cases in Brazil and Abroad, with Effects Both Here and There" (Camargo Corrêa, Votorantim and Cimpor)

The third example derives from an intended complex "merger" between major players in the cement market, Cimpor, Votorantim and Camargo Corrêa, which involved both their positions in Brazil as well as abroad. This is a market marked by horizontal overlapping and vertical integration in various geographic regions in Brazil and this made the analysis much more complex. The end of the transactions would be a corporate structure in which three of the main players in the Brazilian market would be working together/merged.

For the analysis of the potential impact of the merger with respect to Cimpor and Votorantim, investigations were carried out into the possible coordinated effects of approval of the operation, which sought information about the following elements: (i) the characteristics of the markets and firms; (ii) the possible reduction in the number of firms; (iii) the possible existence and elimination of a "maverick" firm; and (iv) the background of collusion in the market, which signaled the presence of all the classic structural elements that allow for and facilitate collusion. The final decision of the authority was not to authorize the deal, with the return to the previous status quo, as embodied in the rights of Lafarge and Votorantim prior to the operation.

The other aspect of the merger involved the positions of Camargo Corrêa and Cimpor, where market shares were not as high as in the first dimension. Even so, competition concerns were identified, which led to corrective intervention, which was concluded by way of an agreement, which isolated or reduced the harmful effects to the market, and which embodied basically the following set of obligations: (i) to dispose of assets; (ii) to break up associations with the Votorantim Group; (iii) to abstain from acquiring a shareholding in concrete companies; (iv) to submit for CADE's analysis and approval each and every association or common enterprise of any type and by whatever legal or factual form in Brazil, with any member of a competitor economic group that might have a direct or indirect relationship with the relevant markets protected in the agreement for the next five years, even if the requirements of Article 88 of Law 12529/11 are not fulfilled; (v) to reduce its participation in trade bodies and associations in the cement and concrete markets in Brazil; and (vi) to comply with investment obligations in R&D&I.

Foreign authorities in places where Cimpor had relevant operations expressed their concerns because of two connected dimensions: Votorantim and Camargo Correa also operated in these markets and the acquisitions also involved taking control via operations in the capital market. So, the Brazilian authority came up against a mass of assets located simultaneously in Brazil and abroad, but with the largest part of the assets and decision centers located inside the country, which culminated in a large amount of tension and the search for all possible information, including that coming from abroad. There was also a constant supply of information to the foreign authorities affected by the transactions. The stance adopted by the authority can be considered to be inquisitive/passive.

4. "Cases in Brazil, with Effects Felt Abroad" (Monsanto-Bayer)

The case was presented as a simple "technology licensing" contract between Monsanto and Bayer for the development, testing, production and sale in Brazil of varieties of soybean seeds containing Intacta RR2 PROTM technology, which is responsible for making plants both glyphosate-tolerant and insect-resistant.

Similar contracts were being routinely presented to the authority. But in this case the degree of information sought was much more pervasive and formal aspects of the contract could be interpreted on the basis of such information, which led to the conclusion that the arrangement was much more than a "simple technology licensing contract;" it was one that in the end allowed for true external corporate control by way of technology licensing. The contract clauses gave Monsanto significant power of influence over Bayer, since (i) they went beyond the legal business scope of the contract, (ii) culminating in the possibility of one being able to control the strategic corporate behavior of the other in areas like new acquisitions, for example, (iii) which resulted in unequivocal anti-competition effects and (iv) did not involve efficiencies that were sufficient enough to distance competition concerns. Approval of the operation was conditional upon the total exclusion of these clauses.

Where the mass of assets and decision centers were located is of reasonable indifference; the central point is the fact that the Brazilian authority showed a greater degree of concern than other authorities and this will therefore lead to companies adapting to a practice that is not routine to them. The level of tension was considered reasonable and this discord should be disclosed and clarified. The stance adopted by the authority can be considered to be inquisitive/active.

5. Conclusion

These forms of strategic behavior by the Brazilian authority point to the following systematized table. If there is some sense in this systematization it may perhaps be useful for preparing questionnaires that allow the authority, at the beginning of its assessment, to perceive what type of situation they are dealing with and direct their scarce resources and their strategies in a more appropriate way.

V. Suggestions for a More Relevant Antitrust Practice: The Old (and Always Avoided) Question of Real Power

The economic policy of competition defense can become more relevant than it has been. To do so I believe that it must be freed from some of the mental and practical maps that limit it too much. The competition defense policy can (i) be more as far as what it proposes today, (ii) be better than is proposed for it today and (iii) be less than is proposed for it today in some axes in order for it to be more powerful and useful for more people.

This exercise in aggrandizement and relevance by the competition defense policy starts first of all with the disarming of two fallacies that are theoretically unsustainable and politically biased: (i) antitrust is technical, not political, and (ii) there is only one path, one way and one alternative: the convergence of models. The former intends to wipe out the past, by stating that the current hyper-rationality models are able to answer all the questions about the best way of organizing competition defense. This, therefore, opens the way for the latter, whose consequence is to erase the future, by denying institutional biodiversity any room for maneuver and implementing a mental monoculture model.

In Brazil, for example, the competition defense policy has constitutional backing. It is one of the legally organized economic policies. Other derivations are imposed based on these principles: (i) it is not possible to treat competition policy as being the only or main policy on which to model the market, and (ii) it is not possible to require convergence along a single path. Countries make their strategic choices depending on variables, like the resources they have at their disposal, the broadening of the democratic base of those who choose and the paths they intend to follow in the future. Democratic pressures can transform a certain asset (a drug considered to be vital) into a need to be suppressed by the State or by someone it chooses, in the same way that technocratic pressures can transform another asset into a monopoly (national security technology). In the same way, such assets in another situation may be explored under conditions of competition. The introduction of the democratic variable to the institutional modeling of economic policies only makes more obvious what the technocratic variable achieved throughout the 19th and 20th centuries in all modalities of "states that drive the economy."

Behavior of Brazilian Authority:

Location of the Assets, Decision Centers and the Search for/Disclosure of Information

Type of case	Prevalence of assets and decision centers	Stance of Brazilian authority as to search for/disclosure of information	Actual example: case/market
Type "a": "cases abroad, with effects felt in Brazil"	Main assets largely abroad/Most important decision centers abroad	collaborative/passive	MACH – SYNINVERSE (telecommunications market)
Type "b": "cases abroad and in Brazil, with effects felt there and here"	Assets abroad and in Brazil; main assets abroad; decision centers abroad and in Brazil; main decision centers abroad	collaborative/active	EMI–UNIVERSAL (recorded music market)
Type "c": "cases in Brazil and abroad, with effects felt here and there"	Assets in Brazil and abroad; main assets in Brazil; decision centers in Brazil; main decision centers in Brazil	inquisitive/passive	CIMPOR–CAMARGO CORRÊA–VOTORANTIM (cement market)
Type"d": "cases in Brazil, with effects felt abroad".	Assets in Brazil and abroad; decision centers in Brazil and abroad; concern of the Brazilian authority diverges from that of the other authorities	inquisitive/active	MONSANTO – BAYER (biotechnology licensing market)

In 2008, North American banks and insurance companies noticed they had taken on rotten loans, which had been passed on to them by other players that were faster and more aggressive; gradually they went to the State to ask for help. After some dubious behavior, the North American State finally decided that it would settle expectations, by taking on (that is to say dividing with the mass of taxpayers, past, present and future) part of the rotten loans, now transformed into debt and potential bankruptcies. Unfortunately, it was too late, and the Brazilian banks had already decreed they were in a state of maximum alert: they would not lend anything to anyone, even more so to people with low purchasing power, who had been recently elevated to the category of crisis causers and were found among those who were defaulting on their mortgages. For a few days the countless private banks operating in Brazil followed the behavior of their leaders, the two giants Itau and Bradesco.

Free competition between banks clearly determined that Brazil was about to enter a crisis due to a lack of credit. This self-announced destiny was interrupted in full flight because of the existence of State-owned banks, which operated in a counter-cyclical direction, by opening up the credit taps, reducing interest rates and obliging private banks to compete. The competition equilibrium that broke the joint strategy of the oligopoly of Brazilian private finance came from the State-owned sector that holds bank reserves and competent distribution channels. The private banks stated in public the same diagnosis and the same consequences. They were obliged to reformulate themselves because of the resources made available by another power that was responsive to democratic policy, which comprised a varied ecosystem of institutional choices. Defense of competition conditions is more complex than the textbooks state. It must incorporate the real world as one of its variables. It must incorporate the world of real power, on the one hand, and democratic demands on the other hand.

1. The Antitrust Policy Being More than It is Today: Seriously Facing Up to the Economic Power of the Financial Sector

A look at the material, institutional and symbolic structure of the antitrust policy with regard to the financial sector, in general, and the banks in particular, leaves no room for doubt: the banks submitted and disciplined the antitrust "threat" in various ways on a different scale. In a series of countries manipulation of the threat of "systemic risk" led to, or threatens to lead to, the insulation of banking regulations in all their dimensions close to the monetary authority, which tends to be captured by the banks.

Another more moderate movement, but still one capable of proving the power achieved by the banks with regard to antitrust objectives, given the prevalence of the symbolic violence of the "systemic risk," says that the banking authority should examine the issues first of all and only then possibly allow others to look at them. Contracts with various names and legal structures practiced by the banks can fulfill the function of subordinating indebted business units, leading to them, in fact, being controlled by the banks, but as a rule, the antitrust authority will be very wary about dealing with such situations. The examples of this "ring-fencing" that the financial sector brings to the competition defense policy might also be extended.

To do more than the antitrust authorities classically propose, this issue should be correctly dimensioned. In this way, we can have a practice that is less alienated in relation to the centers of real power of contemporary economics. So, I consider that there are two questions to be examined: (i) the capacity of financial markets to organize many other markets "from above" and with an intense lack of transparency (the financial entities rule and organize the strategies but are invisible to the authority's eyes; here we face the "invisibility" question); and (ii) the capacity of financial entities to become so big that they are transformed into becoming "too big to fail" (they were allowed to become so concentrated and connected that nowadays they are able to claim an exclusion from the basic economic law of a capitalist economy: if you are not good enough, you won't survive; here we face the "extreme visibility" question).

2. The Antitrust Policy Being Better than Is Proposed for It Today: Seriously Encouraging Technological Innovation and Its Democratization

There is certainly a concern with technological innovation in some antitrust circles. To what extent this is a priority is a complex question; and another more complex question is what its intensity and capacity for being transformed into a decision instrument with empirically verifiable social effectiveness is.

In any event, the grammar of dynamic competition, if the antitrust authority wants to be better than it is today, must inundate the decisions of the authorities, turning them into objective and mandatory criteria. There is an enormous accumulation with regard to how the technological innovation environment functions, which is managed by the neo-Schumpeterian evolutionists and the Latin American economic structuralists. How can this literature cross-fertilize the objectives of the antitrust policy and be transformed into a policy decision that simultaneously encourages the realization of technological innovation (processes or products) and its dispersion throughout the markets? Can analysis of efficiencies, in cases of mergers, incorporate such dynamic competition criteria? Can sanctions, in cases of illegal conduct, incorporate the need for investment in technological innovation and its dispersion, in such a way as to break the structures that encourage occlusive behavior?

In Brazilian law there are commands that allow such interpretations (the Federal Constitution says that "the domestic market must be encouraged in such a way as to make the technological autonomy of the country viable," and the Competition Law states that the criterion of "technological development" must be taken into account when analyzing mergers, for example). They made some decisions, where the cognitive premise was dynamic competition, feasible and this encouraged the rise and dispersion of technological innovation and determined investments in Research, Development & Innovation; or they blocked contractual arrangements that visibly impede the dispersion of innovative behaviors. Such re-interpretation of experiences of the general terms of competition, removing it from the iron cage of static competition, are certainly able to bear fruit in countless laws, allowing the antitrust authority to be better than it is today.

3. The Antitrust Policy Being Humbler and more Generous than It is Today: Allowing "Development as Capabilities" and Public Service Policies

The antitrust authority can reinvent itself and be more relevant (in addition to the two proposals above which involve adequately facing up to the challenges of the economic power of the financial sector and encouraging the existence and democratization of technological innovation, in other words, having a highly effective policy for generating competition). It can also reduce the rhetorical and legal scope, in a humility exercise, opening up space for capabilities and empowerment policies to exist. Here the adversary is any attempt to expand the antitrust rationality to places where it should not go. It does not cease to be a curious fact that it is often the same interpreters or interest groups that both vehemently oppose the expansion of the antitrust rationality in the terms set out above (banks/financial system and dynamic competition) and applaud its expansion to areas where such a policy should not be applied. Being strong with the weak and weak with the strong will not make the antitrust policy any more relevant. It will only make it more of the same.

The assumption that the antitrust policy is just one more among the various economic policies available to societies for resolving their problems is not a new one. If we further consider the limited role with which it is described and experimented nowadays (focused on welfare of consumers "fighting" against sellers who seek higher prices by some form of market distortion), in fact this axis of economic policy provides peripheral economies with solutions for just a limited spectrum of their huge problems.

There are structural problems inside these economies that will be only solved by active policies that focus simultaneously on building economic and social structures and developing and democratizing capacities. An antitrust policy will not solve the problems of the technological development of peripheral economies. It is a very limited instrument for such issues. The necessary policies are of another, much larger, scope. An antitrust policy will not solve the problems of income inequality in peripheral economies. It is a very limited instrument for such issues. The necessary policies are of another scope. An antitrust policy will not solve the problems of Brazil's infrastructure.

Those who say that the State does not need these policies because competition exists and, therefore, so does an antitrust policy, impose a burden on the antitrust system that it is politically, legally and methodologically unable to bear. An antitrust policy may serve to smooth out things so that the efforts of these indicated policies are not unduly captured, which is in itself a very important role. So just to accomplish this "small" mission, in addition to all the efforts already expended, an antitrust policy will have to be reinvented as well.

Brazil's Antitrust Law: Status Quo[1]

Mariana Tavares de Araujo[2]

mtavares@levysalomao.com.br

Partner, Levy & Salomão Advogados

Abstract

In October 2011, the Brazilian Congress approved Law No. 12529, the country's current competition law, which was subsequently signed by President Dilma Rousseff on November 30 that same year and took effect on May 29, 2012. The long expected reform was approved after several years of discussions within the Brazilian government, and of congressional review, during which international fora such as the International Competition Network ("ICN") and the Organization for the Economic Cooperation and Development ("OECD") played a key role in providing support for its approval. Law No. 12,529/2011 (i) consolidated the investigative, prosecutorial and adjudicative functions of the Brazilian competition authorities into one independent agency; (ii) introduced a mandatory pre-merger notification system and new filing thresholds; and (iii) set forth new sanctioning provisions for anticompetitive conduct. This paper will examine the central changes to the country's legal and institutional framework introduced by Brazil's competition law, and the relevant developments and trends in law enforcement since it took effect in May 2012.

---

1 An earlier version of this paper was presented at the ABA Antitrust Conference in Asia: China, in May 2014 under the title "Brazil's Antitrust Law: Two Years On."

2 The author thanks her colleagues Julia Gierkens and Marcos Malvar for their helpful input and overall assistance with this paper.

Executive Summary

This paper will examine the central changes to the country's legal and institutional framework introduced by Brazil's competition law (Law No. 12,529/2011)[3], and the relevant developments and trends in law enforcement since it took effect in May 2012.

Key Aspects: Law No. 12529/2011 (i) consolidated the investigative, prosecutorial and adjudicative functions of the Brazilian competition authorities into one independent agency—the "new CADE;" (ii) introduced a mandatory pre-merger notification system and new filing thresholds; and (iii) set forth new sanctioning provisions for anticompetitive conduct.

Conduct Enforcement: CADE has imposed sanctions in approximately 50 cases in the last 2 years, most of them related to cartel conduct. It has also issued new settlement rules for cartel cases, and for unilateral conduct it has established important precedents regarding Resale Price Maintenance and exclusivity agreements. There is still uncertainty concerning some aspects of the sanctioning provisions, particularly regarding when CADE will impose fines based on the group's revenues instead of only taking into account the turnover of the defendant.

Merger Review: Brazil is now a suspensory jurisdiction, and in August 2013 CADE imposed fines for gun jumping for the first time. The definition of steps that parties are allowed to take prior to the adjudication of the case, however, is still missing. The new thresholds have decreased the number of filings and reduced the average review period. Earlier clearance decisions such as those based on the "effects test" and on the definition of the merging parties "economic group" seemed to indicate that the agency was targeting cases with clear impact on the domestic market. This trend seems to have been overturned more recently.

Recent Developments: In October 2014, CADE published revised merger notification rules. Earlier in 2014, CADE levied a record fine and for the first time imposed structural remedies in connection with a cartel case in the cement sector.

Key Words: antitrust, cartel, resale price maintenance, exclusivity agreements, merger, public consultation, CADE, Law No. 12529/2011, Brazil.

I. Introduction

In October 2011, the Brazilian Congress approved Law No. 12529, the country's current competition law, which was subsequently signed by President Dilma Rousseff on November 30 that same year and took effect on May 29, 2012 ("Law No.12529/2011" or "Competition Law"). The long expected reform was approved after several years of discussions within the Brazilian government, and of congressional review, during which international fora such as the International Competition Network ("ICN") and the Organization for the Economic Cooperation and Development ("OECD") played a key role in providing support for its approval.

---

3 See Law No. 12529/2011 of November 30, 2011 *available at* http://www.cade.gov.br/upload/LAW%20N%C2%BA%2012529%202011%20%28English%20version%20from%2018%2005%202012%29.pdf.

The modern era in competition policy in Brazil began with the antitrust law of 1994 ("Law No. 8884/1994"), which coincided with the country's transition to a market-based economy. Law No. 8884/1994 introduced the institutional framework of the Brazilian Competition Policy System ("BCPS"), which remained in place until Law No. 12529/2011 took effect, comprised of two investigative and advisory agencies, the Secretary of Economic Monitoring at the Ministry of Finance ("SEAE/MF") and the Antitrust Division of the Secretary of Economic Law at the Ministry of Justice ("SDE/MJ"), and a third component, the Administrative Council for Economic Defense ("CADE"), an administrative tribunal in charge of issuing final rulings in both merger and conduct cases. The inefficiencies of that system became apparent fairly quickly, most of them related to its mandatory post-merger review system, the overlapping functions of the three agencies and the lack of resources. As a result, beginning in early 2000, policy makers began proposing amendments to the antitrust statute, but most were not enacted.

Notwithstanding such defects, during the past decade antitrust authorities in Brazil made significant progress. Improvements since 2003 eliminated overlapping functions, so the SDE concentrated on anti-competitive conduct investigations, with special focus on anti-cartel enforcement, and the SEAE on merger analysis. Its anti-cartel program is now widely respected in Brazil and abroad, and merger review was improved through infra-legal measures such as: (i) the introduction of a "fast track" procedure for simple cases; (ii) consent decrees (*Medida Cautelar*) or agreements with the parties (*Acordo para Presevar a Reversibilidade da Operação* or *APRO*) that prevent complex transactions from being closed prior to CADE adjudicating the case; and (iii) the ability of administrative agencies to issue binding interpretations of law issued by CADE with the purpose of ensuring legal certainty regarding the notification thresholds.

The most relevant changes introduced by the Competition Law are related to: (i) the new institutional framework; (ii) a mandatory pre-merger notification system and new filing thresholds; and (iii) sanctions and other specific provisions addressing anticompetitive conduct investigation. Under Law No. 12529/2011, the investigative, prosecutorial, and adjudicative functions of the Brazilian competition authorities were consolidated into one autonomous agency. CADE has been restructured to include: (i) an administrative tribunal composed of six Commissioners and a President; (ii) a Directorate General for Competition ("*Superintendência Geral*" or "DG"); and (iii) an Economics Department. The new DG now performs the former functions of SDE's Antitrust Division and SEAE. SEAE continues to exist but deals exclusively with competition advocacy before the Brazilian regulatory agencies and other governmental bodies. CADE's Attorney General is now in charge of the agency's representation in court and may issue opinions upon request of the Commissioners or of the DG. The Federal Public Prosecutor renders opinions only on cases regarding investigations of anticompetitive conduct. The Competition Law also provides for an additional 200 positions to be held by government employees within SEAE and CADE, preferably.

This paper will examine Brazil's developments regarding merger review and conduct enforcement since the current competition law entered into force. In addition to the brief overview of the Brazilian competition policy system provided in this introduction, section II briefly describes the changes introduced regarding the prosecution of anticompetitive conduct and reviews the authorities' enforcement record since May 2012 and section III provides a summary of the new pre-merger review system and discusses the relevant precedents established during the past two years.

II. Conduct Enforcement

The most relevant features of the Law No. 12529/2011 with respect to anticompetitive conduct are related to the: (i) introduction of a revised list of types of anticompetitive conduct; (ii) applicable fines; and (iii) Leniency Program.

The basic framework for anticompetitive conduct in Brazil is set by Article 36 of Law No. 12529/11.[4] Article 36 deals with all types of anti-competitive conduct other than mergers. The statute did not change the definition or the types of anti-competitive conduct that could be prosecuted in Brazil under the previous law. The law prohibits acts that have as their object or effect (i) limitation, restraint or, in any way, harm to open competition or free enterprise; (ii) control over a relevant market of a certain good or service; (iii) an increase in profits on a discretionary basis; or (iv) engagement in market abuse. Article 36 specifically excludes from potential violations, however, the achievement of market control by means of "competitive efficiency". Under Article 2 of the Competition Law, practices that take place outside the territory of Brazil are subject to CADE's jurisdiction, provided that they produce actual or potential effects in Brazil.[5]

The law is written broadly to apply to all forms of agreements and information exchange of sensitive commercial information, formal and informal, explicit and implicit. One of the changes brought by the Competition Law was a reduction of the fine for anticompetitive behavior, from 1 to 30 percent of the company's turnover in the year prior to the beginning of the investigation to 0.1 to 20 percent of the turnover generated from the sector affected.[6] To date, CADE has not issued secondary legislation clarifying the cases in which the agency will resort to the group's revenues instead of taking into account only the turnover of the defendant. Moreover, managers and directors[7] liable for unlawful corporate conduct may be fined an amount ranging from 1 to 20 percent of corporate fines. In contrast to the previous law, CADE now needs to establish fault or negligence on the part of the directors and executives in order to find a violation.[8]

Pursuant to Article 45 of Brazil's Competition Law, the following shall be taken into account by CADE when setting fines: (i) degree of gravity of the infringement; (ii) good faith of the defendant; (iii) gain obtained or intended by the defendant; (iv) whether the conduct has been consummated or not; (v) degree of actual or potential harm to competition, the Brazilian economy, consumers or third-parties in general; (vi) detrimental economic effects caused by the conduct; (vii) economic situation of the defendant; and (viii) recidivism. Finally, if the defendant was already sanctioned by CADE for antitrust offenses in the last five years, fines must be doubled.

Apart from fines, CADE may also: (i) order the publication of the decision in a major newspaper at the wrongdoer's expense; (ii) prohibit the wrongdoer from participating in public procurement procedures and obtaining funds from public financial institutions for up to five years; (iii) include the wrongdoer's

---

4 See *supra* note 1, at Article 36.

5 See *supra* note 1, at Article 2.

6 See CADE's Resolution No. 3/2012.

7 See *supra* note 1, Article 32. Directors and officers may be held jointly and severally liable with the company for anticompetitive practices performed by the company. Considering the stiff sanctions that have been imposed to legal entities by CADE to date, this provision has been nearly forgotten as virtually no individual would be in a position to be held liable for the sanctions imposed against the company.

8 Other individuals, business associations and other entities that do not engage in commercial activities may be fined from approximately USD 22,200 to USD 885 million.

name on the Brazilian Consumer Protection List; (iv) recommend to the tax authorities to block the wrongdoer from obtaining tax benefits; (v) recommend to the intellectual property authorities to grant compulsory licenses of patents held by the wrongdoer; and (vi) prohibit an individual from exercising market activities on its behalf or representing companies for five years.[9] In terms of structural remedies under the Competition Law, CADE may order a corporate spin-off, transfer of control, sale of assets or any measure deemed necessary to cease the detrimental effects associated with the wrongful conduct.

The Competition Law also includes a broad provision allowing CADE to impose any "any other act or measure required to eliminate harmful effects to the economic order,"[10] which allows CADE to prohibit conduct or impose specific conditions upon the wrongdoer. Given the quasi-criminal nature of the sanctions available to the antitrust authorities, CADE's wide-ranging enforcement of this provision may prompt judicial appeals.

1. Recent Rulings

Since the Competition Law entered into force, CADE has imposed sanctions in connection with approximately 50 investigations of anticompetitive conduct. Although most of the cases reviewed by the Tribunal were cartel matters, important unilateral conduct investigations have also been adjudicated in the past two years. In February 2013, the Tribunal issued a pivotal ruling in a Resale Price Maintenance ("RPM") case, where it sanctioned auto parts manufacturer SKF for setting minimum resale prices.[11] Pursuant to the decision, resale price maintenance will be deemed illegal unless defendants are able to prove efficiencies. An infringement would be found regardless of the duration of the practice (in this case, distributors followed orders for only seven months); the fact that distributors followed or did not follow the minimum sales price; or even the defendant's market share, as CADE considered the conduct illegal by object.

In its decision, the agency majorly also disregarded the efficiency defense. In fact, there is no case in CADE's case law—be it under the merger control system or prosecution of anticompetitive conduct—in which the Brazilian antitrust authority has cleared an anticompetitive merger or dismissed an anticompetitive practice based on efficiency arguments. With this ruling, it seems that CADE has distanced itself from its traditional "rule of reason" approach in RPM cases, to a "modified *per se*" test, in which the conduct is presumed to be illegal, and parties would in theory have an efficiency defense. This change shows an enhanced skepticism or outright disregard of the role of efficiencies in vertical practices, a trend which seems to be at odds with the increasing role played by economics in antitrust analysis.[12]

CADE has also reviewed important exclusivity agreement cases, most of which have been executed between Unimed and local physicians. Unimed—one of the largest medical work cooperative and health insurance companies in Brazil—requires in its contracts with local physicians and hospitals for the provision of health care services that they do not affiliate with any other health plan. CADE prohibited

---

9 The idea behind this provision was to deal with situations in which CADE prohibited the wrongdoer from participating in public procurement procedures and obtaining funds from public financial institutions for up to five years. To avoid this penalty, the parties simply set up a new company and resumed activities in the same sector without being subject to the restrictions imposed by CADE's decision.

10 See *supra* note 1, Article 38 (VII).

11 See Case No. 08012.001271/2001-44.

12 Ana Paula Martinez, Mariana Tavares de Araujo, *Resale Price Maintenance in Brazil: A Moving Target*, CPI Antitrust Chronicle, October, 2013.

such exclusivity arrangements in cases where Unimed held a significant market share (usually around 50 percent). CADE has imposed sanctions on Unimed for the same conduct in over 70 investigations.

Since the current law entered into force, CADE has lived up to its promise to step up sanctions against cartels—it has imposed fines that average 15 percent the annual gross revenues of the defendants. A great number of the decisions issued in cartel cases concerned the fuel retail sector. In 2013, CADE adjudicated the air cargo case, which was one of the first high profile international cartel investigations initiated through a leniency agreement in Brazil in 2006.[13] The parties were fined approximately USD 125 million, the third largest fine imposed by CADE to date.[14] This year, CADE's Tribunal issued a final ruling on the cement cartel investigation, which has been ongoing since 2006. In January, the Reporting Commissioner recommended that the six companies, six individuals and three associations should be found guilty of collusion.[15] The judgment came to an end in May and sanctions included a record-fine of roughly USD 1.3 billion, plus other ancillary sanctions, such as the divestiture of assets and a ban on carrying out transactions in the cement and concrete sector for five years. It was the first time that CADE resorted to this type of sanction, which is relatively unusual in cartel cases. The parties have filed motions for clarification, but no significant changes to the decision are anticipated.

Brazil has a dual enforcement system—certain anticompetitive conduct, such as cartels, is considered both an administrative and criminal infringement. State and federal prosecutors are in charge of criminal prosecution against individuals and, together with the criminal courts, enforce the criminal statute. Law No. 12529/2011 also modifies the criminal sanctions applicable to anticompetitive conduct. The previous provision of the Federal Economic Crimes Law set forth jail terms of 2 to 5 years or the payment of a criminal fine. The Competition Law amends this provision and establishes that anticompetitive behavior may be punished with a jail term of 2 to 5 years plus the payment of a criminal fine. The fact that the criminal fine is no longer an alternative sanction to the jail sentence will prevent individuals from settling the criminal case.

The authorities' interaction and cooperation with public prosecutors also gave CADE the ability to tap into the different investigation tools and resources available through the police and prosecutors—for instance, the use of wiretaps. CADE and the prosecutors have frequently cooperated since the commencement of investigations and have conducted joint dawn raids in several cases. Since 2010, dawn raids were conducted in approximately 15 cartel cases.

2. Leniency Program

Approximately 40 leniency agreements have been signed since 2003, when Brazil's antitrust authorities set forth the prosecution of cartels as its top priority.[16] The majority of the leniency agreements were related to alleged members of international cartels. Brazil's Leniency Program had been introduced in 2000 through an amendment to the previous antitrust law. Two relevant aspects of the program—the disqualification of cartel leaders and the scope of criminal immunity—were modified by the current law.

13 See Case CADE's decision No. 08012.011027/2006-02.

14 The record fine imposed by CADE in connection with a cartel case was roughly USD1 billion for the cartel in industrial gases in 2010. The second largest fine of roughly USD 170 million was imposed in 2005 for the steel bars cartel.

15 See Case No. 08012.011142/2006-79.

16 Since then, more than 400 search warrants have been served to collect direct evidence in cartel cases.

Under Law No. 12529/2011, the DG is the antitrust agency with power to execute the leniency letter. Later on, while adjudicating a case, CADE must verify whether the applicant complied with the terms and conditions provided in the leniency agreement and, if this criteria is met, it must confirm the full or partial immunity granted by the DG.

The applicant must fulfill the following requirements to benefit from full or partial leniency: (i) the applicant (a company or an individual) is the first to come forward and confess its participation in the unlawful practice; (ii) the applicant ceases its involvement in the anticompetitive practice; (iii) the applicant agrees to fully cooperate with the investigation; (iv) the cooperation results in the identification of other members of the conspiracy, and in the obtaining of documents that evidence the anticompetitive practice; and (v) at the time the applicant comes forward, the DG had not received sufficient information about the illegal activity to ensure the condemnation of the applicant.

Companies and individuals will be eligible for full or partial leniency depending on whether the DG was aware of the illegal conduct at issue. If the DG was unaware, the party may be entitled to a waiver from any penalties. If the agency was previously aware, the applicable penalty can be reduced by one to two-thirds, depending on the effectiveness of the cooperation and the parties' good faith in complying with the Program's requirements. Directors and managers of the cooperating firm will be sheltered both from administrative and criminal sanctions if the individuals sign the agreement and fulfill the same requirements.

Under the previous law, leniency was not available to a "leader" of the cartel; such requirement was eliminated by Law No. 12529/2011. The elimination of the disqualification of the "leader" as an applicant in the law does not necessarily mean that the authority will disregard the roles played by each cartel participant in determining whether to grant leniency or not—Article 86 of Law No. 12529/2011 provides that the authority may grant leniency if the program requirements are fulfilled.[17] On the other hand, Brazil's leniency policy already provided that the leadership requirement was interpreted in a very limited way. Therefore, going forward, the authority will not be required to address arguments that a leniency applicant must be disqualified for having been a leader in a conspiracy, but this will most likely not be followed by policy changes resulting in immunity from sanctions independent of the role played by each party.

Further, a grant of leniency under the previous antitrust law extended to criminal liability under the Federal Economic Crimes Law, but not to other possible crimes under other criminal statutes, such as fraud in public procurement. The Competition Law broadens the leniency grant to extend to these crimes, as well. In the past, CADE and the SDE have cooperated closely with the criminal authorities to prevent criminal charges for other conducts from being imposed against individuals that have confessed to participating in a cartel. Still, such amendment significantly enhances legal certainty and therefore tends to increase incentives for the Leniency Program, in particular for individuals involved in domestic bid-rigging cases.

---

17 See *supra* note 1, at Article 86.

3. Settlements

Brazil's Settlement Program for cartel investigations was introduced in 2007, through an amendment to the previous antitrust law. This represented a remarkable improvement as early cooperation on the part of the defendants saves public resources, cuts down on litigation, provides expedited treatment and more certainty and transparency, for the business community. Settling also proves beneficial for the defendant, as it often means a more efficient use of resources on the part of the company.

Over 100 settlements have been executed by CADE since 2007, when CADE issued its revised Settlement Regulation, 15 of which were in connection with cartel investigations. Parties to international cartel investigations, such as the marine hose and the compressors cases, have also settled with CADE. The 2007 Settlement Regulation also included rules on settlements for other types of anticompetitive conduct, which had been in place since 1994.

In March 2013, CADE issued the revised settlement rules, which raised imperative issues for the parties involved on ongoing cartel investigations. One of the most important provisions in the new Regulation refers to the requirement that the parties acknowledge their involvement in the investigated conduct. Such requirement would apply to all cartel cases, and not only to those initiated through a leniency agreement, as it is today. There has been some criticism of preventing defendants from pleading nolo contendere, as it could decrease the incentives for settlements where CADE does not have a strong case, even when it could also be in the government's best interest to do so. The provision does not refer to a "confession" and the requirement "to acknowledge participation" may allow for some flexibility, with respect to its terms, compared to a strict "confession" requirement. Still, since the amendment to the criminal statute, this may prevent individuals from settling with CADE, as "acknowledging its participation" in connection with the administrative investigation may compromise their respective defenses in criminal investigations where the conduct at issue continued after May 29 2012. This situation is specific to Brazil, where there is dual enforcement by administrative and criminal authorities with respect to individuals. This differs from jurisdictions such as the United States where enforcement is purely criminal, or the EU where it is exclusively administrative and the investigated party has to deal with only one investigation in each jurisdiction and does not have to take into account the consequences of its strategy in another parallel case.

The Regulation also introduces a scale of discounts that will apply to the settling sum that defendants that wish to settle are required to pay. Reductions may vary between (i) 30 and 50 percent for the first to propose settlement; (ii) 25 to 40 percent for the second in; and (iii) up to 25 percent for the other parties that come after. For settlement proposals submitted after the DG has concluded the investigation the reductions may be no greater than 15 percent. These discounts are in theory based on the fine that would apply to the parties under investigation for cartel and are supposed to vary according to: (i) the order in which the parties come forward; and (ii) the extent and usefulness of what the parties provide in cooperation (which is also mandatory now) with the authorities. Clearly, the purpose of providing benchmarks is to increase transparency and predictability for the parties, however, since CADE has yet to issue sentencing guidelines, and case law for hardcore cartel cases is still limited, these standards may be of little help.

With respect to the negotiation rules, as it was the case before, defendants can propose to settle at any stage of the investigation, regardless of whether the case is being handled by the DG or the Tribunal. The general rules are: (i) defendants can only try to settle once ("one-shot game"); and (ii) the negotiation period lasts for 30 days, and is renewable for an additional 30 days. The negotiation process may be confidential at the discretion of CADE. The revised Settlement Regulation now provides that the negotiation will take place at the DG for all cases still under investigation, different from before when the entire procedure was conducted at the Tribunal.

Finally, pursuant to the 2007 rules, the investigation was suspended for the parties that settle, for a specified period of time, for the conditions set forth to be fulfilled, after which they would be excluded from the proceedings. Under the new Regulation though, the assessment of whether the parties have or have not fulfilled the settlement conditions will only take place when CADE adjudicates the case, and therefore, just like the leniency applicant, the parties that settle will be bound to cooperate with the authorities until the end of the investigation.

It is too soon to tell how those changes will affect the proposition of settlements—since the new Competition Law CADE has settled over 70 cases, almost 50 of which involved exclusivity agreements by Unimed and did not require the acknowledgement of any involvement in the conduct. Those settlements with Unimed, however, are considered a milestone for CADE, since proceedings related to similar exclusivity clauses accounted for almost a third of the agency's convictions since 1994.

III. Merger Review

Brazil's new antitrust law introduced a mandatory pre-merger notification system, i.e., transactions that meet the Brazilian merger filing thresholds cannot be consummated before CADE's clearance. Penalties for "gun jumping" include fines ranging from BRL 60,000 to BRL 60,000,000 and the transaction may be also declared null and void by the authority. The Competition Law does not specifically determine what constitutes gun jumping, generally stating that "[t]he parties should maintain their physical structures and competitive conditions unaltered until CADE's final approval, being prohibited any transfer of shares or any influence of one party over another' business, as well as the exchange of competitively sensitive information outside of what is strictly necessary for the execution of the relevant binding agreement by the parties." Violations can occur even if the parties to the transaction do not compete in the same markets. In gun jumping cases involving competitors, coordination of competitive activities or detailed information exchanges can also lead to a cartel violation, subjecting the parties to fines from 0.1 to 20 percent of a company's (group of companies' or conglomerate's) gross revenues generated in the "sector of activity" affected by the infringement in the year prior to the initiation of the investigation.

CADE's Tribunal has issued four public decisions regarding gun jumping since the competition law took effect in May 2012.[18] In one of the cases, the discussion was centered on whether the transaction met the mandatory filing thresholds and not on the violation of the mandatory waiting period itself.[19] The three other cases adjudicated by CADE regarded contracts in the market for petroleum and natural gas production. OGX Petróleo e Gás Participações ("OGX") reached a settlement agreement with CADE to close an investigation regarding OGX's alleged violation of the premerger waiting period requirement[20] CADE concluded that OGX had taken steps to prematurely close the acquisition of shares held by Petrobras in a consortium formed to explore pre-salt oil and gas concessions in the city of Santos. OGX agreed to pay BRL 3 million (approximately USD 1.3 million) in fines. The relevant report issued

18 The report issued by the Reporting Commissioner supports CADE's decision in Case No. 08700.007899/2013-39 that there was no gun jumping violation is not public.

19 See Case No. 08700.002285/2014-41.

20 See Case No. 08700.005775/2013-19.

by CADE's Directorate General lists the following elements as evidence that the parties had consummated the transaction prior to clearance from the authority: (i) a contractual provision that established that it would have entered into force before the date the contract was executed; (ii) the fact that the contract did not set forth prior approval from CADE as a condition precedent; (iii) as well as that, prior to CADE having cleared the transaction (a) the payment of the price of the transaction had occurred; (b) the parties had exchanged commercially sensitive information; (c) and the buyer had participated in management decisions regarding the target.

Under the *OGX/Petrobras* decision, regular business activities, such as the payment of bills, acquisition of office materials and hiring of regular services such as maintenance, would not be declared null by the authority, even if the party is found guilty of gun jumping. Conversely, any acts that may potentially affect competition in the market would be void if taken place prior to CADE's approval.

The second case involved Potióleo and UTC and the acquisition of shares in a concession contract to explore an oil field. CADE imposed the minimum fine of BRL 60,000 (approximately USD 28,000) on the companies for gun jumping.[21] The Tribunal's decision makes reference to the same elements established by CADE's DG in the report it issued in connection with the *OGX/Petrobras* case as evidence of gun jumping. Finally, and likewise, when reviewing UTC's and Aurizônia's concession contract to explore an oil field, CADE also imposed the minimum fine against the companies for gun jumping.[22] In this case, CADE found that while there was no change in the management structure, the agreement provided for the payment of installments related to the price of the transaction before CADE's approval. Although none of these decisions establish clear-cut rules on CADE's understanding regarding what constitutes an infringement of the premerger waiting period requirement, in all three cases the authority states that gun jumping in itself is a serious violation, regardless of whether the transaction at issue raises competition concerns or not.

The maximum period to conduct the merger review is 330 calendar days from the day of filing or the day CADE considers the filing to be complete. Many of the cases notified to the Brazilian antitrust authority, however, are reviewed under a fast track proceeding, under CADE's Resolution No. 02/2012, and cases are cleared, on average, in approximately 19 calendar days.[23] In complex cases, the law also allows the Reporting Commissioner to authorize the parties to close the transaction before receiving CADE's clearance, subject to conditions such as the limitations on the freedom of the acquirer to liquidate assets, integrate activities, dismiss workers, close stores or plants, terminate brands or product lines, and alter marketing plans.

1. Filing Thresholds

Brazil's Competition Law requires that a transaction be filed in Brazil if the following criteria are met: (i) each of at least two parties to the transaction meet the turnover threshold; (ii) the transaction amounts to "an economic concentration", as defined by CADE's Resolution No. 2/2012; and (iii) the transaction produces effects in Brazil, as defined by Article 2 of Brazil's Competition Law ("effects test"). In October 2014, CADE approved Resolution No. 8 ("Resolution No. 8/2014"), and No. 9

21 See Case No. 08700.008292/2013-76.

22 See Case No. 08700.008289/2013-52.

23 Cases for which the parties are required to submit the standard notification form have been cleared on average in 86 days.

("Resolution No. 1/2014"), which amended Resolution No. 2/2012 and CADE's internal rules and introduced key changes regarding such criteria, as further discussed below.

The Competition Law also introduces a clawback provision that allows Brazil's antitrust agency to review transactions that fall outside the merger thresholds within one year of its closing. Consumer associations, clients, suppliers, and competitors may file complaints against a transaction before the agency, prompting CADE to act. Also in October 2014, CADE put under public consultation a draft resolution on the procedure for the investigation of mergers that fall outside the statutory filing thresholds. New rules are expected to be published in 2015.

The Competition Law provides for minimum size thresholds, expressed in total revenues, derived in Brazil by each of at least two parties to the transaction. Ministries of Finance and Justice Joint Resolution No. 994/2012 established that one party must have Brazilian revenues in the last fiscal year of at least BRL 750 million and the other BRL 75 million—both acquirer and seller, including the whole economic group, should be taken into account.

Pursuant to CADE's Resolution No. 2/2012, the following entities shall be considered as part of the same "economic group" for the purposes of calculating the group's revenues: (i) entities subject to common control; (ii) all the companies in which any of the entities subject to common control hold, directly or indirectly, at least 20 percent of the voting or total capital stock.

Resolution No. 9/2014 introduced revised thresholds for the notification of private equity transactions, and now the turnover of the following entities shall be taken into account for the purposes of determining whether a filing is mandatory: (i) the economic group of each entity that holds 50 percent or more of the fund; and (ii) portfolio companies controlled by the fund or in which the fund holds a stake of 20 percent or more of the total or voting capital.

Whereas the statutory provisions specifically refer to "concentration acts," it defines those very broadly as when (i) two or more companies merge; (ii) one company acquires sole or joint control of the stock or assets of another, or even a minority shareholding; (iii) an absorption of other companies takes place; or (iv) a joint venture, an association or a consortium is formed. The provisions do not apply to consortia that are formed in connection with public bids.[24]

CADE's Resolution No. 9/2014 defined the following new rules to determine when an acquisition that does not involve change in control is subject to mandatory filing. A filing is now required if: (a) as a result of the transaction, the acquirer becomes the largest individual shareholder of the target company; (b) in cases that do not involve companies horizontal or vertically related, a party acquires at least 20 percent of the voting or total capital stock of the target company, or in cases the party already holds 20 percent of the voting or total capital stock of the target company, if the party acquires at least 20 percent of the voting or total capital stock from the same seller; (c) acquisitions between horizontally or vertically related parties that result in the buyer having at least 5 percent of the voting or total capital stock of the target company. In cases where the party already holds at least 5 percent of the voting or total capital stock of the target company, every time the shareholder acquires an additional stake of at least 5 percent; and (d) acquisitions by the already controlling shareholder, when the controlling shareholder acquires at least an additional 20 percent stake from the same seller.

---

24 The reasoning for this is that the government authority in charge of the procurement will undertake the antitrust authorities' role to ensure that the bids will be competitive.

CADE's internal rules were modified through Resolution No. 8/2014 to waive CADE's clearance for transactions performed in the stock markets and in the over-the-counter market. Only the exercise of rights arising from such transactions is now subject to CADE's approval. Resolution No. 9/2014 also amended CADE's Internal Rules of Proceedings to provide for clearer rules regarding the notification of bonds and securities convertible into stock. Under the revised criteria, a filing will be mandatory only when the conversion of bonds into shares may meet other notification thresholds or allow the investor to (i) indicate members of the company's governing bodies or (ii) veto competition-sensitive decisions.[25]

Finally, the effects test is met whenever a given transaction is wholly or partially performed within Brazil or, if performed abroad, it is capable of producing effects within Brazil. This will be the case if the target to the transaction has a direct and/or indirect presence within the country. Direct presence is achieved through a local subsidiary, distributor, sales representative, etc. Although indirect presence is most commonly established through export sales into the country, we cannot rule out the possibility that CADE would consider third party sales (e.g., via a licensing agreement) as evidence of indirect presence in Brazil.

In a case reviewed under the current statute, the DG cleared a transaction that was submitted for review simply because the buyer and seller fulfilled the Brazilian turnover threshold despite the fact that the target had no activities in Brazil (the target was as international airport in Curaçao).[26] In another case adjudicated in March 2013, the DG concluded that the review was not mandatory given the absence of effects in Brazil as (i) the target had no activities in Brazil; (ii) there were no horizontal or vertical relationships between the parties that could affect Brazil; and (iii) the geographic market was local in scope.[27] Neither decision issued by the DG was reviewed by CADE's Tribunal.[28]

However, more recently, in a case adjudicated in January 2014, the parties argued that, even though they fulfilled the turnover threshold, the transaction was not subject to merger review in Brazil as (i) the transaction did not result in horizontal overlaps or vertical integration; and (ii) the target sales into/in Brazil were "insignificant when compared to the size of the market in Brazil and worldwide." CADE's DG, however, concluded that a filing was required and stated "the Parties seems to place the effects test as the preliminary step in the merger review process, which is a contradiction. The effects of a given transaction can only be verified after CADE conducts a substantive review of the case. And in order to allow the authorities to reach this stage, the transaction must be filed in Brazil."[29] The decision seems to suggest that, as long as the parties fulfill the turnover and the type of transaction thresholds, a filing is always required and CADE would then assess during its review of the case whether the transaction is expected to affect Brazil or not.

---

25 Resolution No. 8/2014 also introduced additional categories of cases that may be reviewed under the fast-track procedure.

26 See Case No.08012.002945/2012-81.

27 See Case No.08700.001204/2013-13.

28 Under the old system CADE took the approach that it had no jurisdiction over some international transactions given the absence of effects in Brazil (see Case No. 08012.003246/2002-86; 08012.009254/2002-36; 08012.006025/2001-89; 08012.005749/2003-77; and 08012.005925/2003-71). The common feature of these transactions was that: (i) the target had no direct presence in Brazil; (ii) the target had low or no sales to Brazil in recent years; (iii) such sales were made on a sporadic basis; (iv) there were no horizontal or vertical relationships between the target and the buyer in the relevant market which affects Brazil. Also, in a 2011 case (Case No. 08012.003505/2011-60, adjudicated by CADE's Tribunal on June 8, 2011), Schneider Electric acquired control over Summit Energy Services, a company that had reported no sales in Brazil and no Brazilian clients. The parties argued that the notification was not mandatory since the transaction did not generate effects in Brazil. CADE, however, considered the notification mandatory based solely on the fact that the parties met the turnover threshold. Moreover, in Case No. 08012.009358/2006-74, the then investigative agency SDE stated that the filing was not mandatory because "the transaction did not involve Brazilian companies and the product at issue is not sold in Brazil." CADE's Tribunal dismissed SDE's opinion stating that "SDE's opinion is based on a partial assessment [of the effects test] . . . in order to assess whether an international transaction does not produce effects in Brazil . . . it is not sufficient to establish whether the transaction involves Brazilian companies or exports into the country." CADE stated that if the target's production capacity is within a relevant market that includes Brazil, a Brazilian filing is mandatory.

29 See Case No. 08700.011324/2013-10.

2. Remedies

CADE has required divestiture undertakings from the parties in 21 cases since the Competition Law entered into force. In addition, it imposed 21 behavioral remedies so as to provide conditional clearance in those cases. In *Mach/Syniverse,* a transaction filed under the old law that involved the market for roaming technology to mobile operators, CADE was concerned about the elevated concentration that would arise from the transaction in the markets of GSM data clearing and Near Real Time Roaming Data Exchange.[30] The parties, then, offered commitments to divest a significant part of Mach's assets that adequately addressed CADE's concerns and the transaction was cleared in May 2013.

The *Ahlstrom Corporation/ Munksjö AB* case was also filed under the former statute. CADE took the view that the transaction would lead to a high concentration in the markets for abrasive paper backings and pre-impregnated décor paper lines with no possibility of new entrants to compete with the incumbents.[31] To address the agency's competition concerns, the parties proposed the divestiture of Ahlstrom's assets in these two markets to a third party. In these two cases, CADE and the parties negotiated divestiture undertakings, which was a tool introduced by the new Competition Law—the Agreement in Merger Control or *Acordo em Atos de Concentracao* in Portuguese. Since the competition law took effect CADE has made use of this tool to set forth remedies in these two cases.

When reviewing the *KPMG/BDO* acquisition,[32] however, which involved the market for auditing services, CADE approved the transaction with restrictions that prohibited KPMG from engaging in other transactions with competitors for twenty four months, through which it would gain access to clients with over BRL 300 million[33] turnover. After this period, KPMG will need to file all transactions involving clients with turnover greater than BRL 300 million. Pursuant to CADE, the rationale for such restriction was to promote entry into the market for auditing services.

3. Avocation Process

In merger cases, the DG is allowed to clear simple transactions without the need of submitting its decisions to CADE's Tribunal. However, the law contains a provision allowing CADE's Tribunal to reexamine any decision issued by the DG, either by the initiative of a Commissioner or any third-party (the so-called "avocation process"). Until now, CADE's Tribunal has resorted to this mechanism three times.

The first case in February 2013 involved the acquisition of the remaining 49 percent shares of Anhembi Morumbi, a private university, by the Laureate Education group, active in the same segment, which already held 51 percent of the target. According to the Commissioner who advocated the case, the Tribunal should conduct a more thorough analysis of the files, due to the concern of possible interlocking directorate between the parties. The transaction was finally cleared by the Tribunal, which nonetheless fined the parties for having omitted information in the notification form.

---

30 See Case No. 08700.006437/2012-13.

31 See Case No. 08700.009882/2012-35.

32 See Case No.08012.002689/2011-41.

33 Approximately USD 132 million (exchange rate = 2.26).

Two other cases involved associative contracts executed between Monsanto and Embrapa[34] and Bayer, respectively. When assessing the cases, CADE's DG took the view that non-exclusive licensing agreements that (i) did not contain non-compete clauses; (ii) did not provide for transfer of assets; and (iii) did not create corporate relationships, would not require antitrust approval in Brazil. CADE's Tribunal, however, avocated the cases and ruled that (i) from a procedural perspective, the criteria to establish whether licensing agreements meet the thresholds are complex and should be further discussed by CADE's Commissioners with the purpose to promote consistency regarding its precedents; and (ii) on substance, the Monsanto transactions were subject to antitrust review in Brazil. New procedural provisions regarding the avocation proceedings were enacted on October 2014, without relevant changes to the material aspects of the analysis.

4. Associative Contracts

The Monsanto cases touch on another gray area regarding Brazil's merger notification system—the types of associative contracts that meet the mandatory filing thresholds in Brazil.[35] Up to now, the agency had been providing some direction through case law, but, in October 2014, CADE issued Resolution No. 10 ("Resolution No. 10/2014") and with that took an important step to increase legal certainty regarding the categories of associative contracts that meet the mandatory filing thresholds, as further explained below.

During the adjudication of the Monsanto cases, CADE's President had stated that "the definition of a licensing agreement as an economic concentration is not related exclusively to the presence of cooperation or collaboration [...] it includes more detailed considerations of the independency between the parties and possible effects that contractual clauses have on the possibility of one party to influence another on relevant contractual decisions and the way the financial risk is shared." In January 2014, CADE's Tribunal cleared the *Monsanto/Bayer* association under the condition that clauses that represent a barrier to entry in the transgenic seed market were excluded from the transaction agreement.[36]

In *Petrobras/MPEC Consortium*,[37] which involved a partnership between the two companies to create a joint venture to offer environmental and risk management services to important consumers of oil products, CADE's DG concluded that a filing was mandatory, highlighting that although the parties would remain structurally and economically independent, they would jointly develop an economic activity and that could lead to the elimination or reduction of competition in the affected markets. Moreover, the transaction agreement included an exclusivity clause preventing the companies from individually providing environmental and risk management services outside the partnership, which was considered a potential antitrust issue by CADE.

Under Resolution No. 10/2014, associative contracts that exceed 2 years where there is a horizontal or a vertical cooperation or a risk sharing arrangement, leading to an interdependent relationship between the contracting parties must be submitted for review, an interdependent relationship is defined as involving: (i) companies with more than 20 percent of the market, in case of horizontal overlap, or

34 See Case No. 08700.006336/2013-23.

35 See Cases Nos. 08700.006706/2012-08; 08700.003937/2012-01; 08700.003898/2012-34; and 08700.006336/2013-23.

36 See Case No. 08700.004957/2013-72.

37 See Case No. 08700.008736/2012-92.

(ii) companies that hold over 30 percent of any vertical integrated market, whenever the agreements contain exclusivity clauses or provide for the sharing of losses or revenues between the parties.

The wording of Resolution No. 10/2014 is less expansive in several aspects than the draft put under public consultation, which shows that CADE continues to open in its engagement with the bar and the business community to address potential concerns voiced regarding proposed regulation. At the same time, it is broader than what had been established by the DG and the Tribunal in cases reviewed under the current statute, and several agreements that raise no competition issues and that do not meet the mandatory thresholds in most other jurisdictions will require antitrust clearance in Brazil.

In the *Vidigal Prado/Yasuda/Marítima* case, CADE for the first time assessed how to calculate the group's turnover in cases involving joint ventures.[38] The parties argued that the acquisition was not reportable since the buyer, the seller, and the target individually considered would not meet the turnover thresholds and that CADE should not include the target's turnover in the economic group's turnover of both the buyer and the seller as this would result in double counting. CADE took a different approach and concluded that since both buyer and seller held over 20 percent of stock of the target, it was part of both economic groups and, therefore, its turnover should be considered for both buyer and seller.

38 See Case No. 08700.001525/2013-18.

Dawn Raids in the EU and China: Fact and Fantasy

FRANK FINE[1]

frank.fine@dehenglaw.com

Head of International Antitrust, DeHeng Law Offices
Executive Director, China Institute of International Antitrust and Investment

Abstract

This paper will analyze some of the fundamental issues for antitrust enforcers and companies relating to dawn raid procedures in both China and the EU. It will be shown (and perhaps surprise the reader to learn) that major concerns relating to Chinese inspection procedures could also be asserted in respect of EU dawn raids. As regards the latter, there are few real constraints on Commission investigators despite all the procedural safeguards in place. For both systems, the interests of public policy in evidence gathering and preventing its destruction is deemed to greatly outweigh the interests of addressees in ensuring notions of "due process."

---

1 The comments made in this paper are strictly personal and are not intended to reflect the views of DeHeng or the CIIAI. The author wishes to thank Hu Tie, a partner in DeHeng's Beijing office, for his helpful comments and suggestions.

I. Introduction

As autumn 2014 begins amid geopolitical, economic and health fears, Western news reports have given ample coverage to recent Chinese antitrust enforcement activity (particularly against Western companies), including the more frequent use of dawn raids[2] by both the National Development and Reform Commission ("NDRC")[3] and State Administration for Trade and Commerce ("SAIC"), which are responsible for price and non-price related infringements, respectively, under the China Anti-Monopoly Law ("AML").[4] In the summer of 2014, Microsoft, Accenture, Qualcomm and Daimler all were visited and searched by the NDRC or SAIC.[5]

It is often reported that antitrust enforcement by these two Chinese agencies and, in particular, their increasing use of dawn raids, are lacking in protections or "due process" for the companies raided. Yet, what does not grab headlines is that the European Union Directorate General for Competition ("DG Comp") has, over the years, been attacked on similar grounds, albeit most of these challenges have been in the European Courts rather than in sensational "EU bashing" news reports. The most recent legal challenge to the EU dawn raid procedure came from *Prysmian*, on 16 September, 2014, when among its various grounds for appealing the European Commission ("Commission") decision in *Power Cables*,[6] it alleged that the Commission unlawfully copied and removed forensic images from the hard disks at its premises.

It may surprise the reader to learn that the Chinese antitrust agencies (including MOFCOM, which deals with merger control) and DG Comp have had regular workshops both in Beijing and Brussels where a fair amount of *savoir faire* is exchanged. Although the public is not invited to these workshops,[7] it is clear that in addition to substantive issues, officials from both sides engage in a fair amount of discussion on investigative procedures, as well as safeguards.[8] One may assume that the Chinese agencies have benefited enormously from these workshops and other bilateral dialogues with EU officials. As a result, it is likely that the NDRC and SAIC are already up-to-date on the techniques that the Commission employs when searching company premises. If the Chinese agencies have not obtained the relevant IT tools from the Commission, they have probably developed their own or obtained them from other sources. It is also clear that DG Comp officials have explained the procedural safeguards that are guaranteed during on-site inspections.

---

2 In this paper, the terms "dawn raid" and "inspection" will be used interchangeably to describe an unannounced compulsory search of premises by antitrust officials.

3 The US-China Business Council claims that from 2008-12, the NDRC launched nearly 20 price-related investigations, whereas in 2013 alone, the NDRC reportedly investigated more than 80 companies. See The US-China Business Council, Competition Policy and Enforcement in China, September 2014, at 7, available at http://uschina.org/reports/competition-policy-and-enforcement-china.

4 As a matter of practice, this division of authority often means that the NDRC takes the lead on cartel investigations, whereas SAIC is concentrating on abuses of dominant position.

5 NDRC and SAIC Regulations adopted in February 2011 empowered provincial and local government authorities to carry out such raids, thus substantially increasing the resources of the agencies to implement such operations and making the recent invasive raids logistically possible. Such raids were probably not foreseen when the AML was adopted. Article 40 of China's Anti-Monopoly Law states, rather innocuously, that when carrying out raids, "there shall be at least two law enforcers [...]"

6 Case AT.39610, Commission decision of 2 April 2014.

7 Materials available at http://www.euchinacomp.org/index.php/competition-weeks.

8 This is not confidential information. Copies of EU Power Points given at these workshops can be downloaded from the Internet.

II. Foundational Requirements

1. Who Must Authorize the Dawn Raid?

In China, a dawn raid may be launched without a court warrant and without probable cause. Article 39 confers authority on the agencies to take measures such as dawn raids when investigating "suspicious monopolistic conduct in accordance with the Law." Before carrying out such raids, Article 39 states that a written report must be submitted to the official-in-charge of the relevant enforcement agency, indicating that the Director General of the antitrust enforcement bureaus of the NDRC or SAIC, as the case may be, must be apprised in advance of any intended raids, suggesting that their explicit or tacit approval of the raid is necessary.

Analogous to the Chinese system, the Commission does not require prior authorization from a court to carry out a dawn raid on business premises. When the Commission is carrying out a dawn raid, a Commission decision is required. Such decisions are not taken by the Commission as a whole. In fact, they are delegated to the Commissioner for Competition, who in turn delegates such power to the Director General of DG Comp.[9] However, unlike the AML, Article 21 of Regulation 1/2003[10] implementing Articles 81 and 82 of the EU Treaty (now Articles 101 and 102 of the Treaty for the Functioning of the European Union or TFEU) requires a court warrant for the inspection of private premises and means of transport.

2. Tension between Evidence Gathering and Specificity of Inspection Decisions

As regard the legal standard or threshold justifying a dawn raid on particular companies, there is a superficial similarity between the Chinese and EU approaches. As noted above, under the AML, the NDRC and SAIC must at least suspect anti-competitive conduct. In the EU, the analysis is more nuanced, but one arrives at virtually the same conclusion. Article 20(4) of Regulation 1/2003[11] states that decisions ordering dawn raids must "specify the subject matter and purpose of the inspection ..." The Court of Justice confirmed in *Dow Chemical Iberica* that it is sufficient, for these purposes, that the agreements and concerted practices concerned are merely "suspected."[12] Recently elaborating on this judgment, the General Court said:

> "To impose a more onerous obligation to state reasons ... would not take not take due account of the preliminary nature of the inspection, the purpose of which is specifically to enable the Commission to establish at a later stage whether, where appropriate, infringements of Community competition law have been committed by the addressees of an inspection decision or by third parties. The wording of the contested decision itself shows that the agreements and concerted practices at issue were not regarded as proved but were merely suspected [...]."[13]

---

9 Commission Rules of Procedure, at article 13(1) and (3); Commission decision of 15 November 2005, OJ L 347/83 (2005).

10 Council Regulation (EC) No 1/2003, 16 December 2002.

11 Id., at article 20(4).

12 See Joined cases 97-99/87, Dow Chemical Iberica v. Comm'n, 1989, ECR 3165, at para 55.

13 See Case T-23/09, Conseil national de l'Ordre des pharmaciens (CNOP), Conseil central de la section G de l'Ordre national des pharmaciens (CCG) v. Comm'n, 2010, ECR II-05291, at para. 41 (citing Dow Chemical Iberica).

To be fair, some EU Court judgments have suggested a more stringent standard. For example, in *Roquette Freres*, a 2002 ECJ judgment, the Court held that the Commission must show in its inspection decision that it has "possession of information and evidence providing reasonable grounds for suspecting the infringement [...]."[14] In the General Court judgment in *Nexans*[15] relating to the inspection decision taken in the power cables cartel investigation, specifically, whether the Commission had sufficiently identified the products to be investigated, the General Court affirmed the *Roquette Freres* standard and wove it into its conclusion compelling the Commission to "identify the sectors covered by the alleged infringement with which the investigation is concerned with a degree of precision sufficient to enable the undertaking in question to limit its cooperation to its activities in the sectors in respect of which the Commission has reasonable grounds for suspecting an infringement [...]."[16]

The General Court judgment in *Nexans* also held that the Commission was not overly broad in its inspection decision by concluding that the inspections covered "agreements and/or concerted practices [which] 'probably have a global reach,'" concluding peremptorily that the inspection decision was "sufficiently precise" as to the geographic scope of the alleged infringements.[17]

This second holding was appealed by *Nexans* to the ECJ, which affirmed the conclusion of the General Court in a judgment dated 25 June 2014.[18] However, in the ECJ's discussion of the relevant case law, the "reasonable grounds" language was dropped entirely and the language on "suspected" conduct reintroduced. Focusing on the preliminary nature of inspections, the Court said that at the time of the inspection decision, "the Commission still lacks [...] precise information to make a specific legal assessment and must first verify the accuracy of its suspicions [...] the aim of the inspection being specifically to gather evidence relating to a suspected infringement."[19]

The above EU case law reveals a palpable tension for the European Commission between the level of suspicion that must exist to justify the raid and the specificity with which the Commission must disclose the scope of its investigation in the inspection decision (a copy of which is tendered to the addressee of the decision at the time of the raid).[20] There is pressure to maintain a lower standard for the former in order to optimize Commission discovery at an early stage of the investigation. However, in order to preserve proportionality and allow the companies raided to ascertain the scope of their duty to cooperate and to assert their rights of defense, there is a counterweight: inspection decisions must state "the subject matter and the objective of the inspection."[21] In particular, the Commission must state the "presumed facts which it intends to investigate [and] indicate as precisely as possible the evidence sought and the matters to which the investigation must relate [...]."[22] For these purposes, it is not necessary for the Commission to disclose all the informa-

14 See Case C-94/00, Roquette Freres SA v. Directeur General de la Concurrence, 2002, ECR I-9011, at para. 61.

15 See Case T-135/09, Nexans France SAS and Nexans SA v. Comm'n, 2012.

16 Id., at para. 45.

17 Id., at para. 97.

18 See Case C-37/19P, Nexans SA and Nexans France SAS v. Comm'n, 2014, ECJ.

19 Id., para. 37. Interestingly, Nexans argued before the ECJ that the Commission failed to show reasonable grounds to suspect a global cartel. However, the ECJ said that as such argument was not raised in its appeal to the General Court, it could not be raised in the ECJ for the first time.

20 See Treaty on the Functioning of the European Union ("TFEU"), 26 October 2012, at article 297.

21 Case C-37/19P, *supra* note 17, at para. 34.

22 Id., at paras. 35-36.

tion in its possession relating to the alleged infringements, to indicate the legal nature of the alleged infringements, to precisely define the relevant markets, or indicate the period of the alleged illegal activity.[23]

In the EU, to ensure that the above-described informational safeguards are met, addressees may appeal inspection decisions to the General Court pursuant to Article 263 of TFEU. Although such appeals have no suspensory effect on the raid, a judgment in favor of the addressee prevents the Commission from using evidence tainted by an illegal inspection. This right of appeal is particularly important given that there is no right of judicial appeal as to specific acts on the part of inspectors once they are on the premises.[24]

In China, the above tension between evidence gathering and disclosure is not yet well-developed. As noted above, Article 39 of the AML requires that before dawn raids are carried out, a written report must be submitted to the Director General of the enforcement bureau of the agency concerned. But it is unclear from the AML what this report must contain. Moreover, on its face, the AML does not require that a copy of this report (or a summary of it), nor a written mandate or oral explanation, be given to the addressee of the inspection so as to alert it as to the subject matter and scope of the intended raid. Yet, as a matter of practice, it would appear that upon arrival at the company premises, Chinese officials give the company a document indicating what they are searching for. But, the fact remains that the administrative decision of the NDRC or SAIC to launch a dawn raid cannot be challenged, whether by means of administrative review or judicial appeal.

It is not for this paper to opine as to whether the administrative measures authorizing a Chinese dawn raids comport with Western notions of due process or best practices. But the situation in China inevitably poses a serious dilemma for addressees of dawn raids—whether they are Chinese or foreign. For better or for worse, they have no legal standing to question the legitimacy of the measures authorizing the raid. They must rely upon the good graces of the Director General for reasonably defining the nature and scope of the raid, and upon his inspectors in carrying out their mandate.

It should be emphasized that while the EU system may penalize the Commission for drafting an overbroad inspection decision by barring the use of the evidence so obtained, there is (i) no effective means of avoiding the raid once the inspection decision has been taken by the Director General of DG Comp (without any oversight whatsoever from a court); and (ii) no legal recourse where dawn raids are carried out against various companies subject to legally valid inspection decisions (often stating highly ambiguous presumed facts and suspicions), and certain of these addressees are later dropped from the final decision or simply not fined. Also, it bears mentioning that until the General Court judgment in *Nexans*, the EU Court has not annulled a single Commission inspection decision, whether in whole or in part. And until now, the Court has never granted interim measures ordering the cessation of a dawn raid, due to the almost insuperable burden on the addressee to show an imminent threat of serious and irreparable harm.[25] For companies operating in the EU, whether they are liable or not, dawn raids are widely considered a cost of doing business.

Despite all of the applicable "due process" safeguards, the EU Courts have been light-handed on the European Commission for decades as regards the legal threshold for carrying out dawn raids and the specificity required of inspection decisions—as well as the Commission compliance with these legal standards. In its September 2013 *Deutsche Bahn* judgment,[26] the General Court adjudicated the issue of whether the absence of a court warrant to justify an EU dawn raid was compatible with the European Convention on Human

23 Id.

24 Such acts may be challenged in the appeal of the final decision. At that stage, the appellant may argue, for example, that some of the evidence used by the Commission was protected by lawyer-client privilege.

25 See e.g., Case 46/87R, Hoechst v. Comm'n, 1987. ECR 1549; Case 85/87R, Dow Chemical Nederland BV v. Comm'n, 1987, ECR 4367.

26 See Joined cases T-289/11, T-290/11 and T-521/11, Deutsche Bahn AG et al v. Comm'n, 2013.

Rights—and the General Court found to the contrary. Indeed, there is growing concern that dawn raids may violate the ECHR.[27] These are all fairly recent developments. Perhaps the Chinese authorities could be forgiven for not having done more during their first five years of antitrust enforcement.

III. The Powers of Inspectors

The powers of the NDRC and SAIC while carrying out dawn raids are derived directly from Article 39 of the AML. This provision authorizes officials to: carry out searches on business premises or "any other relevant place;" require explanations from employees and other parties on the premises as to "the relevant conditions;" examine and copy "relevant documents, agreements, and electronic data" [and] seize "relevant evidence;" and to ask questions regarding the company's bank accounts. And when arriving at the company premises, the officials involved must show their law enforcement certificates.[28]

The powers of EU inspectors are set out in Article 20(2) and 21(1) of Regulation 1/2003.

Article 20(2) empowers EU officials to:

> "(a) enter any premises, land and means of transport of undertakings (b) to examine the books and records related to the business, irrespective of the medium on which they are stored; (c) to take or obtain in any form copies or extracts from such books or records; (d) to seal any business premises . . . [and] (e) to ask any representative .explanations on facts or documents relating to the subject-matter and purpose of the inspection and to record the answers."

Article 21(1) empowers EU officials to inspect by decision "any other premises," including employees' homes and cars, provided that the Commission has a reasonable suspicion that books or other records are likely to be found there. As noted earlier, pursuant to Article 21(3), such searches can only be carried out pursuant to a warrant from the national court concerned.

Before initiating the inspection, the EU officials must present to the addressee a copy of the inspection decision setting forth the subject matter and purpose of the inspection and the penalties for non-compliance.[29]

The powers of Chinese and EU inspectors are broadly similar. In both jurisdictions, business and private premises may be searched; the addressee's employees may be required to answer any questions relating to the subject matter of the inspection; and books and records may be examined and copied—and this applies to electronically stored documents and data. And in both jurisdictions, the penalty for refusal to cooperate is a fine, rather than jail time.

It should be expected, given the periodic workshops and dialogues attended by Chinese and EU officials, that the NDRC and SAIC are on their way to becoming (or are already) fully capable of carrying out the kind of invasive electronic searches that are becoming commonplace in the EU. For example, the Chinese authorities undoubtedly know that the if at the end of its inspection, the Commission has not finished its

27 See discussion in Nicolas Kahn and Christopher Kerse, EU Antitrust Procedure, 3-106-3-109 (2012). See also Imran Aslam & Michael Ramsden, *EC Dawn Raids: A Human Rights Violation?*, The Competition Law Review, Vol. 5, Issue 1, 61-87 (2008).

28 Antimonopoly Law of the People's Republic of China, August 30, 2007, at article 40.

29 TFEU, *supra* note 19, at article 297. See also Reg 1/2003, *supra* note 9, at articles 20(4) and 21(2). However, decisions ordering the inspection of private premises are not subject to a Commission fine for non-compliance.

cull of the relevant evidence, it considers it within its search powers to continue its examination of the copied data on the Commission's premises.[30]

Given the recent flurry of press regarding allegedly intrusive Chinese dawn raids against Western companies, let us review the current state of play in both systems as to the basic procedural safeguards existing under EU law.

1. Privilege Against Self-Incrimination

Under the AML, there is no privilege against self-incrimination as long as the investigation remains administrative in character. Rather, pursuant to the Chinese Administrative Punishment Law, companies must honestly and correctly answer questions put to them during the course of a dawn raid. However, Article 52 provides that if a crime is committed by the addressee in the course of a dawn raid, the company may face criminal prosecution. In these instances, the Chinese Criminal Procedural Law would provide a privilege against self-incrimination.

In the EU, there is such a privilege, but its application is so narrowly restricted in the context of dawn raids that it means virtually nothing—the privilege only applies where the answer to a Commission question amounts to an admission of liability.[31] Otherwise, an addressee may be fined for failing to provide a complete answer to a question, or for providing an incorrect or misleading answer.[32]

2. Right to Counsel

Under the AML, there is no right to have counsel present during a dawn raid. However, current practice suggests that NDRC and SAIC officials may be willing to wait a short while for the arrival of counsel before carrying out an inspection. In the EU, there is a curious paradox: the EU Courts have enshrined the right to counsel present during a dawn raid, but as the result of the 2012 judgment of the General Court in *KVWS*,[33] the presence of an internal or external lawyer is not a precondition to the validity of the inspection. In that judgment, the General Court said the addressee can always "request the advice of a lawyer by telephone. [...]"[34] Indeed, the Commission's concern as to the potential destruction of evidence is so strong that officials are now saying that they are prepared to wait for "about 15 to 30 minutes" for counsel to arrive.[35] In many instances, this is simply not enough time for external counsel to arrive at the company premises. Thus, while the right to counsel exists under EU law, its scope is actually quite limited.

---

30 See Explanatory Note to an Authorisation to Conduct an Inspection in Execution of a Commission Decision Under Article 20(4) of Council Regulation No. 1/3, revised on 18 March, 2013, at point 14, available athttp://ec.europa.eu/competition/antitrust/legislation/explanatory_note.pdf. The legality of this power is now the subject of a pending appeal by Prysmian from the Commission's final decision in Power Cables. See Case T-475/14, Prysmian and Prysmian Cavi e Sistemi v. Comm'n, 2014, O.J. (C315/68).

31 See e.g., Case 374/87, Orkem v. Comm'n, 1989, ECR 3283.

32 Reg. 1/2003, supra note 9, at article 23(1)(d).

33 See Case T-357/06, Koninklijke Wegenbouw Stevin BV ("KVWS") v. Comm'n, 2012, at para. 232. Prior to KVWS, in Case 139/79, National Panasonic v. Comm'n, 1980, ECR 2033, the Advocate General opined that a lawyer's presence is not a precondition to the validity of a dawn raid, a position which obiter in terms of the issues before Court. In that case, the Court held that the addressee of a raid had no right to know in advance of the inspection decision. However, the Commission had already come to the same conclusion as the Advocate General, in its first Explanatory Note regarding the conduct of inspections, which was published in 2008.

34 Case T-357/06, KVWS v. Commission, at para. 232.

35 See Jonathan Faull and Ali Nikpay, The EU Law of Competition, at para. 8.379 (2014).

3. Lawyer-Client Privilege

Under the AML, as an analogue to the fact that there is no right to counsel, there is no lawyer-client privilege, whereas in the EU, this privilege is considered a fundamental right. Before electronic searches became the norm, and the Commission examined and made copies of paper documents, the Commission's "sealed envelope" procedure was resorted to by addressees when even a cursory look at a particular document by inspectors (ideally in the addressee's presence) could not determine whether the document was protected by lawyer-client privilege. By this procedure, which was endorsed by the General Court in *Akzo Nobel*,[36] when a cursory look couldn't resolve the issue, the Commission would place the disputed document into a sealed envelope, which is then tendered to the Hearing Officer for his recommendation as to whether the Commission should adopt an Article 20(4) decision confirming that the document concerned is not privileged.[37] The addressee would then have an opportunity to challenge this decision in the General Court and request interim measures.[38] The Commission has confirmed that it would not open the sealed envelope until the Court of Justice has ruled on the Commission decision.[39]

However, with the Commission moving inexorably to paperless inspections by which documents are searched electronically, there is the risk that the lawyer-client privilege will be eroded. This is due mainly to several factors: first, Commission officials will use IT forensic software and hardware during the search, and deploy keyword search tools to search for relevant evidence, after having copied the data onto their own computers brought to the addressee's premises. There may be very little opportunity during this process for the addressee to assert privilege on any individual documents that are tagged during this search. Second, as already noted, the Commission may decide to bring its copied data back to the Commission's premises for further search. Moreover, the Commission internal guidelines for dawn raids do not grant companies a clear right to attend the follow-up IT search on Commission premises.[40]

The Commission's internal guidelines for the conduct of inspections do not explain how lawyer-client privilege may be effectively asserted and protected during the IT searches. And it is unclear how a judicial challenge or a company's antitrust compliance program[41] may resolve these issues.

---

36 See Joined cases T-125/03R and T-253/03R, Akzo Nobel Chemicals Ltd and Ackros Chemicals Ltd v. Comm'n, 2003, ECR 11-4771, at paras. 84, 96 and 138.

37 Decision of the President of the European Commission on the Function of the Hearing Officer in Certain Competition Proceedings, 13 October, O.J. (L275/29), at article 4(2)(a) *available at* http://eurlex.europa.eu/LexUriServ/LexUriServ.do?uri=OJ:L:2011:275:0029:0037:EN:PDF.

38 Cases T-125/03 R and T-253/03, *supra* note 35, at paras. 81-85.

39 Commission Notice on Best Practices for the Conduct of Proceedings Concerning Articles 101 and 102 TEFU, 20 October, 2011, O.J. (C308/6), at point 54.

40 As stated in Point 14 of the Explanatory Note, *supra* note 29, the data still to be searched on Commission premises would be placed in a sealed envelope with a copy given to the addressee. The Commission "commits to return the sealed envelope to the undertaking *or* to invite the undertaking to attend the opening of the sealed envelope at the Commission premises and assist in the continued selection process." (emphasis added).

41 To preserve their rights, it may be necessary for companies, as part of their compliance programs, to ensure that all privileged documents are stored electronically in a defined location, to clearly mark these folders as privileged, and to be prepared to instruct inspectors that these files are not to be searched electronically. However, these measures may offer scant protection if the documents are recoverable from servers and hard-drives by use of search terms.

IV. Conclusion

Perhaps unwittingly, Western media has been demonizing recent Chinese antitrust enforcement activity and, in particular, dawn raids. These condemnations only relate to investigations of large Western companies. No attention has been paid to the eventuality that the same procedures (or "unfair tactics") might also be deployed against Chinese companies. The press reports also seem uninterested in whether the Western companies concerned might have indeed engaged in the alleged anti-competitive behavior in China, or the fact that some of these companies have already been investigated recently by other antitrust authorities in other jurisdictions for engaging in the same or similar behavior. There is at least the possibility that Western companies may have downplayed the risks of Chinese antitrust enforcement (like other areas of regulatory enforcement) because it was considered lax or immature.

As regards the insinuation that Chinese antitrust enforcers are discriminating against Western companies as part of a wider protectionist strategy, there is no obligation on the NDRC or SAIC to publicly divulge all of its investigation activities—any more than the disclosures that European Commission and other authorities must make. In spite of the normally cautious disclosures of advanced authorities, Chinese Premier Li Keqiang recently stated publicly that only 10% of the current Chinese investigations involve Western companies. Yet, it would not seem that this admission has been taken seriously. Hopefully, the Western media and interest groups will not claim that the NDRC and SAIC have a duty to disclose all companies now being investigated to show the world that they are not discriminating against Western firms—or to end their alleged discrimination by investigating a lot more Chinese companies. One may even imagine the Chinese agencies being asked to disregard their own "enforcement priorities," even though in practice many antitrust agencies, but particularly those of the US and EU, are jealously independent in establishing and implementing their own enforcement priorities.

Finally, global companies would probably concede that dawn raids are intrusive regardless of the jurisdiction in which they are carried out. Even within a single jurisdiction and in the same case, some searches are more heavy-handed than others. Arguably, China is being singled out because it is a relatively new entrant on the world antitrust stage that happens to have the second largest economy. But Western media and interest groups need to know that there are glass antitrust houses everywhere and that throwing stones at China's antitrust enforcement may turn out to be counterproductive.

Merger Remedies of China's Ministry of Commerce[1]

ELIZABETH XIAO-RU WANG

ewang@crai.com

Principal, Charles River Associates

YONG HUANG

huangyong1962@vip.sina.com

Director, Economic Law Department,
University of International Business & Economics (UIBE)

Abstract

Merger remedies imposed by China's merger review agency, the Ministry of Commerce ("MOFCOM"), have received considerable attention in the antitrust community around the world. Among the over 1,000 mergers and acquisitions reviewed by MOFCOM since China's enactment of Antimonopoly Law, it rejected two proposed mergers and approved 24 transactions with conditions, a statistic largely consistent with international norm. The primary feature that sets MOFCOM apart from other competition agencies is its significantly heavier reliance on behavioral remedies. In addition to traditional conduct provisions, MOFCOM has developed a number of behavioral remedies, not typically seen in other jurisdictions, including prohibition from engaging in certain lines of business, continuation of pre-merger practices, hold separate, and interventions on business decisions such as price, quantity, R&D, licensing practices, or contract terms. Furthermore, MOFCOM frequently imposed behavioral remedies not only for vertical mergers, but also for horizontal and conglomerate mergers.

---

1 The views expressed herein are the views and opinions solely of the authors and do not reflect or represent the views of Charles River Associates, the UIBE, or any of the organizations with which the authors are affiliated. This paper builds upon and updates an earlier version of an article by Elizabeth Wang and her co-authors published at CPI Antitrust Chronicle in August 2013 titled "Merger Remedies with Chinese Characteristics."

I. Introduction

Merger remedies imposed by China's merger review agency, the Ministry of Commerce ("MOFCOM"), have received considerable attention in the antitrust community around the world. A number of transactions have involved cross-border mergers in which the Chinese agency imposed conditions while the US or EU regulators approved the same transaction without remedial actions.

When a merger is determined to have anticompetitive effects, competition agencies may choose to approve the merger contingent upon conditions to preserve competition rather than blocking the transaction entirely. These conditions are often referred to as merger remedies. Among the over 1,000 mergers and acquisitions reviewed by MOFCOM as of June 2015, it rejected two proposed mergers and approved 24 transactions with conditions, while approving the remaining 97 percent of the transactions without conditions. These approval rate statistics are largely consistent with those in major jurisdictions like the US and EU.

In general, merger remedies can be classified into two broad categories: structural remedies and behavioral remedies. Structural remedies are aimed at preserving competition by requiring the merged firm to divest certain assets, whether physical or intangible, to a new or existing competitor. Behavioral remedies, as the name suggests, regulate certain future behaviors of the merged firm. A hybrid approach consisting of a combination of structural and behavioral remedies may also be used to prevent harm to competition.

In this article, we analyze the remedies imposed by MOFCOM in the 24 transactions approved with conditions as of June 2015. Table 1 lists the transactions in which MOFCOM has intervened since China's enactment of its Anti-Monopoly Law ("AML") in August 2008.[2] The chart below shows that of the 24 transactions MOFCOM approved with conditions, 15 (62%) involved behavioral remedies, 4 (17%) involved structural remedies, and 5 (21%) involved a combination of structural and behavioral remedies.

The article is organized as follows: Section II looks at MOFCOM's use of behavioral remedies; Section III reviews its use of structural remedies; and Section IV examines hybrid remedies. Section V shares our observations about the unique aspects of MOFCOM's merger remedies.

2 Anti-monopoly law of the People's Republic of China, August 2008 *available* at http://english.mofcom.gov.cn/article/policyrelease/Businessregulations/201303/20130300045909.shtml.

Table 1. MOFCOM Interventions

Case No.	Date of Decision	Transaction	Merger Type	Remedy Type
[1]	11/18/2008	InBev/Anheuser-Busch	Horizontal	Behavioral
[2]	03/18/2009	Coca-Cola/Huiyuan	Conglomerate	NA - Deal Blocked
[3]	04/24/2009	Mitsubishi Rayon/Lucite	Horizontal & Vertical	Hybrid
[4]	09/28/2009	General Motors/Delphi	Vertical	Behavioral
[5]	09/29/2009	Pfizer/Wyeth	Horizontal	Structural
[6]	10/30/2009	Panasonic/Sanyo	Horizontal	Structural
[7]	08/13/2010	Novartis/Alcon	Horizontal	Behavioral
[8]	06/02/2011	Uralkali/Silvinit	Horizontal	Behavioral
[9]	10/31/2011	Alpha V/Savio	Horizontal	Structural
[10]	11/10/2011	GE/Shenhua JV	Vertical	Behavioral
[11]	12/12/2011	Seagate/Samsung's HDD Business	Horizontal	Behavioral
[12]	02/10/2012	Henkel Hong Kong/Tiande JV	Vertical	Behavioral
[13]	03/02/2012	Western Digital/Hitachi	Horizontal	Hybrid
[14]	05/19/2012	Google/Motorola Mobility	Vertical	Behavioral
[15]	06/15/2012	United Technologies Corp/ Goodrich	Horizontal	Structural
[16]	08/14/2012	Wal-Mart/Yihaodian	Conglomerate	Behavioral
[17]	12/06/2012	ARM/Gemalto/Giesecke & Devrient JV	Vertical	Behavioral
[18]	04/16/2013	Glencore International/Xstrata	Horizontal & Vertical	Hybrid
[19]	04/23/2013	Marubeni/Gavilon	Horizontal	Behavioral
[20]	08/08/2013	Baxter/Gambro	Horizontal	Hybrid
[21]	08/26/2013	Media Tek/Mstar Cayman	Horizontal	Behavioral
[22]	01/14/2014	Thermo Fisher/Life Technologies	Horizontal	Hybrid
[23]	04/08/2014	Microsoft/Nokia	Vertical	Behavioral
[24]	04/30/2014	Merck/AZ	Conglomerate	Behavioral
[25]	06/17/2014	Maersk/MSC/CMA CGM	Horizontal	NA-Deal Blocked
[26]	07/02/2014	Corun/Toyota China/PEVE/ Sinogy/Toyota Tsusho	Vertical	Behavioral

Source: Announcements from Anti-Monopoly Bureau, MOFCOM, available at http://fldj.mofcom.gov.cn/article/ztxx/

II. Behavioral Remedies

MOFCOM appears to prefer behavioral remedies over structural ones to address the potential anticompetitive concerns raised by a merger. It imposed behavioral remedies in 15 out of the 24 transactions MOFCOM approved with conditions.

Behavioral remedies are particularly effective in vertical mergers where the merger may raise antitrust concerns by eliminating a key supplier or customer, or by changing the merged entity's incentives towards its upstream suppliers or downstream customers. Behavioral remedies can take a wide variety of forms depending on the individual circumstances of the transaction and the conditions of the marketplace in which the merging firms operate. The following six categories of behavioral remedies have been used by competition agencies such as the US Department of Justice:[3] (1) firewall provisions that prohibit sharing competitively sensitive information within the merged firm; (2) non-discriminatory provisions that prohibit the merged firm from favoring its own acquired firm and disadvantaging its competitors; (3) transparency provisions that require the merged firm to make certain information available to a regulatory authority; (4) mandatory licensing provisions; (5) anti-retaliation provisions (e.g., barring the merged firm from retaliating against customers who enter into contracts with the merged firm's competitors); and (6) prohibition of certain restrictive contracting practices.

Several MOFCOM behavioral remedies follow the international norm and have been imposed to maintain competition following vertical mergers. For example, in its *General Motors/Delphi* decision in September 2009,[4] MOFCOM found that General Motors and Delphi both had leading positions in the auto and auto parts markets, respectively. In particular, Delphi was the sole supplier of auto parts to many Chinese automakers. MOFCOM determined that this vertical merger could reduce competition in both the auto and auto parts markets in China. It required the post-merger Delphi to continue to supply other automakers on a non-discriminatory basis and the post-merger GM to purchase auto parts from multiple sources, without unreasonably favoring Delphi over its competitors. In addition, MOFCOM required that both GM and Delphi could not disclose to one another any trade secrets or other proprietary information obtained from other Chinese automakers.

In addition to traditional conduct provisions, MOFCOM has also developed a number of behavioral remedies, not typically seen in other jurisdictions, to address anticompetitive concerns in both vertical as well as horizontal mergers. The key categories of these remedies include:

1) *Prohibition from engaging in certain lines of business*: For example, in its Wal-Mart/Yihaodian decision in August 2012,[5] MOFCOM observed that Wal-Mart is a world-leading brick-and-mortar retailer with strong brand recognition among Chinese consumers, and Newheight owns Yihaodian, the largest online retailer in China. MOFCOM prohibited Newheight from hosting third-party transactions on its e-commerce platform and prohibited Wal-Mart from online payment processing on its branded website under Yihaodian's license. Another example is in the transaction of

---

3 See US Department of Justice Antitrust Division, Antitrust Division Policy Guide to Merger Remedies, June 2011, para. II.B, *available at* http://www.justice.gov/atr/public/guidelines/272350.pdf.

4 See MOFCOM, Decision clearing the General Motors/Delphi Car Parts acquisition with conditions, September 28, 2009, *available at* http://fldj.mofcom.gov.cn/aarticle/ztxx/200909/20090906540211.html.

5 See MOFCOM, Decision clearing the Wal-Mart/Yihaodian acquisition with conditions, August 14, 2012, *available at* http://fldj.mofcom.gov.cn/article/ztxx/201303/20130300058730.shtml.

Mitsubishi *Rayon/Lucite* in April 2009,[6] in which MOFCOM prohibited Mitsubishi from any further acquisition or any new factory constructions in the relevant markets (methyl methacrylate, specialty methacrylates, polymethyl methacrylate particles and plates) in China within five years.

2) *Continuation of pre-merger practices*: For example, in its Uralkali/Silvinit decision in June 2011,[7] MOFCOM found that the merger between two Russian fertilizer companies would limit competition in the Chinese potassium chloride market. To mitigate the harm to competition, it required the merged firm to maintain pre-merger sales practices and procedures, supply a full range of products in sufficient quantities and continue its pre-merger negotiation processes. Also, in the *Google/Motorola Mobility* decision in May 2012,[8] MOFCOM conditioned its approval on commitments by Google to continue its practice of licensing its Android operating system at no cost on an open source basis and to maintain Motorola's commitments to license its Standard-Essential Patents ("SEPs") on Fair, Reasonable, and Non-discriminatory ("FRAND") terms, among others.

3) *Operation as separate entities, also known as "hold separate"*: By applying the "hold separate" conditions for a prolonged period of time, MOFCOM appears to aim to preserve the competitor that might have been lost in a horizontal merger. For example, in its *Marubeni/Gavilon* decision in April 2013,[9] MOFCOM determined the merger between Marubeni (one of Japan's largest trading companies) and Gavilon (the third-largest North American grain company) would materially increase the merged firm's control of China's soybean imports market and reduce the bargaining power of the downstream Chinese soybean crushing manufacturers. To mitigate the competitive harm of this proposed merger, MOFCOM essentially requested that the parties continue to operate as two separate companies in their exporting of soybeans to China for at least two years after completion of the merger. To assure separate and independent exports to China, the merged entity was required to establish two subsidiaries and to set up firewalls between them.

4) *Interventions on business decisions such as price, quantity, R&D, licensing practices, or contract terms*: For example, in its *Henkel Hong Kong/Tiande* joint venture decision in February 2012,[10] MOFCOM determined that the proposed joint venture would limit competition in the downstream cyanoacrylate monomer market. To reduce the competitive harm to the downstream markets, MOFCOM imposed a number of conditions including requiring Tiande to supply all downstream customers on fair, reasonable and non-discriminatory terms and not to favor its joint venture. In particular, MOFCOM prohibited Tiande from charging "excessive" prices or offering better supply terms to its joint venture. Also, in the Microsoft/Nokia decision in April 2014,[11] MOFCOM imposed a number of conditions on both Microsoft and Nokia. Microsoft is required, among other terms, to continue to license its SEPs on FRAND terms, to continue to grant non-exclusive licenses

---

6 See MOFCOM, Decision clearing the Mitsubishi Rayon/Lucite acquisition with conditions, April 24, 2009, *available at* http://fldj.mofcom.gov.cn/aarticle/ztxx/200904/20090406198805.html.

7 See MOFCOM, Decision clearing the Uralkali/Silvinit acquisition with conditions, June 2, 2011, *available at* http://fldj.mofcom.gov.cn/article/ztxx/201106/20110607583288.shtml.

8 See MOFCOM, Decision clearing the Google/Motorola Mobility acquisition with conditions, May 19, 2012, *available at* http://fldj.mofcom.gov.cn/article/ztxx/201205/20120508134324.shtml; announcement of the decision available at http://english.mofcom.gov.cn/article/policyrelease/domesticpolicy/201206/20120608199125.shtml.

9 See MOFCOM, Decision clearing the Marubeni/Gavilon acquisition with conditions, April 22, 2013, *available at* http://fldj.mofcom.gov.cn/article/ztxx/201304/20130400100376.shtml.

10 See MOFCOM, Decision clearing the Henkel/Tiande joint venture with conditions, February, 9, 2012, *available at* http://fldj.mofcom.gov.cn/article/ztxx/201202/20120207960466.shtml; announcement *available at* http://english.mofcom.gov.cn/article/policyrelease/domesticpolicy/201203/20120308033072.shtml.

11 See MOFCOM, Decision clearing Microsoft's acquisition of Nokia devices and services business with conditions, April 8, 2014, *available at* http://fldj.mofcom.gov.cn/article/ztxx/201404/20140400542415.shtml.

to its non-SEPs to Chinese manufacturers under the same terms it had previously been offering them, not to seek injunctions or exclusion orders against Chinese-produced smart phones that read on Microsoft's SEPs, or to seek injunctions against potential non-SEP licensees unless they failed to negotiate in good faith. Nokia, in turn, is required to continue to honor its FRAND commitments with respect to its SEPs.

Table 2 below lists the types of behavioral remedies employed in each transaction in which MOFCOM imposed one or more such remedies over the last six years.

Table 2. Types of Behavioral Intervention Used by MOFCOM

		Commonly Used Remedies				Less Commonly Used Remedies			
Date of Decision	Transaction	Firewall	Non-discriminatory	Mandatory licensing/ grant access	Prohibit restrictive contracting	Intervention on price, quantity, or R&D	Hold separate	Continue pre-merger practices	Prohibit engaging in certain businesses
11/18/2008	InBev/Anheuser- Busch								x
04/24/2009	Mitsubishi Rayon/Lucite								x
09/28/2009	General Motors/Delphi	x	x						
08/13/2010	Novartis/Alcon				x				x
06/20/2011	Uralkali/Silvinit					x		x	
11/10/2011	GE/Shenhua JV		x	x		x			
12/12/2011	Seagate/Samsung's HDD Business	x			x	x	x		
02/10/2012	Henkel Hong Kong/Tiande JV	x	x			x			
03/02/2012	Western Digital/Hitachi	x				x	x	x	
05/19/2012	Google/Motorola Nobility		x	x				x	
08/14/2012	Wal-Mart/Yihaodian								x
12/06/2012	ARM/Gemalto/Giesecke & Devrient JV		x						
04/16/2013	Glencore Internatioanl/ Xstrata					x		x	
04/23/2013	Marubeni/Gavilon	x					x		
08/08/2013	Baxter/Gambro								x
08/26/2013	Media Tek/Mstar Cayman	x					x		x
01/14/2014	Thermo Fisher/Life Technologies			x		x			
04/08/2014	Microsoft/Nokia		x	x				x	
04/30/2014	Merck/AZ		x		x				
07/02/2014	Corun/Toyota China/PEVE/ Sinogy/Toyota Tsusho					x			

Source: Announcements from Anti-Monopoly Bureau, MOFCOM, available at http://fldj.mofcom.gov.cn/article/ztxx/

III. Structural Remedies

Mergers and acquisitions between rivals, known as horizontal mergers, can reduce competition by eliminating a competitor. Structural remedies aim to preserve competition by divesting assets sufficient to enable a new competitor, or possibly an already existing rival of the merging firms, to maintain the pre-merger level of competition.[12] Therefore, structural remedies can be an effective method to preserve competition that would be lost as a result of the horizontal merger.

Structural remedies generally involve a reduction of equity holdings or a divestiture of assets, and have the advantage of not requiring ongoing monitoring and policing by the competition agency or by courts. Structural remedies are predominant in many major competition jurisdictions. However, only 4 of the 24 cases approved with conditions in China (17%) involved structural remedies exclusively: the *Pfizer/Wyeth* transaction in September 2009,[13] the *Panasonic/Sanyo* transaction in October 2009,[14] *Alpha V/Savio* in October 2011[15] and the *United Technologies Corp/Goodrich* transaction in June 2012.[16] All of these are horizontal mergers where MOFCOM found significant anticompetitive harm.

When divestitures are required, MOFCOM typically allows the merged firm six months to complete the sale of the specified assets to an independent third-party. Parties can request a six-month extension with an appropriate justification. The timing of divestitures appears to be largely similar to that typically required by competition authorities in other jurisdictions such as the US.

Similar to the standard practices in other jurisdictions, MOFCOM requires that a to-be-divested entity operate independently of the merging partner until it is sold to a new owner. Moreover, the independently operated business is typically managed by a trustee. In some cases, the merged firm is required to provide technical support and training to the buyer for a fixed amount of time, varying between one year (e.g., *United Technologies Corp/Goodrich*) and three years (e.g., *Pfizer/Wyeth*). Finally, the merged firms are prohibited from sharing business-sensitive information with each other before the divestiture is finalized.

IV. Hybrid Remedies

To date, MOFCOM has utilized a combination of structural and behavioral remedies (hybrid remedies) in five of the transactions it conditionally approved. The remedies in those cases are particularly complex and detailed. For example, in its *Western Digital/Hitachi* decision in March 2012,[17] MOFCOM stated that the elimination of an important competitor would reduce competition in the Hard Disk Drive ("HDD")

---

12 The differences between structural and behavioral remedies may be quite blurred in some situations. In this article, we define structural remedies to include all the conditions aimed to limit the merged firm's access to assets, including forced divestiture of assets and requirements that the firm reduce its equity stake in another firm.

13 See MOFCOM, Decision clearing the Pfizer/Wyeth acquisition with conditions, September 28, 2009, *available at* http://fldj.mofcom.gov.cn/aarticle/ztxx/200909/20090906541443.html.

14 See MOFCOM, Decision clearing the Panasonic/Sanyo acquisition with conditions, October 30, 2009, *available at* http://fldj.mofcom.gov.cn/aarticle/zcfb/200910/20091006593175.html.

15 See MOFCOM, Decision clearing the Alpha V/Savio acquisition with conditions, October 31, 2011, *available at* http://fldj.mofcom.gov.cn/aarticle/zcfb/201111/20111107809156.html.

16 See MOFCOM, Decision clearing the United Technologies/Goodrich acquisition with conditions, June 15, 2002, *available at* http://fldj.mofcom.gov.cn/article/ztxx/201206/20120608181083.shtml.

17 See MOFCOM, Decision clearing the Western Digital/Hitachi acquisition with conditions, March 2, 2012, *available at* http://fldj.mofcom.gov.cn/article/ztxx/201203/20120307993758.shtml.

market and increase the likelihood of coordination among the remaining HDD suppliers. The key requirements of MOFCOM's remedies included: Hitachi's HDD business shall be operated as an independent competitor with firewalls between Western Digital and Hitachi's HDD teams; Western Digital and Hitachi shall reasonably determine capacity and output based on market demands; Western Digital and Hitachi shall not materially change their current business practices; Western Digital and Hitachi shall maintain the momentum of R&D investment of recent years; and, lastly, Western Digital shall divest Hitachi's 3.5-inch HDD production assets after certain other conditions are met. Of these remedies, the first four are behavioral, while the last one is structural.

In its *Thermo Fisher/Life Technologies* decision in January 2014,[18] MOFCOM found the proposed merger would restrict competition in nine products covering three broad areas, namely cellular and molecular biology, protein biology and cell culture technologies. MOFCOM's structural remedies include requiring Thermo Fisher to divest its global cell culture business line and global gene modulation business, as well as to sell its 51% shareholding in China's Lanzhou Minhai Bioengineering. MOFCOM also imposed behavioral remedies requesting Thermo Fisher to "annually reduce its catalogue price for SSP reagent kits and SDS-PAGE products without reducing discounts given to Chinese distributers; and either provide third parties with SSP reagent kits and SDS-PAGE products by means of an OEM agreement, or offer the third parties perpetual, non-exclusive technology permits for the production of these products (according to the preference of each third party)."[19]

V. The Unique Aspects of China's Merger Remedies

The primary feature that sets MOFCOM apart from other competition agencies is its significantly heavier reliance on behavioral remedies. For a large majority of the transactions that were conditionally approved in the last seven years, MOFCOM imposed some type of behavioral remedy, several of which are highly extensive and restrictive. In contrast, behavioral remedies have been relatively uncommon in other major jurisdictions while the structural remedies are the preferred method to mitigate antitrust risks for proposed mergers.[20]

MOFCOM's heavier reliance on behavioral remedies could be rooted in part in the unique aspects of China's transitional phase from a planned economy to a market economy. For decades, Chinese companies looked to various government administrative agencies to determine what products to produce, how much to produce, and at what prices to sell them for, among other things. As a result, it may be challenging for Chinese regulators to appreciate that, in general, markets rather than regulators are more efficient in allocating the economy's scarce resources during this transition period. Another relevant factor is that

18 See MOFCOM Decision clearing the Thermo Fisher/Life Technologies acquisition with conditions, January 14, 2014, *available at* http://fldj.mofcom.gov.cn/article/ztxx/201401/20140100461603.shtml.

19 Id.

20 For example, the FTC's study of divestiture in 1999 states that "divestitures have continued to be the most common remedy in merger orders" page 3 *available at* http://www.ftc.gov/sites/default/files/attachments/merger-review/divestiture.pdf; UK Competition Commission ("CC") Merger Remedies: Competition Commission Guidelines (Nov. 2008) state that "[i]n merger inquiries, the CC will generally prefer structural remedies, such as divestiture or prohibition, rather than behavioral remedies [...]." pages 14-15 *available at* https://www.gov.uk/government/uploads/system/uploads/attachment_data/file/284415/cc8.pdf. See also Sergio Sorinas, Christine Jorns, *European Union: EU Merger Remedies*, October 1, 2009, *available at* http://www.iflr.com/Article/2324298/European-Union-EU-merger-remedies.html.

AML states that China's merger review shall consider "the effect of the proposed transaction on the development of the national economy,"[21] which may allow MOFCOM to go beyond the traditional competition analysis in its merger review. There is no clear guidance on the extent to which the development of the national economy should be weighted in AML and its related enforcements. As a result, the lines between the function of merger review and other government regulation regarding direct regulation of a firm's conduct are not as clear based on MOFCOM's merger remedies.

Not only has the frequency of imposing behavioral remedies been relatively high in China, but how those remedies were imposed has also been different than other jurisdictions. In particular, MOFCOM frequently imposed behavioral remedies not only for vertical mergers, but also for horizontal and conglomerate mergers. Among the transactions with purely behavioral remedies, approximately half are not vertical mergers.

Structural remedies are an appropriate way to preserve competition in transactions where anticompetitive effects are likely if, and only if, there is a good candidate for the divestiture of the assets causing competitive concerns. A good candidate is a firm or a business that has the experience and skills necessary to restore the pre-merger level of competition in the relevant market. Absent a good candidate for divestiture, structural remedies might not be an option, or may not effectively preserve competition.

Behavioral remedies are generally considered less desirable than structural ones because they require competition agencies (and potentially, courts) to monitor the ongoing behavior of the merged firm. Such activity is costly and if done incorrectly may even create economic inefficiencies. The appropriate option will differ from case to case and will depend on weighing the merger's potential competitive harm, potential efficiencies and the expected effects of the behavioral remedies being considered.

In China's distinct economic and legal environment, it is sometimes impossible to implement structural remedies. In transactions where structural remedies may not be an option, MOFCOM appears to believe that allowing a merger with behavioral conditions to restore competition is generally preferable to blocking a proposed transaction outright. In such situations, one should also evaluate whether the provisions are likely to achieve the intended effects, whether the provisions would result in inefficiencies and how the likely effect on consumer welfare under this approach compares to that under other enforcement options, such as blocking the transaction entirely or approving the transaction without conditions.[22]

Despite these concerns, MOFCOM's March 2013 draft regulation on merger remedies focuses on structural remedies and offers little guidance on the implementation and use of behavioral remedies. We hope that, moving forward, we will see more examples and guidelines specifically regarding behavioral remedies.

---

21 See MOFCOM, Anti-Monopoly Law of the People's Republic of China effective August 1, 2008, section 27(5), *available at* http://fldj.mofcom.gov.cn/article/c/200811/20081105917420.shtml.

22 See Kenneth Heyer, *Optimal Remedies for Anticompetitive Mergers*, Antitrust, Spring 2012, 26(2).

Competition Commission of India: Market Activism, Competition and Development of Markets in India

Geeta Gouri[1]

gouri.geeta@gmail.com

Former Member, Competition Commission of India

Abstract

Competition authorities in their nascent years invariably display market activism in an effort perceived to promote competition. The Competition Commission of India (CCI) is no exception prompting the query: has competitive vigor of the market maintained while limiting unilateral conduct? The paper is a response to this concern. In seeking an answer, the paper traces the process and perceptions in judgments of the Commission pertaining to complex high profile cases of unilateral conduct (stock markets, real estate, virtual markets, automotive). Analysis of market definition and abuse in these decisions on hindsight, suggests that market activism was not merited leaving instead scope for 'Type I' error or "false positive". Legalese interpretation of the market an overhang of the historical anti-monopoly legacy as against a nuanced economic analysis tends to provoke market activism and in so doing blurs the lines between competition and competitive vigor. In appreciating market dynamics and prevalence of competitive constraints the author observes that divergent perceptions lend persuasion towards understanding and appreciating markets. It also underscores the importance of Minority Orders in posing the counterfactual so critical for the maturing of competition authorities

---

1 The author would like to thank her colleagues in the Commission and young competition lawyers for the discussions and debates they have had with her and continue to have, which strengthens the author's conviction that vigor of competitive markets emanates from openness and transparency. The views expressed are personal. The author expresses her gratitude for the help voluntarily offered by Naval, Dinoo and John (Amarchand & Mangaldas) in the tiring job of editing and finding footnotes.

I. Introduction

Competition authorities in their nascent years invariably display market activism in an effort perceived to promote competition. The Competition Commission of India ("Commission"), which was made fully operational on 5 March 2009, is no exception to this general observed trend on market activism. As a market and fair-trade regulator that has been operational for the last five years, the Commission has had over 300 cases in diverse sectors and industries, ranging from stock exchanges, real estate, cement, pharmaceuticals and drugs, State-owned enterprises, hospitals and commodities, involving large multinational enterprises. The cases thus far decided by the Commission cover both antitrust (anti-competitive agreements, including cartels and abuse of dominance) and mergers. Does this market activism by competition authorities in emerging market economies, such as by the Commission, suggest that they are in the process of defining the limits for intervention, in particular, with respect to dominance and its abuse? I am inclined to believe that it is imminently possible provided conditions for differing perceptions on market functioning, for maturing of young commissions, are forthcoming.

The significance of dissenting orders in provoking debate and discourse plays a critical role that can never be underestimated. This belief is not mere wistful optimism of a founding member of the Commission, but based on the understanding that market activism, in the prevailing scenario of market orientation and economic liberalization, does not necessarily ensure competition and market development, which is the primary objective of competition authorities. Markets, with their uncanny knack of shifting contours, leave considerable unease amongst regulators that have been more comfortable with set and defined rules and regulation. Divergent perceptions on market functioning in several high profile cases of the Commission provoke not merely an enquiry into the causes for divergence, but highlight the need for discussion on the more fundamental issue on the role of the State and its intervention in a market-oriented economic policy.

There could be several factors that prompt market activism on the part of the Commission but, primarily, the historical apprehension of monopolies, more so the recent near-monopolies in the private sector, tends to exert considerable influence. Consequently, the Competition Act, 2002 (the Act),[2] framed in legal structures and confined to formalistic rules based on the law, tends to be more supportive of a competition authorities' inclination to intervene in markets much more than the underlying economics of dominance in dynamic markets.

From an economist's point of view, the application of competition law in India is still not fully in sync with the larger market oriented policies ushered in 1991 by the Government of India. Foundations for a mature competition law are predicated by the extent and speed with which rigorous economic analysis, which captures the dynamism of markets, is internalized by competition authorities. Given India's position in the global economy, the rapid transition from a socialist economy, dominated by State-owned enterprises that enjoyed monopolies, to a market oriented economy, having increased competition and the imminent risk of private monopolies or players with significant market power, there is an urgent need to advance the discussion on the role of antitrust intervention by the State. This paper is an attempt to initiate the required discourse on redrawing the avowed boundaries of the market and the State through the prism of the Commission's decisions in cases of "abuse of dominance."

---

2 Competition Act, 2002, as amended by The Competition (Amendment) Act, 2007, available at http://www.cci.gov.in/images/media/competition_act/act2002.pdf?phpMyAdmin=QuqXb-8V2yTtoq617iR6-k2VA8d.

II. Monopoly, Monopolization and Market Activism

In India, there is unease in relation to monopolies and the expectation of abuse of monopoly power, which underlines regulatory market activism and pervades all regulatory bodies and institutions. That such unease tends to linger despite shifts in economic policies towards liberalization and a market oriented economy is not surprising, for change is always difficult to accept, more so when it is against a prevailing ideological conviction. It does, however, suggest that while macro-economic policies are market-oriented, their implementation at the micro-level retains elements of conservatism. Several Indian statutes[3] (with several more in the offing), including the Act, enacted for the implementation of reforms and aimed at a market-oriented economy, reflect the prevailing concern of the State regarding monopoly power. To that end, the regulation of monopolies in pursuit of consumer welfare results in inter alia vigorous market activism.

It may be appropriate at this stage to diverge slightly and take a quick glimpse at the forces that shaped interventions into market functioning. Over the last sixty years, State control and regulation has swung from "control and command" to "regulation," by commissions and other regulatory authorities that are increasingly shaping economic activity.[4] This section is a non-rigorous, but illustrative review of the changing role of the State and the market, as incorporated in economic and industrial policies of the country and in economic laws enacted at every shift in the boundaries of State control over the market place.

1. Economic and Industrial Policies of India

Colonial experience and the prevailing fascination with socialism post-independence gained favor in India, resulting in a strategy of import-substitution with minimal reliance on foreign trade. The unquestioned inevitability of market failures in the mold of socialistic thinking persuaded India to adopt a mixed economy framework (public and private enterprises) as appropriate. "Capacity control and licensing constituted the major planks of industrial policy. Many areas of production were reserved for the State-owned public sector or for small-scale enterprises. As a corollary, the market structures that emerged in most industries were largely an outcome of government policy, not a consequence of free competitive firm interactions" or free market forces. The multitudes of State controlled enterprises lead to fragmented capacity and muted competition. Another corollary was a tight leash on what the private sector could do and where and how it could go about conducting business.[5]

3 Telecom Regulatory Authority of India Act, 1997, available at http://unpan1.un.org/intradoc/groups/public/documents/APCITY/UNPAN025621.pdf; Electricity Act, 2003, available at http://www.cercind.gov.in/08022007/Act-with-amendment.pdf; Insurance Regulatory and Development Authority Act, 1999, available at https://www.irda.gov.in/ADMINCMS/cms/frmGeneral_Layout.aspx?page=PageNo108&flag=1&mid=Insurance%20Laws%20etc.%3E%3EActs. The Securities and Exchange Board of India Act, 1992, available at http://www.sebi.gov.in/acts/act15ac.pdf; Competition Act 2002, *supra* note 1; Petroleum and Natural Gas Regulatory Board Act, 2006, available at www.pngrb.gov.in/draft/807(E)E.pdf.

4 In fact, the present trend in India is aimed at setting up more regulatory authorities in several sectors.

5 See Dr. Geeta Gouri, Making Markets *Work Effectively in India Experience of the Competition Commission*, lecture delivered at the Japan Fair Trade Commission/Competition Policy Research Center International Symposium, Tokyo, Japan, 22 February, 2013, available at http://www.cci.gov.in/images/media/speeches/DrGG.pdf.

In defining the extended role of the State, certain inevitable labyrinths of controls were created, which only grew multi-fold as the Indian economy became more diversified and complex.[6] The starting point was the Industries (Development and Regulation) Act, 1951 ("IDRA Act"),[7] preceded by the Industrial Policy Resolution of 1948.[8] This was followed by the Industrial Policy Resolution of 1956[9], which was considered as the foundation stone of industrial policy in India for nearly forty-five years. The IDRA Act was amended in 1973 and in 1980.[10] The plethora of controls exercised over Indian industry paradoxically resulted in a greater concentration of wealth. The Mahalanobis Committee Report on Distribution of Income and Levels of Living in 1964[11] revealed that the concentration of economic power was over 85 percent in industries and, in response, the first competition law in a developing country, the Monopolies and Restrictive Trade Practices Act ("MRTP Act")[12] was enacted in 1969. The MRTP Act remained in force until its repeal on 1 September 2009, subsequent to the enactment of the Act in 2002.

It was but natural that the dominant thinking, even in academia, during the 50s, 60s and 70s, was one of market apprehension and emphasis on instruments to control monopoly power. A quick survey of economic literature during this period shows that the accepted approach was straight jacketed in terms of efficiency versus equity. It was only by the mid-1980s that scholars started looking at the costs of market sheltered industry and a growing acceptance that states also fail,[13] in the then prevailing Structure-Conduct-Performance ("SCP") paradigm measured by tools of efficiency, such as Total Factor Productivity and Domestic Resource Cost, corroborated by official reports of the Government. Inefficiency of industry and the protected regime brought to the forefront the dimension of State failures vis-à-vis market failure, a hitherto neglected or ignored dimension. The need for competition was asserted, leading to the emergence of India's new economic liberalization policy in 1991. By then, it was well accepted that competition ensured efficiency (operative and allocative) in both the manufacturing and services sector.

Marking a departure from the regime of "command and control," the new industrial policy in 1991 placed reliance on market forces. The so-called "license raj" ended, and protective tariff barriers were brought down. Economic liberalization shifted the divide between private and public enterprises, in favor of a greater role for the private sector through the removal of entry barriers previously erected by the mechanism of licensing. Markets, as the mechanism for resource allocation, replaced licensing. Guided by the objective of improving efficiency, the new policy recognized the need for subjecting Indian industry to the forces of competition and aligning policies accordingly.

Economic liberalization, policies of deregulation and letting markets function, are broad macro policy changes. The ground level intervention of allowing markets to function and, more importantly, to build a body of literature on how they function was left to regulatory commissions. Following the worldwide movement of unbundling the "product from the carriage," the first round at control of monopolies was directed at public utilities in the telecom and electricity (power) sectors to usher in the private sector,

---

6 See Geeta Gouri, Indian Industrial Performance and Policy in Nature, Man and the Indian Economy, at pages 202-229, (ed. Tapas Majumdar) (1993), for an understanding of the forces that necessitated a change in Indian industrial policy towards a more open free-market economy.

7 The Industries (Development and Regulation) Act, 1951, available at http://dipp.nic.in/English/Policies/Industries_act1951.pdf.

8 Industrial Policy Resolution, 1948.

9 Industrial Policy Resolution, 1956, available at http://eaindustry.nic.in/handbk/chap001.pdf.

10 The requirements of funds and allocation of financial resources were also controlled in line with industrial policy, which included taxes, subsidies, administered prices, pricing preferences, interest, capital controls, priority sector lending, saving schemes by individuals and financial institutions, etc.

11 P.C., Mahalanobis, India Committee Report on the Distribution of Income and Levels of Living, 1964.

12 The Monopolies and Restrictive Trade Practices Act, 1969.

13 On privatization, the work by the Institute of Public Enterprise, Hyderabad, was pioneering.

whilst also regulating natural monopoly segments.[14] As ex-ante regulators, the emphasis of these sector regulators was on enforcement rather than on competition, with a marked preference for fixing tariffs and issuing of licenses to permit entry of private players reminiscent of the "command and control" regime.[15] Their respective statutes were framed in the same vein of "command and control."[16]

It was only apposite that the prevailing competition law regime in the country, the structuralist MRTP Act overly concerned with monopoly, had to give way to a new conduct-oriented competition law in alignment with the needs and challenges of the new economic order, but the new competition law was only enacted over a decade later.

2. Competition Law and Policy

The Act was promulgated in 2002 following the Union Budget Speech of 1999, to address the new-market environment in which the State's role was sought to be minimized. The then Finance Minister, Shri Yashwant Sinha, in his speech, clearly drew the lines of difference between the MRTP Act and the need for a new 'competition' law when he said: "We need to shift our focus from curbing monopolies to promoting competition."[17] The MRTP Act was overly concerned with concentration of wealth and monopoly power, laying emphasis on the prohibition of monopolistic unfair and restrictive trade practices. As a predecessor to the Act, the interventions and investigations of the MRTP Commission reflected a rigid and structuralist approach to monopolies and private power.

The differences in the approach in the two competition laws are discernible in their respective preambles. The preamble to the MRTP Act states:

"An Act to provide that the concentration of the economic system does not result in the concentration of the economic power to the common detriment, for the control of monopolies, for the prohibition of monopolistic and restrictive trade practices and for matters connection therewith or incidental thereto."[18]

The preamble to the Act, however, states:

"An Act to provide, keeping in view of the economic development of the country, for the establishment of a Commission to prevent practices having adverse effect on competition, to promote and sustain competition in markets, to protect the interests of consumers and to ensure freedom of trade carried on by other participants in markets, in India, and for matters connected therewith or incidental thereto."[19]

---

14 Liberty has been taken with dates as the intent is on the flavor, with an attempt to be brief and not historical. The Telecom Regulatory Commission was set up in 1998. Reforms in the electricity sector in some Indian states preceded the Electricity Act enacted in 2003.

15 In the electricity sector, retail supply licenses were combined with distribution licenses, enabling regulatory commissions to fix tariffs more often in line with state governments' interest in subsidies and cross-subsidies. Restricted, open access encouraged private generators to sell only to the erstwhile public utility, the distribution companies licensed by regulatory commissions. Utilities with tariffs were fixed by regulatory commissions. In the telecom sector, licenses for network and mobile services were restricted.

16 The emergence of the Competition Commission of India, a predominantly ex-post market regulator, has caused sector regulators to extend their turf by the passing of regulations that govern market size and unilateral effects in their respective sectors. For example, the Telecom Regulatory Authority of India has issued rules and regulations on issues of merger regulation amongst telecom operators. Similarly, the Central Electricity Regulatory Commission has also issued draft Central Electricity Regulatory Commission (Prevention of Adverse Effect on Competition) Regulations, 2012, *available at* http://www.cercind.gov.in/2012/draft_reg/22augdraft-regulations.pdf. The establishment of several more sector regulators are being discussed and are in the offing.

17 See Speech of Shri Yashwant Sinha, Finance Minister, Government of India, 27 February 1999, *available at* www.indiabudget.nic.in/bspeech/bs19992000.pdf.

18 See *supra* note 11, at preamble.

19 See *supra* note 1, at preamble.

The Act, with its focus on economic objectives, defines the role of the Commission as an economic instrument, where dispensation of justice is primarily to promote and sustain competition in markets whilst also protecting the interests of consumers. However, as pointed out by two young competition lawyers, the preamble of the new Act, places more emphasis on the interests of the "common man" than on competitors or the competitive process.[20] Therefore, the onus on the Commission, to protect consumer interest is very heavy. Competition is not defined in the new Act while market power and its abuse leave a vast area for interpretation by the Commission.

The potential for and limits of different interpretations of the Act has caused much discussion on the relevance of economics to competition law. In the debate between law and economics, there are many areas of judgment which are not as clear and obvious, as one would want to believe, on the first reading of the Act. Often a simplistic economic analysis could lead to naive conclusions which defeat the very purpose of the Act and require sharpening of economic tools. The Act is not rigid "*per se*" however, it has been argued that Section 4[21] sets out a *per se* prohibition of an abuse of dominance. Section 4 of the Act states "*No enterprise or group **shall** abuse its dominant position*" (emphasis added). The word "shall," as argued by some legal experts, suggests a per se approach. Such a strict approach would be illogical, irrational and absurd. It would, for example, prevent a dominant enterprise from refusing to supply to a customer who has repeatedly defaulted in payments. Accordingly, the Commission does not believe that a rigid per se approach be applied to unilateral conduct, considers objective justifications and accepts an effect-based approach. Cartels are presumed to be anti-competitive under the provisions of the Act and the burden of rebutting such presumption rests on the alleged cartelizing enterprise.

An effect-based and rule of reason analysis will differ according to the facts and circumstances of each case, in which terms such as "consumer benefits" and "abuse of dominance" may be open to varying interpretations and analytical rigor. As experience now suggests, there are multiple ways to devise rules or criteria for the evaluation of unilateral behavior of firms. A presumption-based approach widens the scope of Type I error (false positives).[22] While the simplicity of per se rules may provide a certain degree of legal certainty, it may deter desirable conduct and adversely affect consumer welfare.

The key challenge stems from the fact that the theories of harm of foreclosure and/or restrictions of competition are often not robust or, even if they are, empirical validation or quantification gets severely constrained due to a host of factors. Following the black letter of the law may not fully meet the ends of ensuring competitive markets. A more nuanced, layered economic analysis at the Commission level may reveal that consumer benefits may not really be as apparent as suggested in the first instance, and a precipitous analysis may risk distorting competition and market functioning.

The underlying understanding is that dominant companies have the potential to distort competition. The Act does not frown on dominance *per se*,[23] but through the provisions of Section 4, imposes a "special responsibility" on a dominant company to ensure that its behavior does not impair undistorted competition.

---

20 See Naval Satarwala Chopra and Dinoo Muthappa, The Curious Case of Compulsory Licensing in India, Competition Law International, Vol. 8 No. 2., August 2012.

21 See supra note 1, at para. 4.

22 A false positive occurs where a competition authority incorrectly holds pro-competitive behavior as abusive. The fear of false positives is that when pro-competitive conduct is erroneously found to contravene antitrust rules, it may result in "chilling competition."

23 Interestingly, in Tata Engineering & Locomotive Co. Ltd., Bombay v. Registrar of the Restrictive Trade Agreement, New Delhi ((1977) 2 SCC 55), the Supreme Court held that the "rule of reason" is to be applied in evaluating certain types of agreements relating to restrictive trade practices, and the subsequent Mahindra & Mahindra Ltd. v. Union of India ((1979) 2 SCC 529) decision referred to various US antitrust judgments. The Raghavan Committee (constituted by the Indian Government to recommend a suitable legislative framework relating to competition law), in this framework, emphasized the importance of the "rule of reason" as against a pure "per se" approach in framing the provisions of the Act.

Section 4 of the Act sets out types of unilateral exclusionary and exploitative conduct which, if engaged in by a dominant enterprise, would be illegal and prohibited.[24] Thus, the types of conduct listed under Section 4 would be otherwise considered legal if engaged in by non-dominant players. Dominance is defined in the Act itself, along with conditions and factors that establish dominance.[25]

Through a strict interpretation of Section 4, it appears that if a dominant enterprise engages in conduct that falls within any of its sub-sections, it is automatically presumed that the dominant enterprise has abused its dominance and that the only exception to this is a "meeting competition" defense to the imposition of unfair and discriminatory conditions or prices, including predatory prices.[26] To a question posed earlier in the day:[27] could the same issues be addressed as "unfair business practices" without having to show dominance? The answer is no.

Before turning to the orders of the Commission on unilateral conduct, we shall look at a few features specific to the Act, only in India, that will help us to appreciate the Commission's readiness to act as a market activist. First, for all issues concerning competition and market abuse, the right of redress lies only with the Commission and not the courts. Once a complaint or "information" is filed alleging anti-competitive activity, no retraction by the informant is permissible. The fee for filing information is low for individuals at INR 5000 (less than $100). Therefore, at a low price, an informant is guaranteed a final decision on whether or not there has been a breach or contravention of the Act.

Second, the Act is agnostic as regards the identity of an informant. Any person(s) can file information under Section 19(1)(a) of the Act. The Commission is bound by the law to initiate an investigation, provided a *prima facie* case of a contravention of the Act exists. Dismissal of a case by the Commission under Section 26(2) of the Act, where the case is not considered as meriting investigation, is appealable to the Competition Appellate Tribunal ("COMPAT"). The private right of action is limited to only filing the information, as once information has been filed, the Commission is mandated to issue an order and a make a decision based on its merits.

Third, under Section 49 of the Act, the Commission is mandated to participate in "competition advocacy."[28] Agnosticism and advocacy incorporated in the Act by legislative intent, have granted legitimacy to a market

---

24 See supra note 1, para. 4 of the Act provides that: "(1) No enterprise or group shall abuse its dominant position.

(2) There shall be an abuse of dominant position under sub-section (1), if an enterprise or a group;

(a) directly or indirectly, imposes unfair or discriminatory—(i) condition in purchase or sale of goods or service; or (ii) price in purchase or sale (including predatory price) of goods or service [...]

(b) limits or restricts—(i) production of goods or provision of services or market therefor; or (ii) technical or scientific development relating to goods or services to the prejudice of consumers; or

(c) indulges in practice or practices resulting in denial of market access [in any manner]; or

(d) makes conclusion of contracts subject to acceptance by other parties of supplementary obligations which, by their nature or according to commercial usage, have no connection with the subject of such contracts; or

(e) uses its dominant position in one relevant market to enter into, or protect, other relevant market."

25 Explanation (a) to para.4 of the Act defines a dominant position as "a position of strength, enjoyed by an enterprise, in the relevant market, in India, which enables it to(i) operate independently of competitive forces prevailing in the relevant market; or (ii) affect its competitors or consumers or the relevant market in its favour." Section 19(4) of the Act sets out factors that the Commission shall have due regard to in determining whether an enterprise enjoys a dominant position.

26 Explanation to para.4(2)(a)(ii) of the Act provides: "For the purposes of this clause, the unfair or discriminatory condition in purchase or sale of goods or service referred to in sub-clause (i) and unfair or discriminatory price in purchase or sale of goods (including predatory price) or service referred to in sub-clause (ii) shall not include such discriminatory conditions or prices which may be adopted to meet the competition [...]."

27 As per the question raised by Harry First, Professor, New York University in a note circulated prior to the conference.

28 See *supra* note 1, para. 49(3) of the Act provides "The Commission shall take suitable measures for the promotion of competition advocacy, creating awareness and imparting training about competition issues."

oriented economy, perhaps even foreclosing the need for further legislative interventions or policy documents. The success of economic reform hinges on competition and efficient markets being everyone's concern. These two statutory provisions (Sections 19 and 49) place a heavy responsibility on the Commission. There is no competition policy as yet in India—the law and its implementation have preceded the policy.

Fourth, the Commission is empowered to levy significant levels of penalties and issue behavioral remedies for contraventions of the Act. In cases of abuse of dominance, the Commission may additionally impose structural remedies.[29] This requires the Commission's orders to be "transparent" and follow "due process."

Fifth, the Act is "competition neutral." Competitive neutrality is a term used in the application of competition law to public sector companies and describes how competition authorities can implement and ensure neutrality and a "level playing field" between public and private enterprises. The Act makes no distinction between public and private sector enterprises. Even government departments engaged in commercial activities are within the purview of the Act[30] and the Commission can aim to ensure competitive neutrality and a level playing field among all market participants, irrespective of private or government ownership.

Sixth, as an ex-post regulator, the Commission can issue guidelines for rectifying market distortions only if a contravention of the provisions of the Act is established.

Finally, the Commission has set time limits by way of a recommended time frame for issuing of decisions.

29 See *supra* note 1, para. 27(b) of the Act empowers the Commission to: "impose such penalty, as it may deem fit which shall be not more than ten per cent of the average of the turnover for the last three preceding financial years, upon each of such person or enterprises which are parties to such agreements or abuse: [Provided that in case any agreement referred to in section 3 has been entered into by a cartel, the Commission may impose upon each producer, seller, distributor, trader or service provider included in that cartel, a penalty of up to three times of its profit for each year of the continuance of such agreement or ten per cent of its turnover for each year of the continuance of such agreement, whichever is higher]."

30 See *supra* note 1, para. 2(h) of the Act states that: "enterprise" means a person or a department of the Government, who or which is, or has been, engaged in any activity, relating to the production, storage, supply, distribution, acquisition or control of articles or goods, or the provision of services, of any kind, or in investment, or in the business of acquiring, holding, underwriting or dealing with shares, debentures or other securities of any other body corporate, either directly or through one or more of its units or divisions or subsidiaries, whether such unit or division or subsidiary is located at the same place where the enterprise is located or at a different place or at different places, but does not include any activity of the Government relatable to the sovereign functions of the Government including all activities carried on by the departments of the Central Government dealing with atomic energy, currency, defense and space."

III. Market Activism, Competition and Development of Markets

Several complex and, in some instances, unique cases of unilateral conduct came up early before the Commission for adjudication. The complexity of these cases demanded a layered and nuanced approach in comprehending competition issues and, for a young competition authority, posed a challenge to borrow a phrase: "How and When to Limit Unilateral Conduct Without Suppressing Competitive Vigour."[31] Critiques of the Commission's market intervention in unilateral conduct cases have been many and have typically posed the following questions. First, how was the relevant market defined and why? While lawyers look at "how," it is often more important to understand "why." Second, whether the abuse which flows from a given market definition is sustainable in terms of inter-temporal and inter-group costs and benefits. The Act, whilst it defines a consumer and, as mentioned above, refers to consumer welfare in its Preamble, raises the issue of which consumer was focused on in the respective order. Lastly, was the Commission's intervention in the market a mechanism aimed at maintaining competitiveness and demarcating between competition and competitive vigor?

The first step in allegations pertaining to abuse of dominance is to define the relevant market. The scope for competition and market development devolves on how the relevant market is defined by competition authorities, so as to analyze dominance within the relevant market and its abuse. Equally important is how abuse is perceived and assessed. The existence of market power and its abuse hinges on defining the relevant market.[32] The orders of the Commission on defining the market have been critiqued as being too narrow and inconsistent.[33] A narrow market definition suggests that dominance is inevitable, while inconsistency hints at a subjective rather than objective criteria being taken into account in defining the relevant market. The criticism also hinges on the fact that the widely accepted test for delineating the boundaries of a relevant market, the "hypothetical monopolist" test, more commonly referred to as the Small but Significant Non-transitory Increase in Price ("SSNIP") test has not always been utilized in defining the relevant market. On the aspect of abuse, unease has been expressed with regard to "who is the consumer" and in assessing consumer harm, whether the harm occurs both spatially and temporally.

Valid as these criticisms are, the Commission's approach on these issues are based on a set of assumptions and reasoning which need examining before arriving at any conclusions. Of particular significance is that several decisions of the Commission, passed on the basis of a majority, that have been disputed, and the arguments on market definition which have differed in various dissenting orders passed by different Members of the Commission. Dissenting orders provide the counterfactual to the given line of thinking reflected in majority orders.[34]

---

31 Title of panel discussion moderated by AZB & Partners at the American Bar Association Conference Antitrust in Asia: Developments in India's Competition Regime, New Delhi, November-December 2012.

32 See OECD Policy Roundtables, *Market Definition*, Directorate for Financial and Enterprise Affairs, 2012, at page 11, *available at* http://www.oecd.org/daf/competition/Marketdefinition2012.pdf.

33 See Nishith Desai Associates, *Competition Law in IndiaJurisprudential Trends and the way forward*, 2012, at page 42, *available at* http://www.nishithdesai.com/fileadmin/user_upload/pdfs/Research%20Papers/Competition%20Law%20in%20India.pdf; and Samir Gandhi, AZB & Partners, *Enforcement trends in India under the Competition Act 2002*, *available at* http://uk.practicallaw.com/2-532-3777.

34 Id., at *Competition Law in India - Jurisprudential Trends and the way forward*, page 9, which provides that up to February 2013, in almost 20% of the Commission's cases, Members have issued either separate or dissenting orders.

The relevant market is defined with respect to two parameters—product market and geographic market. Delineation of the relevant market is to specify the product and geographic scope within which the alleged anti-competitive effects of particular business conduct are to be assessed. The Act defines these markets respectively in Sections 2(r), (s) and (t),[35] and Sections 19(6) and (7) provide factors that should be considered in such market determination. A relevant product market is defined in terms of inter-changeability and substitutability as discerned by consumers, by reason of characteristics, price and their intended use. The Act lays emphasis on assessing substitutability from the demand-side. A relevant geographic market is the obverse of the product market where defining a relevant geographic market involves identifying competitive pressure of substitutes (whether of products or competing suppliers), located outside the focal area. The analysis is aimed at identifying competitive constraints of one area on another (whether such constraints are exercised by products or suppliers located in such areas). According to the words set out in the statutory definition, emphasis is given to the homogeneity of conditions of competition for the supply of the product/service and accessibility to consumers. The Commission has, thus far, typically defined the relevant product market from the demand-side, and has also considered supply-side substitutability in a few cases. The relevant geographic market, however, has been routinely been defined as "India."[36]

From the Commission's decisions in unilateral conduct cases, three sectors have been selected: (i) stock-exchanges, platforms and networks; (ii) real estate; and (iii) Internet and virtual markets. In addition, passing references to two other cases which raise pertinent issues to the present discourse.

1. Stock-exchanges, Platforms and Networks

A controversial but interesting case of "abuse of dominance," that came up early in the Commission's establishment, in terms of the abuses of predatory pricing and leveraging, involved two major stock exchanges in India. MCX Stock Exchange Ltd. ("MCX-SX"), a public limited company and a recognized stock exchange for trading in the Currency Derivatives ("CD") segment, filed the case against the National Stock Exchange India Ltd. ("NSE"), DotEx International Ltd. ("DotEx") and Omnesys Technologies Pvt. Ltd. ("Omnesys"), alleging an abuse of dominant position in the market for stock exchange services in India under Section 4 of the Act.[37]

It was alleged that transaction fees, the principal source of revenue for stock exchanges, were waived off by NSE for the CD segment. Further, it had been alleged that NSE kept membership deposits unjustifiably low and waived the admission fee entirely for the CD segment. Since NSE was not charging transaction fees for the CD segment, MCX-SX was unable to levy such a zero fee for its only segment, i.e., the CD segment, leading to significant losses. It was also alleged that NSE was subsidizing its losses in the CD segment from its revenues in the cash futures, options and wholesale debt market segments, thus leveraging its dominant position in the market for stock exchange services to protect its position in the CD Segment, in violation of Section 4(2)(e) of the Act.[38] As per the allegations leveled by the informant, various fee

35 Para. 2(r) of the Act states that the: "'relevant market' means the market which may be determined by the Commission with reference to the relevant product market or the relevant geographic market or with reference to both the markets;" para. 2(s) of the Act states that the: "'Relevant geographic market' means a market comprising the area in which the conditions of competition for supply of goods or provision of services or demand of goods or services are distinctly homogenous and can be distinguished from the conditions prevailing in the neighbouring areas;" and para. 2(t) of the Act states that: "'Relevant product market' means a market comprising all those products or services which are regarded as interchangeable or substitutable by the consumer, by reason of characteristics of the products or services, their prices and intended use."

36 See *supra* note 60, for a discussion on the geographic market in the Prints India v. Springer case.

37 Case No. 13/2009, MCX Stock Exchange Ltd. v. National Stock Exchange of India Ltd., et al, decided on the 23 June 2011, *available at* http://www.cci.gov.in/May2011/OrderOfCommission/MCXMainOrder240611.pdf.

38 See *supra* note 1, at § 4(2)(e).

waivers and other concessions in the CD segment have been adopted by the NSE as an exclusionary device to kill competition and competitors, and NSE has therefore used its dominant position in the relevant market to eliminate competition and competitors.[39]

a. Defining the Relevant Market

In the *MCX-SX v. NSE Stock Exchange* case,[40] the product under consideration was the Currency Derivative or CD segment. In India, before the CD Segment came into being, this service was being provided by banks only and for a hidden charge. Banks, however, are not trading platforms and cannot provide for diversity of options for hedging risk. Derivatives can be traded either in an exchange or in the Over The Counter ("OTC") market.[41]

Both the Commission's orders in this case (majority and minority) defined the market as "the stock exchange services in respect of [the] CD segment in India [...] "[42] rather than stock-exchanges services as a whole, as had been defined by the Director General ("DG") in its investigation report. The minority order differed slightly in treating the stock exchange as a platform (CD segment a vertical on the platform). The CD segment can be a vertical on a stock exchange platform or it can be a stand-alone platform. Transaction platform(s) facilitate executing trades with different options and thus provides a two-sided market.[43] And, in this difference, the analysis of abuse between the two orders varied.

The market definition was surmised on the consideration that services on a stock exchange maybe similar, but the product, CD, cannot be said to be interchangeable or substitutable with the other instruments traded on a stock exchange,[44] namely equity, debt instruments, etc., which are the underlying assets. In terms of Section 2(t) of the Act, the CD segment cannot be regarded as "interchangeable or substitutable by the consumer, by reason of characteristics of the products or services, their prices and intended use [...]."[45] Other factors, such as regulatory trade barriers and participants/members conducting currency derivative trades, also contributed to the Commission's determination that the CD segment is a separate product market.[46]

---

39 See *supra* note 37, at para. 2.10.

40 See *supra* note 37.

41 See Case No. 13/2009, MCX Stock Exchange Ltd. v. National Stock Exchange of India Ltd., et al, dissent order, decided on the 3 June, 2011, available at http://www.cci.gov.in/May2011/OrderOfCommission/MCXDissentOrder240611.pdf, paras. 6.3-6.4 states that: "[t]he stock exchanges in India offer the facility to trade in the following major segments: equity, equity futures and options, interest rate futures, exchange traded funds, debt, currency derivatives, among others . . . Stock exchanges, as the name implies, are meant to provide trading platforms for stocks." A stock exchange is a platform where currency derivatives may be a vertical or a CD segment can be a separate platform by itself. In either case, the existence of two sides enables network economies to be realized and is an important factor to be considered in their pricing policies.

42 See *supra* note 37, at para. 10.25.

43 See *supra* note 41.

44 See *supra* note 41, at para. 5.6.

45 See *supra* note 34.

46 Trading in derivative products in India has to be approved by Securities and Exchange Board of India ("SEBI") and the Reserve Bank of India ("RBI"). The uniqueness of currency derivative and the lack of interchangeability and substitutability with other market segments is based on the Report of the RBI-SEBI Standing Technical Committee on Exchange Traded Currency Futures, 2008, available at http://rbidocs.rbi.org.in/rdocs/PublicationReport/Pdfs/84986.pdf,on whose recommendations a separate segment (i.e., the CD segment) was considered appropriate and introduced into the country. In fact, the report clearly advocated the need for a separate CD segment from other segments on which securities are traded. Moreover, as the majority order states, the information having been filed by MCX-SX, competition concerns should relate to the market in which the informant operates (i.e., the CD segment) and cannot be in the context of a market (i.e., for all stock exchange services) which does not concern its operation.

NSE (a multi-trading stock exchange) commenced trading on the CD Segment from 29 August 2008; the Bombay Stock Exchange ("BSE") followed suit on 1 October, 2008;[47] MCX-SX was given permission by SEBI to start trading in currency derivatives only, as it did not adhere to certain regulations. It commenced trading on the CD Segment on 7 October 2008.

On appeal, the COMPAT, in its order, defined the relevant product market as "stock-exchange services"[48] (in agreement with the relevant market definition adopted by the DG) and not the CD segment.

b. Dominance and Its Abuse

The dominance of NSE, in the majority order of *MCX-SX v. NSE*, was based not on NSE's market shares in the CD segment as defined, which was marginally lower than that of MCX-SX, rather it premised on the dominant position of NSE in stock-market services derived from the explanation of "dominant position" provided under Section 4, supported by an assessment of the factors set out in Section 19(4) of the Act. Explanation(a) to Section 4 of the Act defines a dominant position as:

> "dominant position" means a position of strength, enjoyed by an enterprise, in the relevant market, in India, which enables it to:
>
> (i) operate independently of competitive forces prevailing in the relevant market; or
>
> (ii) affect its competitors or consumers or the relevant market in its favour."

Allegations of unfair pricing and leveraging were *non-sequitur* outcomes of NSE's dominance. Factors of revenue, joint membership and scale of operations were considerations that confirmed NSE's dominance and, in turn, NSE's ability to indulge in unfair pricing by way of charging zero transaction costs for trading on the CD segment. While the allegation pertained to predatory pricing, the Commission preferred to refer to zero transaction costs as "unfair."[49] "Unfair" as the competitor, a new entrant, would not be able to sustain itself in the market without the advantage of "leveraging"—NSE was able to enter and sustain the CD segment.

The minority order was premised on the peculiarities of pricing on a platform and the economics of network industries. The contention of unfair or predatory pricing on the stock exchange platform (which does not follow the traditional profit maximization rule or marginal cost pricing) was found to be unsubstantiated given the dynamics of network industries.[50] The need to deepen markets in the nascent CD segment, which prompted the NSE to adopt an introductory zero pricing model for the benefit of consumers, is valid in this framework. It also raises issues on the myriad of pricing strategies open to new entrants more so in a two-sided market. The COMPAT (Appellant Tribunal) upheld the majority's view.[51]

---

47 In April 2010, the BSE suspended operations in the CD Segment in light of its strategic alliance with the United Stock Exchange ("USE"). USE commenced operations in the CD Segment on 20 September 2010 with BSE as a shareholder. In 2013, BSE re-entered the CD segment.

48 Appeal No. 15 of 2011, The National Stock Exchange of India Ltd. v. Competition Commission of India and MCX Stock Exchange Ltd., Competition Appellate Tribunal, at paras. 21. 54, *available at* http://compat.nic.in/upload/PDFs/augustordersApp2014/05_08_14.pdf.

49 Predatory pricing would require assessing the recoupment period for compensation of loss of revenue incurred during the period of zero transaction costs.

50 In network industries, there are externalities that operate across two groups of customers. A skewed pricing structure is a feature of two-sided markets—to be able to attract both sets of customers, platforms usually structure their pricing in a manner that one group pays less than the other or one group is paid to participate (for example, radio or newspapers). Selling any product or service much below production costs or much higher than production costs may traditionally raise antitrust issues, but in network industries, this may not necessarily result in anti-competitive harm and may be aimed at increasing efficiencies.

51 See *supra* note 48.

2. Real Estate and Services of Builders

Yet another high profile unilateral conduct case by the Commission was in the real estate sector. The informant alleged unfair conditions meted out by a real estate player, DLF Limited ("DLF"). The real estate market has been in the limelight for several controversies in a country where demand for affordable housing is high and land acquisition a cumbersome process.[52]

It was alleged that DLF had imposed arbitrary, unfair and unreasonable conditions on apartment allottees of the housing complex "the Belaire" situated in DLF City, Phase-V, Gurgaon, being constructed by DLF, and that DLF had abused its dominant position in violation of Section 4 of the Act. The informant in this case was Belaire Owners' Association, an association formed by the apartment allottees of Belaire.

a. Defining the Relevant Market

The relevant market in DLF was the real estate developer services ("services" as defined under Section 2(u) of the Act).[53] The point of determination was whether these services, provided by DLF to the informant, are of a distinct nature "by reason of characteristics [...] their prices and intended use" as stipulated in Section 2(t) of the Act. The Commission noted from the DG's investigation report that the nature of service being provided by DLF in the context of the instant case was described as services of developer/builder in respect of "high-end" residential accommodation in Gurgaon.[54] Thus, there were two important components to the service market definition with regard to characteristics of the underlying physical asset (product) that required interpretation, i.e., the "high-end" nature of the product and the fact that these services were provided by DFL for "residential accommodation." The third component of "Gurgaon" related to the relevant 'geographic' market.

Terms such as "high-end," "premium" or "affordable" are relatively subjective and therefore it was felt necessary to establish a clear and logical interpretation of the term "high-end." The Commission noted that "high-end" is not a function of size alone. It is a complex mix of factors, such as, size, reputation of the location, characteristics of neighborhood, quality of construction, etc., that qualify a dwelling unit as "high-end" or otherwise. However, the most significant characteristic of a "high-end" dwelling unit has to be the characteristics desired by actual customers and, amongst all objective differentiators of a customer's preferences, his or her capacity to pay—as demand is desire backed by the ability to pay. Apart from physical attributes, these categorizations also take into account income or expenditure levels of the customer base. Together, these factors create a distinctly identifiable residential unit that is not substitutable in an economic sense.

Users/buyers of "high-end" accommodation demand quality and the ambience of a distinctly higher level, and are willing to pay significantly higher prices to meet their requirements. "Taking into account the current prices of HIG (High Income Group) accommodation provided by the development authorities in India, as also the demands and paying capacity of the growing upper middle and rich classes in society, from the cost perspective, (the Commission found) it is quite logical to accept an apartment costing between Rs.2 - 2.5 crores (20-25 million (dollars)) as "high-end" in the Indian socio-economic reality."[55]

---

52 Case No. 19/2010, Belaire Owner's Association v. DLF Ltd., Haryana Urban Development Authority, and Department of Town and Country Planning, State of Haryana, 12 August 2011, available at http://www.cci.gov.in/May2011/OrderOfCommission/DLFMainOrder110811.pdf.

53 See *supra* note 1.

54 The services under examination in the DLF case were similar to the services provided by stock exchanges. The Commission drew a distinction on the underlying product offered by DLF as against those offered by other builders.

55 See *supra* note 52, at para. 12.31.

The Commission's distinction between "high-end" and "mid-group" as constituting separate markets based on price and consumer preferences has come under considerable criticism,[56] primarily on account of the data used by the Commission to distinguish between the two markets on the basis of value rather than stock. No SSNIP test was attempted. In a differentiated product market, consumer surveys are no doubt important for distinguishing between different types of residential apartments. The importance of consumer surveys and the constraints placed on defining a relevant product market rigorously are now slowly appreciated by the Commission.[57]

Geographic market definition was also an important factor in the *DLF* case. The informant had argued that the relevant geographic market was the National Capital Region, of which Gurgaon is a part. The Commission opined that based on the facts of the case, Gurgaon was seen to be the relevant geographic market. "A decision to purchase a high-end apartment in Gurgaon is not easily substitutable by a decision to purchase a similar apartment in any other geographic location. Gurgaon is known to possess certain unique geographical characteristics, such as its proximity to Delhi, proximity to the Airports and a distinct brand image as a destination for upwardly mobile families."[58]

Contentious relevant geographic markets, which first arose in the *DLF* case in terms of defining a market that is exclusive and non-interchangeable or substitutable, has raised a lively debate in the Commission with regard to defining geographic markets. Several dissenting orders passed at the *prima facie* stage reflect the contentions that have arisen in relation to relevant geographic market definitions in the real estate sector.[59]

b. Dominance and its Abuse

Dominance in a relevant market that is defined within the geographic boundaries of "Gurgaon" can be claimed to be axiomatic. The shortcomings of such a narrow geographic market, as pointed out by critics, was that defining market boundaries needs to be based on a more rigorous consumer-based data set and estimation of SSNIP, to rule out the substitutability of neighboring areas upon a 5 percent to 10 percent increase in the price of a residential apartment. The Commission discussed several of these issues prior to defining the relevant market. The dominance of DLF was assessed in respect to residential apartments in the market so defined. DLF, on account of historic factors, was the first real estate developer in and around Delhi (including Gurgaon), reflected in its large land bank. More significantly, the abuse inherent

---

56 See *supra* note 32, at pages 49-50. See also the show The Firm's video entitled DLF Case: Consumer Commission Of India, *available at* http://thefirm.moneycontrol.com/story_page.php?autono=580702; and SmeekshaBhola, India: *Determination of Relevant Market–'Easier Said Than Done,' available at* http://www.mondaq.com/india/x/295618/Trade+Regulation+Practices/Determination+Of+Relevant+Market+Easier+Said+Than+Done.

57 In Case No. 01/2010, GKB Hi-Tech Lenses Pvt. Ltd. v. Transitions Optical India Pvt. Ltd., majority order, 16 May, 2012, involving photo chromic lenses, the importance of consumer surveys was emphasized to draw distinctions between glass photo chromic lenses ("GPL") and plastic photo chromic lenses ("PPL"). The case was filed by GKB Hi Tech Lenses Pvt. Ltd. against Transitions Optical India Pvt. Ltd. (a joint venture in India between Transitions Optical Holdings B.V. and Transitions Optical Inc.). The case related to an abuse of dominance by Transitions, an international lens manufacturer. The Commission, upon analysing characteristics of the products, factors relevant to demand decisions, such as price and lack of competitive constraints reflected by price differences between PPL and GPL, observed that "in highly differentiated product markets and consequent high differences in prices, the continuum exists on an intra-product basis and not inter product bases and exclusivity prevails. Behavioral economics also seem to suggest that price differences do not act as a competitive constraint, as the perception of higher quality of PPL may not be in proportion to the differences in prices," at pages 27-28. The Commission concluded that the market for PPL or Plastic Photo chromic Lenses was the relevant product market and not the larger market of lenses (glass and plastic lenses).

58 See *supra* note 52, at 12.36.

59 Case No. 21/2011, Mr. Jagmohan Chhabra and Mrs. Shalini Chhabra v. M/s Unitech Ltd., Gurgaon, dissenting order, 8 November, 2011, *available at* http://www.cci.gov.in/May2011/OrderOfCommission/MrJagmoha%20Dissenting8Nov2011.pdf; Case No. 27/2011, Jagmohan Chhabra and Mrs. Shalini Chhabra v. M/s Unitech Ltd., Gurgaon, dissenting order, 8 November, 2011, *available at*http://www.cci.gov.in/May2011/OrderOfCommission/Mr.%20J%20ChabraDissenting8Nov2011.pdf; Case No. 67/2011, Geogi Kuruvilla, Chennai & Others. v. M/s Hirco Developments Pvt. Ltd., Mumbai & Others, dissenting order, 9 February, 2012, *available at* http://cci.gov.in/May2011/OrderOfCommission/Case67of2011DissentingOrder.pdf; and Case No. 55/2011, Kolkata West International City Buyers Welfare Association, Howrah v. Kolkata West International City Pvt. Ltd. & Others, dissenting order, 24 January, 2012, *available at* http://www.cci.gov.in/May2011/OrderOfCommission/kolwestDissentingOrderfeb12.pdf.

in the unequal agreement between buyers of apartments and the real estate developer was clearly anti-competitive. Criticism that a "one sided" agreement entered into by a dominant enterprise with its customers is anti-competitive in itself tends to prevail.

The *DLF* case spawned a large number of complaints in the real estate industry to the Commission. This suggests that the debate on defining the relevant market (in particular, the geographic scope of the market) and its abuse in the real estate sector has yet to evolve rigorous, consistent tools of analysis and measurement, as evidenced by several minority orders of the Commission in this sector.

3. Internet and Virtual Markets

The first case of internet-based markets faced by the Commission was in the publishing industry. It brought to the forefront the difficulty of drawing market boundaries within the confines of political boundaries of a nation state. Publishing is now an online business and each business house is a platform that connects authors and readers worldwide. Changing models of business always present a challenge to competition authorities, as was in the *Prints India v. Springer* case.[60] The concept of markets on the Internet and the definition of monopoly and abuse of dominance was the central focus of the Commission's order in this case. Prints India, a distributor of Scientific, Technological and Medical ("STM") journals, alleged an abuse of dominance by Springer India Private Limited ("Springer," a venture of Springer Verlag) that had entered the business of publishing, editing and distribution of academic journals in India, both at the print level and online. Springer's entry into the Indian market was very successful and Springer quickly took over the publication and distribution of various "must have" journals in India. Being web-based, Springer provided various value additions, such as, peer review, editing etc., on the Internet, apart from providing the exclusive "right to publish" to authors. Springer is part of a well-known publishing group with a much sought after reputation by scholars seeking to publish their articles. Their publications are prestigious and fall into the category of "must have" journals for libraries and scholars. Demand is not price responsive where "must have" journals are concerned.

The allegations ranged from violations of Section 4(2)(a)(i) (imposition of unfair conditions in sale of goods—margin squeeze) and Section 4(2)(a)(ii) (unfair pricing) to Section 4(2)(c) (denial of market access, a violation which was found by the DG). Prints India also alleged that Springer, as a distributor, had entered into anti-competitive agreements Section 3 with other academic institutes for the co-publishing of certain journals.

a. Defining the Relevant Market

The relevant product market was defined as the market for publishing STM academic journals in English, both online and in print.[61] The Commission opined that supply-side substitutability should be taken into account in defining the relevant product market, taking note of the European Commission's merger decision in the *Candover* case.[62] The relevant market defined as STM academic journals, in English, in India is perhaps acceptable as regards the product market for print journals but, for the purposes of online journals, it is difficult to define the geographic demarcation of such a market. To restrict the market to India would require data on "hits" of readers

60 Case No. 16/2010, Prints India v. Springer India Private Limited & Others, 3 July, 2010, *available at* http://www.cci.gov.in/May2011/OrderOfCommission/CaseNo16of2010MainOrder.pdf.

61 Id., at page 31.

62 Id., at page 28-29.

in India alone and, more specifically, for readers of STM journals in India alone. Moreover, the conditions stated in Section 19(6) of the Act (listed below) are not applicable for internet/virtual markets:

> "19 (6) The Commission shall, while determining the "relevant geographic market," have due regard to all or any of the following factors, namely:
>
> (a) regulatory trade barriers;
>
> (b) local specification requirements;
>
> (c) national procurement policies;
>
> (d) adequate distribution facilities;
>
> (e) transport costs;
>
> (f) language;
>
> (g) consumer preferences;
>
> (h) need for secure or regular supplies or rapid after-sales services."[63]

b. Dominance and Its Abuse

The measurement of dominance in the *Prints India v. Springer* case involving online journals was based on the impact factor or "must have" nature of the journal, which can be quantified on the basis of "hits." The DG's data, submitted by the informant, estimated that Springer's market share in terms of "must have" journals was 31 percent for STM journals (as Springer published 47 out of 150 STM journals) and 64 percent in terms of circulation numbers (as Springer circulated 35,000 STM journals out of a total of 55,000 STM journals in the country).[64] In a supplementary report, the DG examined the revenue of top international publishers, which showed that Elsevier had a market share of 15.4percent against which Springer's market share was only 4.65percent.[65] This data, however, did not include all journals in the STM category.

The dominance of Springer was not established on the basis of inter alia market share. A factor that weighed against the dominance of Springer in online journals was not only the prevalence of competitive constraints in terms of the number of established publishers in the STM segment itself, but also the growing presence of open publishing models that act as a competitive constraint and impose countervailing power on Springer. The allegation of abuse of dominance did not stand the scrutiny of the Commission. Dominance remained undefined.

A quick reference to the allegation of "unfair agreements" in a presumed vertical relationship between the informant and its co-publishers (8 Academic Institutes) by Prints India by way of determining the sale price, controlling the supply of journals, imposing unfair conditions, sharing the market between print and online and seeking confidential information was found not to be anti-competitive. The Commission opined that the arrangement between Prints India and Springer was not a vertical relationship. The activities performed were held to be similar to an assembly line production in the manufacturing sector.[66]

---

63 See *supra* note 1, at para. 19 (6).

64 See *supra* note 60, at page 6.

65 See *supra* note 60, at page 34.

66 See *supra* note 60, at page 36.

4. Passing Reference Cases

As mentioned earlier, a passing reference to two other Commission cases which pose challenges to antitrust authorities is briefly covered. The first is the unease of competition authorities in dealing with dominant players who are exposed to competitive constraints. The second relates to the spare parts market euphemistically classified as the aftermarket.

The characteristics of competitive constraints and their prevalence, where there are no entry barriers, was the Commission's concern in *HNG Float Glass v. Saint Gobain Glass, Chennai*.[67] SaintGobain is an international market leader in the manufacture of glass products, including float glass. The technical requirements of continuous production, firing of kilns and also the quality of input required, has made this industry oligopolistic worldwide. India is no exception to this trend. HNG, a manufacturer of float glass in India, alleged anti-competitive pricing practices by SaintGobain. The majority order examined the competitive constraints exercised on SaintGobain, both in pre-conduct and post-conduct scenarios. If there are no entry barriers, the sector is always open to competition and dominance is not an established or consistent feature for any enterprise operating in the sector. There was, however, a dissent order.

The definition of substitutability, whether from the demand-side or supply-side, comes into focus when defining the "aftermarket," a concept popularized by lawyers in the US. The recent order of the Commission on automotive spare parts, in a similar vein, defines an "aftermarket" for spare parts as a separate market from the (primary) car market.[68] The issue here revolves on how to define the aftermarket using Section 2(t) of the Act. The case revolved on the availability of or access to spare parts for the independent repair shops or service garages not authorized by vehicle manufacturers, after the car has been purchased. In India, there are at least fourteen car manufacturers also referred to as Original Equipment Manufacturers or OEMs. Parts which are specific to particular models of an OEM are sub-contracted for production to Original Equipment Suppliers ("OES"). The spare parts market constitutes: (i) genuine parts which are available often in authorized show rooms, but are priced high; (ii) pirated products or fakes in India; (iii) generic products, such as tires, fuel pumps, batteries, etc., produced by several companies including multinational enterprises; and (iv) service centers which cover a wide range of garages from large mechanized garages to small mechanics. The first category of spare parts is specific to the car model where the design of the spare part belongs to the car manufacturer. These are a part of a production platform contracted out to OES and are bought entirely by the parent car company, OEM, under given designs and maybe patent restrictions. The spare parts for car A cannot be substituted by spare parts for car B. As per Section 2(t) of the Act, none of the categories of spares parts are substitutable between cars of different brands or even cars of different makes or designs of the same brand. The lack of substitutability, as per Section 2(t), will be part of the car market and not a separate market. In the case of generics market substitutability is also limited, and as regards fakes or pirated version their classification is within the "grey market". By process of elimination, pure substitutability is only relevant in the services market.

---

67 Case No.51/2011, M/s HNG Float Glass Ltd. v. M/s Saint Gobain Glass India Ltd., majority order, 24 October, 2013, *available at* http://www.cci.gov.in/May2011/OrderOfCommission/266/512011.pdf.

68 Case No. 03/2011, Shri Shamsher Kataria v. Honda Siel Cars India Ltd. & Others, 25 August, 2014, at page 20.5.54, *available at* http://cci.gov.in/May2011/OrderOfCommission/27/032011.pdf.

Furthermore, would the relationship between OEMs and OESs be considered as a vertical relationship under Section 3(4) of the Act?[69] An OES, as a company, constitutes an "enterprise," but is it at a different stage or level of the production chain in "different markets"? If spare parts are part of the car market where sub-contracting is often resorted to by a manufacturer, on account of labor costs, can the agreements between OEM and OES be classified as falling under Section 3(4) dealing with vertical restraints? The overlap of dominance in a market (or even its abuse) through agreements, with either downstream or upstream enterprises, is now an on-going concern.[70]

5. Points for Introspection

Criticism regarding the Commission's analysis of market definition in dominance and monopolization cases has revolved around the lack of analytical economic tools used in defining the market, suggesting a subjective rather than an objective delineation of markets. This criticism is based on the fact that the SSNIP test has not been utilized, a criticism that has consistently been made as regards the orders of the Commission. The SSNIP test is no doubt an important tool for arriving at demand-side substitutability and for defining the boundaries of the relevant geographic market. The cases reviewed above suggest that when defining "substitutability" itself, there has been some liberty in the market definitions adopted, often supported by referring to factors listed in Sections 19(6) and 19(7) of the Act.

In the *MSX-SX v. NSE* stock exchange case, it is obviously clear that CDs cannot be substituted by equities or stock. If sufficient data over a period of time was available, substitutability between the CD segment and the OTC segment as one market could have been assessed. The majority order has gone into detail regarding the relevance and feasibility of applying the SSNIP test. Under prevailing data constraints, the fact that prices for trading were not charged by stock exchanges and since the CD segment was set up only in August 2008, the order voicing the apprehension that without a referral price, employing the SSNIP test to quote loosely could result in the "Cellophane Fallacy" to include false substitutes and exaggerate the market definition.[71]

The contraventions of the Act and their assessment by the Commission in the *MCX-SX v. NSE* case is interesting, in that dominance was not based on market share but rather on the Commission's understanding that NSE enjoyed the ability to operate independently of others. The criticism, therefore, for not using the SSNIP test in this case is perhaps not a sufficiently robust argument.

---

69 See *supra* note 1, at para 3(4) "Any agreement amongst enterprises or persons at different stages or levels of the production chain in different markets, in respect of production, supply, distribution, storage, sale or price of, or trade in goods or provision of services, including—

(a) tie-in arrangement;

(b) exclusive supply agreement;

(c) exclusive distribution agreement;

(d) refusal to deal; and

(e) resale price maintenance

shall be an agreement in contravention of sub-section (1) if such agreement causes or is likely to cause an appreciable adverse effect on competition in India."

70 See *supra* note 60, in Prints India v. Springer, in relation to production and distribution in the publication industry, the Commission observed that "[t]he vertical nature of the enterprise does not emerge clearly as far as publication is concerned. The different activities performed during the publication process are synonymous with assembly line production in a manufacturing sector."

71 See *supra* note 37, at para 10.16. However, inappropriate the reference to "Cellophane Fallacy" the intent was more to highlight the limitations of SNNIP test is cases where substitutability is well known.

The significance of market definition in this case lies more in understanding the effects of network economies. In fact, the product market definition in the *MCX-SX v NSE* is to be credited for having opened the debate on how to view a platform and to appreciate the dynamics of network economies of a platform. The minority order refers to a vertical (CD) on the platform of the stock exchange for executing trades for several requirements. Platforms, such as mall's and stock exchanges, are used for providing space and whether these spaces are open only to interchangeable products as in the NSE stock market suggests that that use of SSNIP and other econometrics tests is important. The observation that the platform (i.e., the stock exchange) over which services are delivered is largely composed of relatively larger and substantial fixed/sunk costs, and very little or negligible variable costs which may be attributable to a single or batch of transactions. In network industries, there are externalities that operate across two groups of customers. A skewed pricing structure is a feature of two-sided markets—to be able to attract both sets of customers, platforms usually structure their pricing in a manner that one group pays less than the other or one group is paid to participate (for example, radio or newspapers). Selling any product or service much below production costs or much higher than production costs may traditionally raise antitrust issues, but in network industries this may not necessarily result in anti-competitive harm, and may be aimed at increasing efficiencies.

In the *DLF* case,[72] a SSNIP test would have demarcated the boundaries of the product market (whether "high-end" or otherwise) and the geographic market (whether "Gurgaon" or wider), sharply facilitating the critical factors that go into valuation of real estate. Major criticism and unease with the Commission's decision in the *DLF* case has been on the non-application of the SSNIP test. A perception that a small 5 percent to 10 percent increase in the price of an apartment in Gurgaon would not make a person shift his preference to an outlying area of the National Capital Region needs to be further substantiated.

A booming and upwardly mobile young population and rapid urbanization places considerable pressure on housing, both for residence and investment. To zero down on the factors that influence the real estate market, consumer surveys are important. The dissenting orders passed in later cases in the real estate sector point to this lacuna. For example, the dissenting order passed in *South City Group Housing Apartment Owners Association v. Larsen & Tubro & Others*[73] emphasized that the geographic location in the real estate sector has to be analyzed by taking into account historical and social features. Again, the project related to a large upper-end residential block in South Bangalore, where the relevant geographic market was defined as the entire city of Bangalore. Redefining the market for real estate must borrow from urban sociological movements. The history of "[u]rban settlements historically have seen shifts in location of habitats (villages, townships, cities etc.), defined by conditions of employment, trade, conveniences et al forces that have been well documented by sociologists. Similar patterns at a perhaps [more basic and] simplistic level, can be observed in the shifts in movements of housing areas for residential apartments in growing cities and often in pockets."[74] In the *DLF* case, Gurgaon was a village just two decades ago, while in the *South City* case, as argued by the informant, the project was outside the city but closer to the newer emerging urban areas in Bangalore. Real estate developers keep track of these trends as reflected by their upcoming projects. The geographic market which defines the product/service could be just a road. Defining markets in real estate requires a nuanced approach which includes an assessment

---

72 See *supra* note 52.

73 Case No. 49/2011, South City Group Housing Apartment Owners Association v. Larsen &Tubro& Others, 23 October, 2013, *available at* http://www.cci.gov.in/May2011/OrderOfCommission/267/492011.pdf.

74 See *supra* note 73, at page 4.

of the particular circumstances of the area under consideration and the impact of space and time on consumer preferences to purchase real estate in such areas.[75]

Substitutability in virtual markets in defining the geographic market raises another concern in cases of unilateral conduct. This is of greater significance than demand-side substitutability. The publishing business of Springer was the first case where the Commission faced the problem of defining the relevant "geographic market." It was also the first case that started the process of assessing the relevant market in terms of substitutability, from both the demand and supply side, where the geographic market factors outlined in Section 19(6) of the Act demonstrated demand and impact on the price of a product. The economic understanding of product and geographic dimensions of a relevant market is still mired in legal interpretations of judiciary reach. The order in the prevailing tradition of the Commission defined the geographic market as limited to India as the Commission is of the view that since "dominant position" is defined to mean "a position of strength, enjoyed by an enterprise, in the relevant market, in India [...]" the geographic marked cannot be widened beyond the territory of India.[76]

Defining relevant markets for competition law in the virtual market remains a challenge and will become more relevant because of the increasing commercial activities carried out on the Internet, where access expands beyond national boundaries or political demarcation of markets. The nagging doubt that continues to remain is restricting the relevant geographic market to India on the legal argument that Explanation (a) to Section 4 of the Act requires a determination of a dominant position in India. Would the factors of Section 19(6) of the Act apply in case of Internet and virtual markets? Applicability of the Act is different from defining the boundaries of a relevant market which is broadly an economic assessment of the conditions of competition defined by consumer preferences for certain products/services and, in turn, the measurement of market shares for an individual country. This concern was voiced in several cases currently under investigation by the DG. One group opined that the relevant market for the use of Internet services had to be delineated as the market for online search advertising in India. The other group drew attention to the need for defining and determining the relevant geographic market in cases of virtual markets.

This unease stems from the fact that internet-based services do not recognize national boundaries, but the Act defines dominance within national boundaries. However, in view of the increasing number of economic activities that function on the internet that are similar to economic activities of the real world, application of competition law and its principles will need to be relooked.

Similarly, there still exists a gap in defining substitutability itself, even when the weaker term of "interchangeability," a term of law, is used. The aftermarket and its definition of "what constitutes a substitutable product" still pose a challenge, and raises the question of defining aftermarkets for spare parts used for replacing/repairing a machine, be it a computer, washing machine, an automobile or an airplane. Are these aftermarkets amenable to be part of agreements in a vertical arrangement?

In markets where a product is differentiated by quality and price and in the absence of consumer surveys, due regard should be given to distinctions between quality and price ranges, as has been noted by the Commission in *GKB v. Transitions Optical*.[77]

---

75 See *supra* note 59, Case No. 21/2011; Case No. 27/2011, Case No. 67/2011; Case No. 55/2011. Case No. 29/2012, DGCOM Buyers & Owners Association, Chennai v. M/s DLF Ltd., New Delhi & Others, dissenting order, 27 November, 2012, *available at* http://cci.gov.in/May2011/OrderOfCommission/292012R.pdf, where it was argued that old Mahabalipuram Road in Chennai is the new popular area for building apartments, especially since the building of apartments is no longer permitted in old residential areas of Chennai.

76 See *supra* note 60.

77 See *supra* note 57.

Defining the relevant market is not only predicated on "how" a market is demarcated but also on "why" a market should be defined. Market delineation, in trying to identify the contraventions of the Act in the context of the information filed with the Commission, without robust economic analysis (elasticity measures), could be misleading in comprehending the contravention and in hindering the emergence of competitive vigor. In the cases analyzed above, the companies and businesses involved were leading private corporations Competition amongst stock exchanges is always limited. Defining the market as the CD segment, but examining dominance based on strengths in the stock exchange market, hints at the concern that the informant, MCX-SX, may exit the market, reducing the already limited number of competing stock exchanges in the country. Strategies of entry and exit vary among players in such markets, and that a new player strategizes to make entry is difficult to accept for a regulator. The emphasis on strategic behavior in a platform, and pricing in a two-sided market, was the central argument of the minority order in this case. The minority order drew attention to different pricing strategies that were followed by players, drawing attention to the risk that a static definition of unfair pricing, as alleged, would fail to capture the dynamism of platform and network markets. The concept of network economies of platforms is more relevant in emergent markets today. As more activities take place on the web, an accurate examination of Internet based platforms and discussion of externalities in two-sided markets will become increasingly important.

In the *DLF* case, the "abuse of dominance" arose from the one-sided nature of the agreement, which is considered normal practice in the real estate sector. The concern of the Commission in the *DLF* decision was not in redrafting what maybe an equitable agreement between real estate companies and apartment allottees, but in enabling competitive constraints to emerge in the real estate business where consumers can exercise their choice.[78]

This also brings to fore the question of who is the consumer? In the *MSX-SX v. NSE* case, even if the end consumers are customers seeking a derivative hedge for their foreign exchange transactions, the argument of the majority order is that consumer benefits will accrue from competition. Yet, the argument that zero transaction fees benefit consumers, more so when the transaction fees constitute an insignificant part of the costs of trading of an exchange, was not considered as relevant. The consumer in this case was the competitor. The follow up exercise lies in measuring "consumer harm," both inter temporally and spatially. Intervention by the market regulator should be aimed at protecting competition and not protecting competitors.

V. Conclusion

In concluding the one important question that needs to be answered: has the competitive vigor of the market maintained while limiting unilateral conduct? The question gains greater credence under the conditions that the Commission is vested with the difficult task of not merely assessing markets and of competition, but of defining the limits of intervention. Not often, market activism is merited. Orders of the Commission suggest that the scope for Type 1 errors or "false positives" is imminent. Developments in economic theory have made it apparent that a presumption-based approach widens the scope for such errors and may deter the desirable conduct and adversely affect consumer welfare. Presumptions that a

78 The Commission issued a decision on modifications to be made to DLF's Apartment Buyers Agreement, pursuant to the COMPAT's order dated 29 March, 2012 in Appeal No. 20 of 2011, M/s DLF Limited v. Comm'n, 12 August, 2011, *available at* http://compat.nic.in/upload/PDFs/mayordersApp2014/19_05_14.pdf, directing the Commission to pass an order under Section 27(d) of the Act specifying the extent and manner in which the terms and conditions of the agreement needed modification.

nascent competition authority may commit suggests: firstly, the obfuscation between competition and competitors. As more and more cases of dominance relate to markets where a dominant player operates, competitors enter by "firing from the shoulders of the Commission" is a constant possibility. Defining competition under dynamic conditions underlines the need for simulating strategic behaviors of entry and exit. Prevalence of competitive constraints rather than numbers defines dynamic markets.

Secondly, consumer benefit and maximizing consumer welfare gains clarity when harm is assessed spatially and temporally. The essence of competition and competitive markets is to harness the benefits of efficiency emanating from new technology, product innovation and productivity increases. Thirdly, softer instruments of intervention that include advocacy and advice to Government often rectify a distorted market without impairing competition. The issue of guidelines and regulations that hinge upon finding contravention under the Act do not reflect lack of competition, but point towards synchronization of macro policies and their micro effects. Lastly, the luxury of recourse to formal legal structures, without the underpinnings of complex economic analysis, is something emerging market economies can rarely afford. Competitive markets often do not emerge.

The learning curve for a young competition authority is invariably steep. The need to intervene, seen in the vigorous market activism of the Commission, could be a process of learning or it could indicate that apprehensions of monopoly and abuse of dominant power run deep. However, divergent perceptions and different views expressed in minority or dissenting orders of the Commission suggest that this is the process of maturing. The different levels of statutory appeal to assess contraventions held, along with the intervention of competition lawyers, will help this process. The most significant factor is that external macro policies of economic liberalization and the growing emphasis of market orientation, big business and globalization, would hasten the maturing of the Commission much earlier than expected.

Making Markets Work in Developing and Emerging Economies: Has Competition Law and Policy Played Any Role? Some Notes and Observations on the Case of India

R. Shyam Khemani[1]

shyam.khemani@skpgroup.com

Former Advisor, Competition Policy, The World Bank Group
Special Advisor, Competition Policy, SKP Group

Abstract

Since the early 1990s, a large number of countries—mainly developing and emerging market economies—have enacted competition legislation. There are now nearly 130 plus jurisdictions with specific competition law-policy to address anticompetitive problems that arise from enterprises engaging in price-fixing and other forms of cartels, dominant or monopolistic market positions, and large mergers and acquisitions that result in high concentration of industry and weaken competition. Initially, there were active debates as to whether such laws were necessary, especially with the advent of deregulation, liber-

---

1 I wish to thank Mr. Manas K. Chaudhari (Khaitan & Co, Delhi, India), and Ms. Nisha Kaur Uberoi (Cyril Amarchand & Shroff, Mumbai, India) for helpful comments and inputs on an earlier draft of this paper. Any errors and views expressed are my own.

alized trade and investment, and globalization of markets—which it was argued would make it unlikely for enterprises to engage in anticompetitive business practices. Also whether having a competition law-policy in countries with inadequate administrative capacity and institutions not lead to unnecessary government interventions, economic distortions and possibly corruption and bribery. However, liberalized trade and investment is not necessarily sufficient to foster competitive markets. Also, the experience of the past two or more decades has not revealed the alleged problems on any notable scale. Against this background, this paper discusses the implementation of India's new Competition Act, which while enacted in 2002, came into full effect in 2009. Although there have been institutional and legal challenges, the administration and enforcement of the Act has broadly been moving in the right direction. However, greater application of economic analysis, consistency in legal interpretation, reduction in staff turnover at the Competition Commission of India, and issuance of interpretation and advisory guidelines, among other such measures, would be desirable. It would reduce unnecessary business uncertainty, transaction and legal costs imposed on the private sector.

I. Introduction

Among the various issues debated by the World Bank Group ("WBG") during the early 1990s, relating to the promotion of "second generation policy reforms" in developing and emerging market economies, was whether or not the governments of these economies should enact and implement competition (antitrust/anti-monopoly) law as part of their economic policy framework. In particular, the following questions/concerns were raised:

(i) Can such economies, with lack of or weak administrative capacity, effectively administer competition law-policy, which entails applying fairly sophisticated economics?

(ii) Would having such a law-policy in the hands of governments, with limited capacity, not become another form of intervention, distort markets, impose a heavy regulatory burden, and/or act as a vehicle for corruption and bribery?

(iii) Since competition can exist without having specific competition law-policy, and having such a law/policy does not necessarily result in competition, are regulatory reforms and trade and investment liberalization not more effective policy instruments for promoting competition and market driven economic development?

In the context of the theme of this conference, it is worth revisiting these debates and evaluating the experience of implementing competition legislation in an economy such as India. The ensuing discussion is organized as follows: section II briefly re-caps some of the "drivers" for enacting competition laws in developing countries generally, and the time-sequence of key events and the institutional structure relating to India's Competition Act; section III provides a brief-overview of the administration of the Competition Act, especially in reference to the above questions/concerns; and section IV presents some conclusions and recommendations.

II. The "Drivers" for Enacting Competition Law

Different factors have driven governments at different times to enact competition legislation. In Canada, for example, "An Act for the Prevention and Suppression of Combinations formed in Restraint of Trade"[2] was enacted by parliament in 1889, primarily to address the "combinations" (mergers and acquisitions) by large grain traders and storage facilities against farmers. In the United States, the catalyst for enacting the Sherman Act in 1890 was to counter the extensive economic power and anticompetitive business practices wielded by large "trusts" (viz., combinations) in, among others, the oil and transportation (railways) sectors.

In connection with developing and emerging market economies, it may be re-called that during the early 1990s, there were approximately 35 jurisdictions—mostly western industrialized nations—with specific competition laws. The subsequent adoption of competition legislation by many other (currently 130 plus) countries has been driven by a range of factors: large and persistent fiscal deficits that limited the ability

2 An Act for the Prevention and Suppression of Combinations Formed in Restraint of Trade, 1889.

of governments to impose further taxes or borrow from capital markets, and provide basic infrastructure and other services. This generated pressure to downsize the public sector, privatize state enterprises, deregulate markets and avoid policy interventions that resulted in high costs and poor economic performance. Also, the globalization of markets and its impact on the flow of trade and investment, left governments with few policy options or room to maneuver. The Uruguay and other rounds of trade negotiations/agreements, and the creation of the WTO, as well as regional trading blocs, resulted in greater measures against state aids such as subsidies, and the erection of tariff and non-tariff barriers in international trade. In addition, countries with poor infrastructure facilities, inefficient and under-developed domestic capital markets, found that their relative competitive position in exporting was getting quickly eroded. Also, increased competition amongst nations to attract foreign investment by fostering a more market friendly business environment.

When India enacted the Monopolies and Restrictive Trade Practices ("MRTP") Act in 1969,[3] which was administered by an independent MRPT Commission, it was largely viewed as being a highly interventionist piece of legislation, particularly the provisions relating to preventing the "concentration of economic power."[4] This provision in effect impeded if not completely prevented M&As as a means for business expansion, and corporate re-structuring. As a consequence, Indian enterprises faced significant hurdles in exploiting available business synergies and economies of scale and scope. As a result, if they wish to grow and utilize internal earnings, and became increasingly conglomerations of unrelated economic activities through essentially forced diversification, this coupled with other provisions relating to "regulation of monopolies [...] and monopolistic restrictive and unfair trade practices"[5] which extended to regulating production, terms of sale, including prices and fixing of standards for goods and services, imposed a heavy regulatory burden on industry. The MRTP Act along with licensing, foreign investment and ownership restrictions, "reserve" sectors for small and medium sized enterprises, and an exclusive list of industries for "public sector undertakings," were among the plethora of government economic policies that contributed to the poor and inefficient performance of the Indian economy. As part of the 1991 economic reforms, the government amended the most restrictive provisions of the MRTP Act, which included a complete deletion of the provisions relating to concentration and limits on firm size.[6]

It would be fair to say that the Government of India and its senior economic policy-makers did not suddenly have an "awakening" that converted them to the merits of promoting free markets and competition. From 1985 onward, India had persistent balance of payments problems that by the end of 1990 culminated into a serious economic crisis. The foreign exchange reserves dwindled to barely being able to finance three weeks' worth of imports. The government was close to default—a country heavily dependent on imports of, among other vital goods and services, oil, industrial equipment and food—and it had to air-lift part of its national gold reserves to the IMF in exchange for a loan to cover its BOP debt. A small cadre of pro-market government officials backed by the Minister of Finance successfully pushed for changes that included reductions in import tariffs, deregulation of markets, reduction of taxes and greater foreign investments. These measures are credited for contributing to India's subsequent (until recently) high economic growth.

---

3 Monopolies and Restrictive Trade Practices Act, 1969, available at http://indiacode.nic.in/rspaging.asp?tfnm=196954.

4 Id., at para. 1.

5 Id.

6 Exemption of Government Companies (called the Public Sector Units or PSUs) from the ambit of the MRTP Act was initially a 'reasonable restriction' on application of the law when considered in context of economic development objectives such as market failure whereby the private sector did not invest or failed to assume risks. But later, it became a serious Constitutional issue besides an economic issue, particularly after the economic liberalization of the Indian economy in 1991 the national industry associations were challenging exemptions for PSUs.

What role did competition law play in this regard? Precious little as far as the current Competition Act is concerned, which was enacted in 2002, a decade after the initial reforms, but came into full effect in only 2009.[7] Perhaps the removal of the most interventionist provisions of the MRTP Act played a benign, but certainly not an active or direct, role in fostering competition. In addition, it is important to note that although many senior Indian Government officials recognized the merits of competition and competition law, for several years they were reluctant to support the enactment of a modern competition law—hence the decade long process. In part, the fears were that the entrenched Indian bureaucracy would opportunistically misapply the law to intervene in the newly liberalized markets, and engage in corruption and bribery. The internal debates at that time countered that the same arguments applied to having a police force, or tax collection, so then should government abolish such institutions/policies? The response to this reinforced the exact point that was being made; the Indian police and tax collection system were notorious for corruption and bribery. These arguments only highlighted the importance of having an effective institutional design, with built-in checks and balances, technical assistance and cadre of qualified and well-paid officials. Also, it was pointed out that worldwide there were few examples or allegations of corruption and bribery involving competition authorities and its officials.

The Congress Party led government, historically known for its socialist-command and control economic policies, lost the elections in 1998, and the National Democratic Alliance led by the Bharatiya Janata Party ("BJP") formed the new government. Known for its free market policies, it established a "High Level Committee on Competition Policy and Law" comprising of selected public and private sector officials drawn from law, economics and business communities.[8] The Committee's Report was submitted in 2000,[9] which gave impetus and laid the groundwork for the current Competition Act (2002) discussed further below.

In contrast, the 1991 economic reforms took place under duress. These reforms are widely credited for subsequent economic development in India. However, they are a clear example that competition can be fostered without necessarily having an effective competition law in place. This is not to say that competition law is not important in this regard. Having such a law in place deters egregious anticompetitive business practices, and safeguards the competitive process. Moreover, through its advocacy function competition authorities can also draw attention to, and contribute to, reforming economic policies and regulations that unnecessarily impede competition. Also, limit or expose rent-seeking behavior, non-transparent government-business relations, corruption and bribery, thereby creating a more market friendly and predictable business environment.

Although hard evidence on the impact of effective competition law enforcement on economic development and growth is generally lacking, studies/analysis by, among others, the World Bank Group, show a clear association between high intensity of competition in domestic markets and higher levels and rates of growth in per-capita GDP; entry of firms; and less dominance by large enterprises. These are features that are prevalent amongst countries that rank high on the world business competitiveness index and have a competition law in place. In addition, enforcement of competition laws in individual industries/markets have often led to changes in business conduct, prices and output—especially in the case of cartels.

---

7 The Competition Act, 2002, as amended by The Competition (Amendment) Act in 2007.

8 The author served as a special advisor to the Committee.

9 Report of the High Level Committee on Competition Policy and Law, 2000.

III. The Administration of the Competition Act

As briefly mentioned above, while India's Competition Act was enacted in 2002, it did not come into full effect until 2009. Shortly after enactment, the law was subject to legal challenges on structural issues and partly due to the lack of sufficient separation between the adjudication and regulatory functions of the Competition Commission of India ("CCI"). The Supreme Court delayed the implementation of the Competition Act for little over one year, and the government another four and half years, which finally led the government to introduce several amendments, many of them beyond the subject matter of the challenge before the Supreme Court of India. These were:

(1) Reduction in the size of the Competition Commission from 11 to 7 members;

(2) Establishment of the Competition Appellate Tribunal ("CAT") chaired by a senior judicial member with two non-judicial members;

(3) Compulsory notification of mergers and acquisitions above a certain size threshold;

(4) Waiting period for completion of M&A transactions extended from 90 working days to 210 calendar days.

The Supreme Court also enunciated that the Competition Act has four major functions viz., (a) adjudicatory; (b) regulatory; (c) advisory; and (d) inquisitorial (enforcement); and that the Government of India may consider amending the law in such a manner that it meets the challenge of the petitioner. The Court further observed that besides the CCI there has to be a separate Appellate Body to oversee the orders of the CCI by way of first appeal, and the final appeal on points of law will continue to be governed by the Supreme Court.

The CCI statutorily came into effect with the appointment of the chairperson and initially two members in 2009 (required quorum of minimum three members). Subsequently, CCI reached its full complement of seven members, but at the staff level remains to this date significantly undermanned. Most of the staff has been "seconded" from other government departments, especially taxation and revenue, which has generated questions and issues regarding the quality of legal/economic analysis in a number of enforcement cases. Since many seconded staff are appointed for limited time periods, this has also contributed to high staff turnover, adversely impacting on the timeline for completion and quality of the casework. The resultant institutional memory and experience loss both of the CCI and the DG offices has hardly been addresses much less arrested till date—imposing significant uncertainty and legal costs on the private sector. In addition, in some cases, CCI has taken action against alleged infractions of the law for periods when the law was not in effect.

The Competition Act is a fairly comprehensive and modern piece of legislation reflecting principles of global "best practice." As one would expect, it contains provisions prohibiting anticompetitive agreements relating to production, supply, distribution, storage, acquisition or control, as well as prices, terms of sale, division of markets, among others; the abuse of dominant market position, and combinations that cause or are likely to cause appreciable adverse effects on competition. While the sections of the Competition Act dealing with horizontal and vertical agreements, and market dominance came into effect in 2009, the regulation of combinations with mandatory notification requirements became operational in 1 June, 2011. The CCI can initiate investigations based on complaints, its own decision (viz., *suo moto*) and/or on reference by the Central or State Government or a statutory authority. In the case of combinations, it is restricted from investigation after one year after the combination has come into effect.

To date, there have been 367 investigations,[10] 8 of which have been "*suo moto*." In the case of the latter, the products/markets investigated are wide ranging, including, among others, onions, sugar mills, diesel locomotive spare parts, LPG cylinders, chemist and drug suppliers. A tally from the CCI website indicates it has issued 590 orders[11] (including clearances) in cases falling under the following sections of the Competition Act:

(1) 54 percent of cases relating to prohibited anticompetitive business practices and various agreements that may *prima facie* appreciably adversely affect competition. Of these, 41 percent of the cases were subsequently discontinued on the grounds that there exists no *prima facie* case.

(2) 8 percent related to cases investigated under the abuse of dominance provisions.

(3) 37 percent relating to notified M&A transactions, the vast majority of which have been cleared within the mandatory 30-day review period (adjusting for "clock stoppages" relating to additional information requests).

As would be expected of an economy such as India, where historically markets have been insulated from both domestic and international competitive pressures, many of the cases have pertained to cartels, bid-rigging and unfair and discriminatory practices. Enterprises found in violation of the law can be fined up to 10 percent of the turnover for the preceding three years, or up to three times their profits. In a high profile cartel case relating to cement, CCI claimed that 11 companies met regularly to fix prices and imposed a fine of approximately USD 1 billion.[12] The parties have appealed to the CAT. In another case relating to supply of LPG cylinders to various public sector oil companies, the manufacturers were charged with bid-rigging and fined approximately USD 30 million.[13] High fines have been imposed in similar cases: a real estate developer was fined approximately USD 100 million (viz., CCI vs DLF)[14]; a USD 425 million fine was imposed in a case involving auto parts;[15] and in explosives manufacturing, the leading company was fined USD 5.5 million.[16]

With respect to combinations (M&A transactions), the initial concerns raised in both the domestic and international business community—that the mandatory pre-notification requirements would impose a heavy regulatory burden, lead to significant delays, adversely impact on much needed corporate re-structuring, and on domestic and foreign investment in India—have not materialized. The CCI has reviewed about 210 merger filings in a timely and efficient manner, the great majority cleared within the 30 day first review time period. There have been only 3 "Form II" cases, which entail the provision of more detailed information by the transacting parties, and longer review time periods. This is broadly in keeping with the experience of more industrialized nations. Thus far, there has been no litigated M&A transaction.

---

10 According to communication received from the law firm Amarchand Mangaldas & Shroff (Mumbai), which includes merger filings.

11 There can be more than one "order" per case, such as dissenting views by one or more of the CCI members hearing a case.

12 Case No. 29/2010, Builders Association of India v. Cement Manufacturers' Association & Others, 20 June 2012, *available at* http://www.cci.gov.in/May2011/OrderOfCommission/292011.pdf.

13 Case No. 3/2011, In re: suo-motu case against LPG cylinder manufacturers, 24 February 2012, *available at* http://www.cci.gov.in/May2011/OrderOfCommission/LPGMainfeb2.pdf.

14 See www.cci.gov.in, for further details on this and other cases cited.

15 See details regarding the fine *available at* http://www.cci.gov.in/May2011/PressRelease/PressRelease032011.pdf

16 Case No. 6/2011, Coal India Limited v. GOCL Hyderabad & Others, 16 April 2012, *available at* http://cci.gov.in/May2011/OrderOfCommission/062011.pdf.

However, the Sun-Ranbaxy case is the first Phase II case since third party interventions have for the first time been resorted to by the Commission in a merger control matter.[17]

Although the CCI was fully established and the Competition Act came into effect in 2009, in the period since 2002, it has engaged extensively in "competition advocacy."' In collaboration with the World Bank and other donors, a number of sector specific competition assessments were conducted for: cement, manufacturing, pharmaceuticals, banking, intercity bus transportation, trucking, domestic passenger airline services, and other areas such as anti-dumping, public sector undertakings and intellectual property. Competition advocacy initiatives have continued with meetings between competition law/policy officials and various sector specific regulators, departments and ministries at the Central and State levels, including, among others, Road Transport and Highways, Materials Management-Ministry of Defense, Department of Pharmaceuticals, Health & Welfare, and Procurement.

Through its law enforcement and competition advocacy functions, awareness of CCI and the Competition Act has certainly been heightened as can be adjudged by: increased business press reportage, growth in private sector law and economics consulting firms, and increased business compliance programs.

1. Emerging Issues/Lessons from the Indian Experience

The number of investigations initiated by the Commission is quite high—even netting out the number of mandatory merger notifications/filings over which it has no direct control. The Commission has not articulated what constitutes "*prima facie*" grounds for initiating an investigation. There are cases where investigations have been launched on the basis of a single complaint. In one matter relating to alleged abuse of dominance and discriminatory/unfair trade practices by the Board of Control for Cricket in India ("BCCI"), the complainant disappeared/could not be found after the investigation. Moreover, the complainant did not appear to have any direct commercial interests or dealings in the industry, or even indirect interests as a purchaser of tickets for cricket events. At most, he might have been a TV couch potato watching broadcast matches. In another case, the complainant was also not a customer or directly affected party of the automobile spares part and servicing in question.

The basis on which fines have been determined and imposed by the CCI is not clear. In some cases, such as cement, the fines appear to be disproportionately high, while in other cases such as in Mulitplex Film Distribution, quite low. In any case, while recognizing that the terms "high" and "low" are relative and should be benchmarked, in some cases CCI has used profits, and in others turnover, to determine fines, and the periods over which the computations have been made tend to vary, not necessarily corresponding to the time period over which the alleged infractions have taken place. In the case of the alleged bid rigging by LPG cylinder manufacturers,[18] the entire profits of the companies were used as a basis for imposing fines, without adjustments for profits earned from other unrelated commercial activities.

While the CCI record on review of combinations/M&A transactions is commendable, thus far no guidelines or statements on how it assesses the competitive effects of a transaction, that could usefully guide

17 Phase II can be different from Form II filing since not all Form II lead to a Phase II investigation/hearing. For further details on this case see www.cci.gov.in.

18 See *supra* note 10.

business, have yet to be issued.[19] There also remain inconsistencies between definitions of control under the merger provisions and the Indian takeover laws as to how options and convertibles are computed, specifically, in terms of the 25 percent limit specified in the Competition Act but not in the takeover laws. Earlier, there was also confusion on the notification requirements of intra-group amalgamations that had no effect on the competitive landscape, which to the Commission's credit was subsequently clarified by providing a partial exemption.

In most cases/orders, economic analysis has been lacking. The CCI has adopted a legalistic approach in its non-merger investigations and decisions. All these cases/decisions have been appealed to the CAT or "stayed" through District High Courts. The various fines levied have yet to be collected—in some cases, it has been required that 10 percent of the fines are deposited while appeals are pending. Thus there is considerable legal uncertainty with respect to the final outcome in various cases.

As an indicator of the lack of economic analysis in the cement case,[20] the approach to defining the "relevant market" was based on administrative reporting/regional zones specified by the government when the product was under public sector control—instead of analyzing the relevant market in terms of demand-supply related factors, in-outbound shipments by firms, geographic segmentation, entry of new firms, etc. —which is highly questionable. Also, of the total number of 49 cement companies, with 173 plants, 11 have been charged and fined for cartelization of the market, without putting forward an analysis or "theory of the case" as to how the cartel could be maintained with some major firms stated by the Commission as not being members of the cartel.

Moreover, not all of the 11 companies operated in the same zones let alone appropriately defined markets. In addition, the Director General for Investigations relied on price correlations without correcting for and taking into account other relevant factors influencing prices—especially since electricity is a critical input for all companies, the price of which has been increasing. Similar questions arise in the (lack of) economic analysis in the bid-rigging case against LPG cylinder manufacturers.[21]

> However, more importantly, the CCI in this case failed to leverage the analysis and charge the public sector enterprises such as the Indian Oil Company and Bharat Petroleum among others in abetting, if not participating, in the anticompetitive arrangements. Essentially, these enterprises would invite tenders for the supply of LPG cylinders, select and often further negotiate down the lowest bid, and negotiate and allocate production quotas and markets to *all* the qualified bidders for the supply of LPG cylinders. Among the consequences was that costs of production and therefore prices were higher than necessary as most of the manufacturers were operating with underutilized capacity. CCI seemed to have missed an opportunity to alter the manner in which these public sector enterprises administered tenders and also to act as a catalyst for efficient restructuring of the industry. Besides, the lack of application of economic analyses, the Commission and also the COMPAT (or CAT) have not maintained consistent legal approaches, such as in the absence of 'fining guidelines' or other guidelines on how different factors are being

19 There have been various other guidelines/statements, at time at the eleventh hour relating to "local nexus" thresholds in case of multi-jurisdictional transactions that require notifications were issued. However, some questions remain as to the reporting thresholds for "groups" vs. buyer/target firm. Notwithstanding such concerns, the reporting thresholds under the merger control provisions of the Act are deliberately set high. Also, as its experience has grown, CCI has introduced various amendments to the merger regulations, and is open to suggestions by the business community.

20 See *supra* note 9.

21 See *supra* note 10.

considered. These inconsistencies cause serious impediments in the proper growth of jurisprudence in India on competition law.[22]

IV. Concluding Remarks and Recommendations

The preceding discussion provides a very brief overview of India's experience with the implementation of the Competition Act. In reference to the questions posed at the outset, it can be confidently stated that despite some initial stumbling blocks on the institutional design of the competition regime, especially relating to the separation of the adjudication and regulatory functions, the implementation of the Competition Act is broadly going in the right direction.

Commentators have pointed out that unlike other "regulators," CCI has been applying the law and concluding matters in a timely manner. However, there are no doubt areas where administrative and other procedures would benefit from streamlining, and greater articulation and application of guidelines. Administration of competition law is in part an evolutionary process, and in the Indian case there have already been changes/proposed amendments. However, greater transparency is desirable in regards to what constitutes a "*prima facie*'" or other basis for decision-making in investigating matters, case selection, determination and imposing of fines, and economic analysis used to assess competition, among other areas mentioned above. Concerns relating to corruption, bribery, and misuse or overreach of bureaucratic power, procedural and other delays, imposition of regulatory burden on business etc., have not materialized. There have been some unofficial allusions made by some law practitioners of corruption relating to investigations conducted, but no formal or documented cases have been presented.

In terms of administrative capacity, the CCI faces challenges in recruiting and retaining qualified multidisciplinary staff, with emphasis in the fields of law, economics and business. The interim measures of staff temporarily seconded from other parts of government is unsatisfactory. Aside from loss of acquired learning and experience due to staff turnover, there have been inconsistencies in the quality of casework. The World Bank had recommended that the staff of CCI be paid well to attract the best within and outside the public sector. Unfortunately the recommendation was only partly adopted—the salaries and other benefits of the members of the Commission were raised and are considered to be relatively high, but at the staff level the salaries have remained unchanged. In regards to the latter, there are no incentives for seconded staff to pursue careers in CCI and give up tenure and seniority in their "home" departments.

However, senior civil servants from other ministries, many within 3-4 years of retirement, have sought positions to become members of the CCI. To date, no member of CCI has been appointed from outside the government civil service cadre. At the design stage, it was hoped that CCI would at least have members drawn from the legal, economics, academic and business communities. Such diversity would certainly contribute to more informed decision-making.

Despite being short staffed the CCI has investigated a fairly high number of cases (excluding mandatory M&A notifications), that has led to questions whether it is over extending itself and is "'hyper-active,"

22 For example, fines were reduced by the COMPAT in almost all cases but it refused to apply its own principles in the DLF and NSE cases. In another case, CCI held cartels may have been formed but if the same remained in operation for a week or so it may not have impacted the market for long enough period, hence exoneration was ordered.

which adversely impacts on the quality and consistency of the case analysis, and may in some areas unnecessarily impose high costs on business to respond to unsubstantiated allegations. Hence greater selectivity and setting priorities of the cases to be investigated would be recommended. In addition, the law does not have provisions for negotiating with undertakings and implementing consent orders—which contributes to unnecessary administrative and business costs. Apparently, the decision to not incorporate such a provision was not a design flaw, but a deliberate decision to minimize opportunities for possible corruption and bribery and/or interventions in markets.

Has the implementation of the competition law strengthened and fostered competitive markets? It is too early to state this to be the case—as in many other jurisdictions, including advance industrial economies—no post case/investigation analysis has been conducted. However, business has definitely and increasingly taken cognizance of the application of the Act, and hopefully this has led to appropriate changes in their conduct. One indicator is the growth in business compliance programs offered by various law firms to their clients. The increased competition in the Indian economy is in large due to the 1991 reforms and subsequent trade, investment, ownership and other market liberalization and regulatory reforms. The role and challenges for the CCI will be to ensure that these measures are maintained, if not further accelerated (through competition advocacy), and counter pressures from both the public and private sector entities lobbying for exemptions and exceptions from the law as has already been attempted in individual cases.

Making Markets Work in Southeast Asia

R. Ian McEwin

mcewin@me.com

Khazanah Chair of Regulatory Studies, University of Malaya
Visiting Professor of Law, Chulalongkorn University

Abstract

Practicing lawyers are not normally interested in examining why or how laws originate, but rather with identifying which institutions make and adjudicate the law and the way those institutions actually make and apply the law. But to properly understand competition law across borders a lawyer should why competition laws were introduced; why competition laws and their associated institutions were designed the way they were; what forces impact on the way competition law operates in practice; whether competition laws are strongly enforced or not; and, if they are enforced, whether there are there any enforcement biases towards special interest groups. Southeast Asian countries are diverse in a number of respects yet are integrating economicallyand to some extent politically. This chapter provides some historical and economic background to the introduction of competition laws in Southeast Asiaa region in which all countries have committed to introducing competition laws by the end of 2015.

I. Introduction

> "[T]he Southeast Asian economy is the product of a relationship between political and economic power that developed in the colonial era and was sustained, with a different cast of characters in the post-colonial era. In this relationship, a political elite grants to members of an economic elite monopoly concessions, normally in domestic service industries, that enable the latter to extract enormous amounts of wealth, without a requirement to generate the technological capabilities, branded corporations and productivity gains that drive sustainable economic development."[1]

Whether competition law is introduced, its form and whether it is enforced at all ultimately depends on the political-decision making institutions in a country. Southeast Asian countries share some similarities. All, with the exception of Thailand, were colonies of European powers—and it can be argued that Thailand replicated colonial institutions as part of its modernization and as a defense to its own possible colonization.

One of the legacies of colonization was a high degree of government intervention.[2] Colonial powers were mainly interested in economically exploiting their colonies and brought in manpower from China and India as people were seen as the major regional resource constraint. An important legacy of this is that ethnic Chinese (and to a lesser extent ethnic Indians) now dominate business in Southeast Asia. Mostly they gained this dominant position by collaborating closely with government and indigenous political elites—obtaining monopoly licenses and concessions, tax-farming (where they collected taxes on behalf of the monarch), etc.

Also important to the introduction of competition law and its impact are local business conditions. In Southeast Asia, business networks among ethnic Chinese (usually based on the region where that came from in China) were an important reason for their business success. Being able to find out the prices of commodities in different countries more quickly than locals allowed for speedy arbitrage. In the absence of effective legal institutions, they benefitted from trust between members of their own extended family or clan group that allowed for secured lending between them and also a greater willingness to be involved in long-term contracting. This gave them a considerable advantage over indigenous businesses, but also resulted in well-developed networks and collaboration.

Asian crony capitalism is sometimes used to describe both the links between government and business and the inter-firm networks that make up business groups. Collusive ties between rulers/bureaucrats/business both in setting and enforcing property rights and rules are common throughout Asia. Failure to prosecute "big blokes" or "khon yai" is usually a reflection of networks. In hierarchical societies people lower down the hierarchy are forced to take the blame.

The term crony capitalism is applied to business groups such as the keiretsu in Japan, the chaebol in South Korea and the overseas family-owned business groups and conglomerates in Southeast Asia. Cronyism among business groups refers to the practice of firms in the group owning each other's shares and lending money to each other on the basis of the relationship rather than on economic merit. As Hamilton puts it:

---

1 See Joe Studwell, Asian Godfathers: Money and Power in Hong Kong and Southeast Asia, XIII, (Grove Press, 2007).

2 See William Case, Politics in Southeast Asia: Democracy or Less (Routledge Curzon, Oxford, 2002).

> "It is at this point that the analysts begin to equate cronyism with *guanxi*, that ubiquitous term meaning, in Chinese, relationship or connection. Equating cronyism and *guanxi* implies that networks based on interpersonal associations look a lot like market distorting cartels."[3]

Imposed competition law impacts on elite business dominance and their networks. An important reason why ethnic Chinese groups were given concessions such as monopolies was because they posed no political threat to indigenous rulers/elites. The concessions could easily be taken away with little political consequence. So ethnic Chinese business needed to guard against expropriation—as they previously needed to do in China. One way to protect against confiscation is to form conglomerates in many different markets. This allowed for parts of the group to be taken without necessarily impacting on the remainder. It also allowed for secrecy about company control and operations—which has implications for competition law enforcement.

Another legacy of their colonial past in Southeast Asia was their relatively late industrialization. Colonial powers exported manufactured goods to their colonies in return for commodities. Post-independence industrialization was usually slow as countries continued with their colonial past—exporting mainly commodities and importing manufactures. As a result, much of the elite family wealth created in Southeast Asia has been in commodities, finance, real estate and hotels. These sectors require little investment in technology and skills—but relationships were important.

Political elites determine whether competition law is introduced or not and its shape. A country with a stable political elite is unlikely to give up its self-serving privileges. Crouch and Morley argue that: "a long-established cohesive elite can often obstruct political change even when other factors are pushing in the direction of change."[4] So we would expect that competition law is likely to be introduced only where the existing political elite is unstable and so there is disagreement about the sharing of state provided rents between different elite groups.

Practicing lawyers are not normally interested in examining why or how laws originate, but rather with identifying which institutions make and adjudicate the law and the way those institutions actually make and apply the law. But to properly understand competition law across borders a lawyer should understand several aspects of the legal and cultural background, including: why competition laws were introduced at all; why competition laws and their associated institutions were designed the way they were; what forces impact on the way competition law operates in practice; whether competition laws are strongly enforced or not; and, if they are enforced, whether there are there any enforcement biases.

Different jurisdictions may interpret similar, or even the same, competition law differently due to differences in attitudes towards competition, differences in goals, differences in interest group influences, differences in legal reasoning and institutions, differences in likely economic effects in different markets as a result of the same anti-competitive conduct, and differences in the competence and effectiveness of administrative, legal and judicial processes. But there is an increasing convergence in competition law around the use of economics—with jurisdictions deciding similar fact situations in ways that improve economic outcomes, not other social objectives.

---

3 See Gary Hamilton, Asian Business Networks in Transition: or, What Alan Greenspan Does Not Know about the ASIAN Business Crisis in The Politics Of The Asian Economic Crisis Cornell 47 (T.J. Pempel, University Press, 1999).

4 See Harold Crouch and James W. Morley The Dynamics of Political Change in Driven by Growth: Political Change in the Asia Pacific Region, 299, (James W. Morley ed., M.E. Sharpe, 1993).

II. Southeast Asia Political Patronage

While Southeast Asia's countries are considerably diverse, the political systems, reflecting traditional political governance, operate in similar ways. As mentioned earlier, much of the private wealth in Southeast Asia comes from state-sponsored monopolies. The following scenario is representative:

> A monarch (sultan or king) or elected politician (usually a President or single-party government)—both called here the ruler—centralizes control over the (often competing) elites via a patronage system. But money is needed to do that. Money to support a patronage system can come: from foreign investors; foreign aid; selling domestic production or import licenses or concessions; for making decisions advantaging one party over another in a dispute, from money obtained from the appointment, promotion and retirement of senior military officers, ministers and senior members of the bureaucracy or by appointments to state-owned bodies; or control over the revenues of state-owned enterprises, particularly banks. The ruler might also centralize control of all state-awarded contracts in a body directly under his control.

One of the means for doing the above could include the setting up of a non-audited, tax-free "foundation'" to accept donations from all those who benefit from military or bureaucratic appointment and promotion, the awarding of lucrative contracts for construction or licenses for importing or producing usually in monopoly or highly concentrated markets. The ruler can impose "levies'" on the profits of banks, conglomerates and state-owned enterprises in exchange for minimizing competition—particularly from foreign financial institutions. The foundation can then distribute money to family and friends either as gifts or as loans to buy property on advantageous terms or shares in newly privatized, monopolized corporations.

Of course, the whole patronage structure is extended and reinforced by senior military or bureaucrats also going into business with their children, and setting up their own patronage networks. Children could then move in politics, allowing for further deals between elite families to further extract money from the general population. Ethnic Chinese may be favored in business patronage networks because they cannot challenge the ruler politically. Of course, colonial powers also awarded monopolies to their own nationals—hence limiting indigenous economic prospects. With independence there was a major rush to replace foreigners with locals.

While the economies in Southeast Asia differ, all are mostly dominated by large, state-owned enterprises (closely linked to politicians) and/or have private sectors dominated by large conglomerates owned by a relatively few very rich families—usually of Chinese ethnic origin—who are also closely linked to politicians.

III. Everyone Wants to Be a Monopolist

Southeast Asia sits on the maritime routes between China, India, the Middle East, Africa and Europe. Southeast Asian exports included products such as "clove, nutmeg, sandalwood, sappan wood, camphor, and lacquer [which] found their way to world markets even in Roman and Han times."[5] China dominated trade in the area up until the 17th century. Chinese emperors saw themselves as emperors of the whole world—and so relations with other countries were not seen as equal but rather tributary. The Confucian contempt for merchants and a belief that China did not need goods from overseas meant that any trade that occurred was seen as a tribute—that is, gifts to the Emperor. Benevolent emperors eventually allowed trade as a favor to foreigners and, in 1685, the previous ban on foreign trade was lifted and customs houses established in several provinces.

China's nomination of favored "tributary states" in Southeast Asia, for example, the maritime Malay kingdom of Sri Vijaya, in Sumatra, in Indonesia during the Tang Dynasty (618-907) lead to increased trade between China and Southeast Asia. During the Ming Dynasty (1368–1644), China greatly increased its demand for Southeast Asian products through "official" trade. Southeast Asian production was stimulated though trading expeditions—for example the Mong Emperor Yongle (1402-24) sent six trading expeditions to Southeast Asia. As Reid notes:

> "If one moment must be singled out for the beginning of Southeast Asia's 'age of commerce,' the first state trading mission under the eunuch admiral Zheng He, in 1405, is the best candidate."[6]

Through the tributary system and a ban on private overseas trade, Ming Emperors tried to monopolize trade. However, in 1576 China began licensing junks to trade legally in Southeast Asiahelping certain ports to prosper.

Before the Europeans, local rulers wanted to monopolize trade. The rulers in Southeast Asia were absolute—some claiming supernatural status (derived from Indian, mainly Brahman influences). Rulers regulated markets directly and claimed the right to confiscate the land and wealth of their subjects. Reid notes:

> "As a result of its exceptional exposure to global commerce, Southeast Asia [...] shared the experience of Western Europe and Japan more closely than did most of continental Asia. The differences between Southeast Asia and other regions in the early modern era are equally instructive. In relation not only to Europe but to most other parts in Asia, the absence of clear safeguards got private property below the winds inhibited the development of financial institutions and discouraged the development of fixed capital [...]. By the latter stages of the age of commerce, and still more in the eighteenth century, Europeans had little doubt why Southeast Asians did not become rich. They blamed the rapacity of rulers for the failure of a propertied middle class to develop [...]."[7]

> "One of the most striking differences between Southeast Asia and most other parts of the Eurasian continent was the intimate relation between power and commerce. Rulers and their ministers participated fully in trade, and their literature appreciated its importance. Successful merchants

5 Anthony Reid, Southeast Asia in the Age of Commerce, 1450-1680 Vol 2: Expansion and Crisis, 1, (Silkworm Books, Yale University, 1993).

6 Id., at page 12.

7 Id., at page 268.

necessarily evolved into power-holders, either by allying with an existing court or forming a new one."[8]

The sixteenth century was a good time for monopolists everywhere. In England, during the reign of Queen Elizabeth I (1558-1603) lobbyists paid royal courtiers to sponsor their petitions for monopolies. As a result, as Bindoff puts it:

> "[T]he restrictive principle had, like some giant squid, fastened its embracing tentacles round many branches of domestic trade and manufacture," and "in the last decade of Elizabeth's reign scarcely an article in common use—coal, soap, starch, iron, leather, books, wine, fruit—was unaffected by patents of monopoly."[9]

Lobbyists paid royal courtiers to present petitions to the Queen for domestic monopoly grants. Once granted, search warrants and the courts were used to eliminate competition and so allow the monopolist to fix price and quality. Foreign trading companies also were granted monopolies. The Muscovy Company formed in 1555 was granted a monopoly of all English trade between Russia and Asia through the Russian White Sea port of Arkhangelsk. Later, it also held a monopoly on trade with North America (and a monopoly charter for the colonization of Virginia). Elizabeth granted further monopolies to the Barbary, Eastland and Levant companies—associated with the same men as the Muscovy Company—the Levant Company having a monopoly over trade through the Levant and Persia with India. In 1600, the East India Company was chartered with a monopoly over all trade with the East Indies.

As demand for spices grew in Europe, Portugal, Holland, and to a lesser extent England and Spain, fought for control of the market. Up until the 15th century, Southeast Asian goods were transported to Europe via the Red Sea and Persian Gulf ports to the Mediterranean. As they developed the sea route around the Cape of Good Hope, the Portuguese also started to disrupt trade along the traditional route at the end of the 15th century, by sinking Muslim and Indian trading ships.

Between the 15th and 17th centuries, England, Holland, Portugal and Spain all fought to control the spice trade to Europe. England set up the East India Company in 1600. In order to limit harmful competition between Dutch ships, the Verenigde Oostindische Compagnie ("VOC") was set up in 1602 with the exclusive right to trade east of the Cape of Good Hope. The Dutch focused on pepper and spices in Southeast Asia, whereas the Portuguese mainly focused on the West coast of India.

The VOC had been set up to become a monopoly.[10] The Dutch, with the help of local Muslims, drove the Portuguese out of Ambon in 1605 and obtained a monopoly of the cloves grown there. Jan Pieterszoon Coen was appointed Governor-General in 1619 and used force to try and establish trading monopolies. In 1621, he conquered the five nutmeg producing islands of Banda, killing almost all the population of 15,000 and taking the rest into slavery. The islands were re-populated with Dutch settlers who sold their nutmeg to the VOC.

While the Portuguese went east, the Spanish went west. When Ferdinand Magellan died in 1521, in the Philippines, and four of his five ships lost, the remaining ship still brought sufficient spices back to make the overall voyage a financial success. During the 16th century, Holland gained control of shipping in Northern Europe and they entered the spice trade gradually taking over from the Portuguese. After conquering Malacca in 1641 and gaining control of the cinnamon and spice trade in India and Ceylon, the Dutch also controlled

---

8 Id., at page 270.

9 See S.T. Bindoff, Tudor England, 228, (Penguin Books, 1950).

10 Id., at page 274.

the spices in Indonesia. The Dutch tried to keep prices high by restricting output by, for example, burning trees etc. While the French did not play a major role in the spice trade, they reduced the economic hold the Dutch held by planting cloves, cinnamon and nutmeg on their own islands in the Indian Ocean.

IV. Business Is Different in Southeast Asia

As Witt and Redding [11] put it: "Asian business systems (except Japan) cannot be understood through categories identified in the West." If business does not work the same way then are business practices identified as anti-competitive in the EU or USA anti-competitive or not in Southeast Asia? Will competition law intervention have the same effect? Are competition authorities likely to work in the same way?

Competition policies and laws have the potential to have a major impact on the economic development of Southeast Asia, but there are powerful losers. Some countries in Southeast Asia see competition law as complementing market-driven industrial policies. If competition law is introduced to help speed up economic development for countries at low or middle-income levels, then decisions of competition regulators and courts will reflect economic development goals. As well, competition law decisions may have to take into account the effects of their decisions outside the relevant market(s). Decisions on price-fixing, etc., can have a considerable impact on ways of doing business that have existed for centuries. In countries with limited social security to deal with the impacts of economic change, competition law decisions may also have greater social consequences and so placing greater importance on economic fairness may result in order to avoid social instability—stability being an important goal of all Asia societies. Practicing lawyers cannot assume that competition law decisions made in Southeast Asia will follow the jurisprudence of other countries, even though most competition laws in Asia are based on those of Europe.

V. The Asian Financial Crisis – the Trigger for the Introduction of Competition Law in Southeast Asia

In 1999, Indonesia and Thailand were the first countries in Southeast Asia to adopt competition laws—as a direct result of the 1997 Asian Financial Crisis. But their subsequent enforcement experiences have been quite different. While Indonesia has been active in enforcing competition law, Thailand has not successfully imposed a single penalty despite several high profile investigations.[12]

11 Michael A. Witt & Gordon Redding INSEAD Working Paper No. 2013/05/EPS/EFE, Asian Business Systems: Institutional Comparison, Clusters, and Implications for Varieties of Capitalism and Business Systems Theory. Socio-Economic Review 11, 2, page 4 *available at* http://www.insead.edu/facultyresearch/research/doc.cfm?did=51658.

12 See R. Ian McEwin, Designing Competition Law under Financial Crisis—Indonesia and Thailand Compared, Competition Policy International Journal Volume 10 No. 1, 2014, at 248-280.

Institutions matter for economic growth. Institutions create incentives either for general economic advancement or for economic and/or political elites to become rich at the expense of the rest. It cannot be assumed that rulers or governments act in their country's interest. Acemoglu and Robinson[13] argue that poor economic growth results from bad institutions—which are the result of political systems that create private gains for elites even if everyone else is made worse-off. Growth, they argue, comes from having "inclusive" societies —which open up economic and political systems—and which deprive elites of their rents. But, of course, elites have an interest in retaining their "extractive" institutions and will fight change. North, Wallis and Weingast[14] similarly argue that lack of development comes from "limited access order" where a rent-seeking coalition restricts access to the political and economic systems and which elites have an interest in maintaining. Economic growth for them also comes from opening up economic and political institutions.

But what institutions are necessary for good economic growth? Acemoglu and Robinson argue that inclusive economic institutions include effective property rights and legal and court systems. Inclusive political systems mean liberal democracies. However, rule of law may be more important than democracy. Too much participation can impede infrastructure developments due to legal suits and political demonstrations.

North, Wallis and Weingast also argue that the natural state of political affairs is the "limited access pattern" where government is centralized and operates without the consent of those governed and where society is organized by personal relationships and dynasties. The next phase is an economy that grows more quickly, has many civil organizations, a decentralized government and where social relationships are mainly impersonal, governed by the rule of law, secure property rights and greater fairness and equality. An important part of this is the need to transform personal privileges into "'impersonal rights.'" Rather than privilege creating rents, open access erodes rents through entry.

North, Wallis and Weingast argue that the move to an open access system came with the American and French revolutions that legitimized competition both in politics and the economy. Acemoglu and Robinson similarly argue that:

> "The reason that Briton is richer than Europe is because in 1688 [...] England [...] had a revolution that transformed the politics and thus the economics of the nation. People fought for and won more political rights and used them to expand their economic opportunities. The result was a fundamentally different political and economic trajectory, culminating in the Industrial Revolution."[15]

The Asian Financial Crisis in 1997 can be seen, similarly, as a "revolution" that has started to break down the systems of "extractive" or "limited access" governments in Southeast Asia. Before 1997, centralized governments in Southeast Asia emphasized bureaucratic capacity. Creating legal rules with independent adjudication impeded "efficient" central development planning and also rent-seeking. Foreign investors did not care as long as they could gain access, often through their embassy, to the bureaucrats that counted to get licenses and resolve problems. This strategy worked as long as economic growth continued—after all, leaders could argue that no one else could replace them (a common theme even in Singapore). However, weaknesses in institutions such as in legal and judicial systems soon became apparent as bureaucrats and

---

13 See Daron Acemoglu and James A. Robinson, Why Nations Fail: The Origins of Power, Prosperity and Poverty (Crown Religion, 2012).

14 Douglas C. North, John Joseph Wallis and Barry R. Weingast, *Violence and Social Orders: A Conceptual Framework For Interpreting Recorded Human History* (Cambridge University Press, 2009).

15 See *supra* note 13, at page 4.

their political masters' greed became more transparent and the benefits of impressive growth were not widely shared.

Competition law can be seen as part of the opening up of economic and political institutions. But how does competition law help the move towards an "open access order" or "inclusive system"? Coupled with other microeconomic policy reforms, competition law can help to create the conditions for new entry into markets and ensuring only efficient firms are able to prosper. Cartels restrict entry not only into the cartel but also into the market—through threats of boycott. Breaking up restrictive cartels not only reduces high prices but also allows for greater potential entry. Similarly, attacking dominant firm predatory conduct that excludes efficient competitors also allows for greater entry of new firms. As governments have commonly restricted access to markets, reducing entry barriers also reduces the source of rents to economic and political elites so helping to ensure economic prosperity.

Is competition law a pre-requisite for inclusive growth? Simply reducing tariffs or market entry barriers is not enough. Barriers to trade and entry can be resurrected through collusion and abuse of market power. Competition law is necessary to stop former public barriers to competition being replaced by private barriers. The economic success of the United States can be attributed, in part, to the delegation of industrial policy to competition law. That is, the emphasis is not on an "extractive" industrial policy where government consciously promotes (and protects) specific industries or sectors via "national champions" and where legislation is "captured" by vested interest groups. Instead, competition law can be seen, using Acemoglu and Robinson's terminology, as more "inclusive" in that impersonal rules about competition are enforced by an independent court system. However, moving from an "extractive" to "inclusive" system is not easy. Many paths may be taken and roadblocks erected.

VI. Recent Southeast Asian Growth

Southeast Asia has had remarkable economic growth over the last 50 years. Initially, industrialization followed the normal path of developing import-substituting industries. But Asian economies were reluctant to go too far down this path. Japan from the 1960s built its industrial capacity on exports and all major Asian economies subsequently followed this export strategy. While South Korea followed the Japanese conglomerate industrialization model (through the Chaebols), Taiwan pushed the development of small and medium industries. In Malaysia, the Philippines and Thailand, emphasis was initially placed on agricultural exports such as rubber, sugar, coconut and palm-oil products and textiles. This soon changed to promoting labor-intensive export industries such as clothing, footwear and electronics assembly.

In 1997, Thailand had one of the best economies in Southeast Asia. But Thailand had pegged its Baht to the US dollar for years. In 1997, selling pressure from speculators and bankers triggered the collapse of the Baht, which led to the 1997 Asian financial crisis. Subsequently, competing devaluations in other Southeast Asian countries led to foreign capital flight and economic recession. The economic collapse saw countries review their economic policies. While economic growth started to recover quickly in 1999, economic growth in Indonesia, Malaysia, the Philippines and Thailand has not matched pre-1997 levels.

An important cause of the crisis was financial sector weaknesses that included "relationship-based lending practices, excessive risk-taking, and inadequate financial supervision and regulation."[16] Further, as Tran Van Hoa put it there is:

> "[T]he presence of nepotism or favoritism in many Asian countries under which investment and loans were given to people or companies with close connections to government officials or the ruling class. The nepotism is more pronounced in Indonesia where monopolies even for staple foods or commodities have been created for the benefit of the elitist and highly connected business people."[17]

In summary, while governments were important in promoting the high levels of growth in Southeast Asia for the last few decades of the 20th century, they were also largely responsible for the historic economic collapse in 1997. The crisis, in part, was due to a political inability to move away from the old ways of running things. As Robison notes:

> "Rather than a convergence towards free markets and liberal forms of democracy and legal rational forms of authority, there is also a convergence where neo-liberal ideas about the market state are accommodated within highly illiberal forms of political authority and within forms of regulation that see the market in terms of the interests of its most powerful players."[18]

As a result of the crisis, some affected governments in Southeast Asia collapsed either through elections (Thailand) or through varying degrees of turmoil (Indonesia had four presidents in five years and the Philippines threw out its corrupt president).

The first competition laws in Southeast Asia followed the Asian Financial Crisis (Indonesia and Thailand in 1997). To understand why competition laws were (and are being) introduced in Southeast Asia requires some background knowledge of the way governments work in the region. Competition laws are the product of political elite competition—whether between elite groups within and between political parties in democracies or elites within single party governments. Due to differences in the way elite competition is played, inevitably there will be differences in competition laws reflecting differences in political factors, the importance of vested interests, attitudes to competition and the stage of economic and institutional development in a country.

In most of Southeast Asia, personal enrichment is an important motivator for seeking political and bureaucratic power. Aspinall and Van Klinken, in the Indonesian context, point out that it is:

> "essential to understand illegality by state officials through a political, rather than merely a legal lens . . . .[I]llegality almost invariably occurs as part of collective, patterned, organized and collaborative acts, linked to the competition for political power and access to state resources. Understanding illegality in this way is helped by viewing the state less as a bureaucratic machine and more as a field of power characterized by competition and insecurity." [19]

---

16 See David A. Hollingsworth, The Rise, the Fall and the Recovery of Southeast Asia's Minidragons: How Can Their History Be Lessons We Shall Learn During the Twenty-First Century and Beyond? 15 (Lexington Books, 2007).

17 See Tran Van Hoa, Causes and Prescriptions for the Asian Financial Crisis in The Causes and Impact of the Asian Financial Crisis 11-25, 17 (Tran Van Hoa and Charles Harvie ed., Palgrave Macmillan, 2000).

18 See Richard Robison, Strange Bedfellows: Political Alliances in the Making of Neo-liberal Governance in Governance and the Depolitization of Development 27 (Wil Hout and Richard Robison ed., Routledge, 2009).

19 Edward Aspinall and Gerry Van Klinken, The State and Illegality in Indonesia 23 (KITLV Press, 2010).

VII. The Competition Law State of Play in Southeast Asia

The ASEAN Economic Community ("AEC") Blueprint provides a roadmap for establishing a "single market" by 2015. The intent is to create a single economic market and production base as well as to enhance the competitiveness of the region and improve its attractiveness as a host location for foreign direct investment. Relative to the European Union ("EU"), ASEAN's notion of a "single market" represents loose integration. However, even this requires countries to move beyond trade liberalization. As a result, the AEC Blueprint has set goals in a number of policy areas including competition policy (here limited to competition law).

Since there is no multilateral or plurilateral competition regime, every ASEAN member state has agreed to enact a national competition statute prior to 2015, and most have already done so. ASEAN has opted to move mainly toward coordination of competition laws. The ASEAN Economic Community ("AEC") Blueprint states that: "The main objective of the competition policy is to foster a culture of fair competition,"[20] but does not say what "fair competition" means. ASEAN has set fairly modest goals for itself in the area of competition law and policy.[21] First, not all ASEAN countries have competition laws but they have all committed to introducing them by 2015. Secondly, ASEAN sought to develop regional guidelines on competition policy by 2010 and did so. Thirdly, it seeks to enhance capacity building in the area of competition law. Lastly, it seeks to establish a network of national competition law enforcement bodies—the role of the network being to "discuss and coordinate" competition policies. There is no commitment to harmonize competition law and policies across countries.

Cambodia is the only country in Southeast Asia without any competition law or laws with competition provisions. Indonesia, Malaysia, Singapore, Thailand and Vietnam have general competition laws. In the Lao People's Democratic Republic, competition law takes the form of a decree issued by the Prime Minister's Office in 2004, but it has not been implemented as yetit is currently being revised taking into account mainly Vietnamese competition law.[22] The constitutions of Myanmar and the Philippines contain anti-monopoly and fair competition provisions. Myanmar passed a competition law in February 2015. The President of the Philippines signed a new competition law into effect in July 2015, Brunei Darussalam does not have a general competition statute as yet (some have noted that the law has been passed but it has not been publicly disclosed at the tine of writing), but there are various competition provisions in sector-specific regulations on telecommunications. As would be expected, countries that do have general competition laws have taken a variety of approaches and some are more comprehensive than others. It is important to emphasize, however, that the differences between statutes are stark and while in some instances countries have competition statutes, they appear not to acknowledge the primacy of markets in allocating resources. Instead, priority is accorded to the State and the (economic) interests of the State (and their elites).[23]

---

20 Asean Economic Community Blueprint 2008, page 18 *available at* http://www.asean.org/archive/5187-10.pdf.

21 Association for Southeast Asian Nations, Roadmap for an ASEAN Community 2009-2015 32 (2009).

22 A new Lao PDR competition law was passed towards the end of July. At the time of writing this chapter an English translation was not available.

23 This will be discussed in McEwin Competition Law in Southeast Asia forthcoming.

Competition in Kenya and Its Impact on Income and Poverty: The Case of Sugar and Maize[1]

JONATHAN ARGENT

JArgent@worldbank.org

Economist, Trade and Competitiveness Global Practice, World Bank Group

TANIA BEGAZO

TBegazo@worldbank.org

Economist, Trade and Competitiveness Global Practice, World Bank Group

Abstract

Competitive, well-functioning food markets are necessary to enhance consumer welfare. In Kenya, a variety of factors conspire to distort market prices upward in key food markets (sugar and maize). Distortionary factors include import tariff policy, nontariff barriers, potential anticompetitive conduct by firms, and direct state intervention in markets. Changes in sugar and maize prices are shown to have significant welfare effects on consumers. In the case of sugar, relaxing trade barriers and increasing efficiency in the domestic industry are expected to allow sugar prices to fall. A 20 percent price reduction could reduce poverty by 1.5 percent. Similarly, adjusting government interventions in the maize market, which have been shown to inflate maize prices by 20 percent on average, could reduce poverty by 1.8 percent. In both cases, more competitive prices have a larger average effect on the poorest households in urban and rural areas, supporting the relevance of effective competition policies for poverty reduction strategies.

---

1 Martha Martinez Licetti, Senior Economist, Team Lead, Competition Policy Thematic Group provided useful guidance. Valuable input and comments were provided by Paul Brenton, Tanja Goodwin, Andrew Karanja, John Keyser, Johan Mistiaen, and Peter Ormosi. The Competition Authority of Kenya provided valuable input for this paper.

I. Introduction

This paper shows that through appropriate policy action to support well-functioning markets, Kenya can improve the welfare of consumers and reduce poverty. Current wholesale sugar prices in Kenya are almost three times world prices. We show in this paper that relaxing trade barriers to allow sugar prices to fall by even 20 percent could reduce poverty by 1.5 percent. Similarly, adjusting government interventions in the maize market, that have been shown to inflate maize prices by around 20 percent on average, could reduce poverty by 1.8 percent. More competitive prices have a larger effect on the poorest households in both urban and rural areas. While the estimated effects for maize are larger than those for sugar, there is much larger scope for reduction in sugar prices, and as such potential welfare effects relating to sugar reform are likely larger.

This paper builds on a strand of literature that focuses on the welfare impacts on the poor associated with competition problems.[2] For example, Urzua (2009) showed that the welfare cost from monopoly power in Mexico was borne disproportionately by the poor. Work by Creedy and Dixon (1998) analyzed 14 commodity groups using household survey from Australia and concluded similarly that welfare losses from monopoly power were heavier among lower income than higher income groups.

There is a considerable literature that examines the effects of food prices on welfare, and this has expanded rapidly since the global financial crisis. Pioneering work by Deaton (1987, 1989) and Ravallion (1990), among others, developed the analytical and econometric tools for assessing the welfare impacts of changes to food prices using survey data, at a time when these were already at the forefront of development debate. Even at that time, Ravallion (1990) observed "The welfare effects in a food producing economy of changes in the price of food have been central issues in numerous debates on development policy.[3] " While a substantial literature of welfare analysis of food prices already existed, recent global food crises have generated further expansion of this kind of work,[4] although the policy recommendations have not always been consistent.[5]

This paper investigates the link between competitive, well-functioning food markets and consumer welfare. The paper explores two key food markets in Kenya—sugar and maize—and argues that a variety of factors conspire to distort market prices upwards. Distortionary factors include import tariff policy, non-tariff barriers, potential anticompetitive conduct by firms and direct state intervention. We link the changes in prices to the associated welfare effects on consumers, using the most recent available representative household survey data—the Kenya Integrated Household Budget Survey ("KIHBS") 2005/6.[6] In the case of maize, where there is significant production by smallholders captured by KIHBS, we are able to integrate the effects of price change both on the value of household production and consumption, to estimate net welfare effects. This builds on more general work by the World Bank, proposing broader level reforms for driving growth for shared prosperity in Kenya.[7]

---

2 See OECD, Competition and Poverty Reduction Background Note. Global Forum on Competitiveness (2012), *available at* http://www.oecd.org/officialdocuments/publicdisplaydocumentpdf/?cote=DAF/COMP/GF(2013)1&docLanguage=En.

3 M. Ravallion, *Rural Welfare Effects of Food Price Changes Under Induced Wage Responses: Theory and Evidence for Bangladesh 574* (Oxford Economic Papers, 1990).

4 See for example Benson et al. (2008), Ivanic and Martin (2008), Ivanic, Martin and Zaman (2012), Porto (2012).

5 See Swinnen (2011) for a review of how policy recommendations have not always been consistent in their approach to high or low food prices.

6 While consumption patterns are doubtless changing in Kenya, annual data from FAOSTAT shows that relative consumption of food is changing very slowly, supporting the validity of using the 2005/6 data to draw inferences on household behavior that are applicable to Kenya today.

7 See Fengler et al (2013).

II. The Sugar Sector

Sugar is one of the most widely consumed products in Kenya. It is, surprisingly perhaps, more frequently purchased than any other good reported in the last household survey (KIHBS of 2004/5). At least 89 percent of households regularly consume sugar (80 percent of Kenyan households purchased sugar in the week prior to the interview and a further 9 percent consumed sugar from their own stocks). Average annual household consumption of sugar at the time of the survey is estimated 16.3kg per adult equivalent.[8] This corresponds to a average annual household expenditure on sugar of KSH1,084 (USD 15) per adult equivalent from the same source.[9] To put this into context, the annual per adult equivalent poverty lines for rural and urban areas at the time were KSH18,746 (USD 256) and KSH34,954 (USD 477) respectively. So, the average household's sugar expenditure is roughly 3 percent of the urban poverty line and 6 percent of the rural poverty line. The same level of consumption at current retail prices would cost approximately KSH2,147 (USD 25).[10]

This paper is concerned only with white or brown sugar for human consumption – not industrial sugar, or sugar that still requires further processing for consumption. For clarity, our analysis covers all consumer sugar except for industrial refined sugar, as this is not a substitute for consumers – industrial sugar can only be imported for industrial purposes by firms listed in the East Africa Community ("EAC") Gazette, with a remission of duty (to 10 percent). When we refer to "raw" sugar we are following the EAC Common External Tariff ("CET") definition,[11] which includes all refined or partially refined brown sugar. Raw imports into Kenya are brown sugar that is ready for human consumption, not "raw" sugar that must still be milled.[12]

Consumers do not typically adjust their consumption of sugar much in response to price changes–together with the high expenditure on sugar this implies significant welfare costs from high prices. In other words, the elasticity of demand for sugar is quite low–people are reluctant to adjust their consumption of sugar much in response to prices. This means that sugar is sufficiently important to consumers that they are prepared to make sacrifices in the consumption of other goods to soften their reduction of sugar consumption in the face of high prices. As a consequence, sugar prices are important for household welfare in Kenya (and particularly that of the poor, who spent a larger fraction of their income on sugar). High sugar prices result in lower consumption of other goods, rather than just sugar.

Given how important sugar prices are for household welfare, it is worth considering reforms in the sector to drive price decreases. As we will see in the next sections, policies that aim at shielding the domestic sugar industry from competition keep Kenyan sugar prices considerably above world prices, with substantial welfare effects as a consequence. The sugar crisis of 2011 is a case in point. In light of these findings, it is worth reflecting on long-term policy action that will allow for a better balance between the profits of domestic sugar producers and the costs to Kenyan households. Restrictive trade policies are

---

8 For all the estimations here we have trimmed outliers that are more than five standard deviations above the mean. This is the general rule followed for dealing with outliers in this paper.

9 The expenditure is that reported in the survey. Converted to USD terms using the average exchange rate of 73.35 KSH/USD from July 2005–June 2006.

10 Change in cost calculated by dividing by average prices between July 2005 and June 2006 and multiplying by prices as of January 2013. Converted using the average exchange rate of 86.86 KSH/USD as of January 2013.

11 EAC Tariff Book, Common External Tariff 2012 Chapter 17 specifies that raw sugar includes all "sugar whose content of sucrose by weight, in the dry state, corresponds to a polarimeter reading of less than 99.5°" *available at* http://tradehelpdesk.eac.int/tf/index.php?id=04&ChapterID=17.

12 See Monroy et al. (2013).

not only depriving families from welfare gains but also disrupting incentives for increased efficiency in the domestic sugar industry.

This section gives an overview of the sugar market in Kenya, analyzes the sugar crisis of 2011 in particular and examines the impact that price changes in sugar have on the welfare of Kenyan consumers. We show that even a modest price decrease of 20 percent (far smaller than the current difference between Kenyan and world sugar prices), would have a significant impact on real incomes, particularly among the poor.

1. Government Intervention and Market Structure of the Sugar Industry

Kenya's sugar market is insulated from international competition by trade barriers. Kenya's sugar industry has long been highly protected and even liberalization within the Common Market for Eastern and Southern Africa ("COMESA") has been restricted. Historical import tariffs have been at the higher of an *ad valorem* rate of 100 percent or a specific duty of USD 200/MT, where they remain today. It is indicative of the limited capacity of the domestic sugar industry that there were still significant imports through the 1990's despite such barriers to trade–imports averaged 26 percent of domestic production from 1993 to 2000.[13] Starting in January 2001, Kenya's market was opened to foreign competition within the COMESA Free Trade Area ("FTA"), dropping the tariff to zero for member states.[14] However, as cheaper imports from COMESA "flooded" into the Kenyan market, the Government responded quickly with the addition of a quota on COMESA imports in February 2002. This " safeguard" measure was subsequently extended (multiple times) until 2008 (with varying quota size); after which the COMESA out-of-quota tariff was to fall progressively (70 percent, 30 percent, 10 percent) to 0 percent in 2012 while the quota simultaneously increased.[15] However, further extension was granted to keep the out-of- quota rate at 10 percent through until 2014. Kenya has recently been granted another extension of the current quota of 350,000 metric tons through until 2015.[16]

The COMESA quota has generally been underutilized,[17] reportedly due to non-tariff barriers ("NTBs") that allow discretionary blocking of sugar imports. The Kenyan Government has upon several occasions, including 2011, locked out COMESA imports due to various disputes.[18] Mandatory import permits for sugar are required by the regulations under the Sugar Act of 2001,[19] through which the Kenya Sugar Board has complete control over imports. Although licenses are issued annually, every shipment of sugar requires pre-import approval. For this reason, it is unclear whether the duty free COMESA quota will be used in full. Other NTB's such as clearing fees and informal payments[20] may also play a role in

---

13 Author calculations from ISO (2000) data as quoted in the Structural Aspects of the Sugar Industrial in East and Southern Africa available at http://www.iuf.org/sugarworkers/wp-content/uploads/2012/07/Africa-2002-Basic- Structure.pdf. Some of this import volume is likely accounted for by industrial refined sugar, which Kenya does not produce, and which have been removed from all of our own calculations.

14 See Structural Aspects of the Sugar Industrial in East and Southern Africa (2002).

15 See KSB (2010).

16 See FAS (2014).

17 See FAS (2009, 2011). Between 2002 and 2006 the quota of 200,000MT was never completely used according to KSB (2010) data. FAS (2011) noted that only about 40 percent of the quota was used in 2010.

18 A COMESA lockout occurred between October 2008 and July 2009 surrounding disagreements between Kenya and COMESA regarding the auctioning mechanism (FAS, 2010). FAS (2012) claims that the Government of Kenya allowed few imports in 2011 due to a pending lawsuit regarding imports from COMESA.

19 The most recent iteration of the regulations is The Sugar (Imports, Exports and By- Products) (Amendment) Regulations, 2013.

20 See FAS (2009).

increasing the price of COMESA imports, but these are likely superfluous in comparison to the discretionary control. More recently, high world prices of sugar making preferential access to other markets (such as the European Union ("EU")) more attractive and occasional export bans from key COMESA exporters[21] have reduced the availability of imports from COMESA. It is doubtful whether this last factor has had significant impact, given the dominance of the discretionary controls mentioned above.

Barriers to competition from COMESA imports mean that these imports have a limited effect on Kenyan sugar prices. The barriers mentioned above have prevented imports in sufficient quantities to drive down the local price of sugar towards the levels in cost-leading COMESA countries. Kenya has a structural deficit in sugar production relative to consumption of roughly 200,000MT per annum at current prices. The amount of imports allowed is just such that the market clears at the current (high) prices, but there is no threat of sufficient imports to undercut prices due to the NTBs in place. Without these barriers, cheaper imported sugar should lead to decreases in the local price, all things held equal. With the insulation from competition provided by NTBs, local price variation is driven by local production, supplemented by limited imports from COMESA.[22] International landed prices form a loose upper bound to Kenyan prices. Section 2.2 below expands on this Government ownership in the sector remains large, despite higher relative efficiency in the private sector and long term plans for privatization. While some privatization has taken place over the past decade, government-controlled factories held a 37 percent production share,[23] with additional non-controlling shares in other firms. Part of the argument in favor of privatization is the relative efficiency of production in private mills over those controlled by government.[24] Plans to privatize the industry, with the hope of inspiring more investment and efficiency,[25] have been topics of discussion since joining COMESA, with little real action. Cabinet has approved the privatization of 5 state owned mills, but this has yet to occur. The latest information from the website of the privatization commission claims that the latest proposal is under consideration by parliament.[26]

The local sugar milling market is quite concentrated, and combined with the barriers to trade, this suggests that the largest players have significant power over prices. Mumias, the largest sugar company had a market share of 38 percent of domestically produced sugar in 2011, lower than its typical market share due to cane shortages.[27] Combined with the government-controlled share of the industry, this implies that essentially two entities control at least 75 percent of local production.[28] The shares of local producers in domestic market sales vary quite widely depending on period, as the volume of imports fluctuates a great deal. For example, Kenya Sugar Board data from the first two quarters of 2012 shows imports were approximately 33

---

21 For example Egypt in late 2009 (FAS, 2010).

22 Imports of non-COMESA raw (brown) sugar are negligible and may actually be zero—they are so low they may represent data errors. Trademap data, author calculations. Illegal imports, either undeclared or coming in falsely under the auspices of COMESA (see for example CGD Bills Digest (2005), http://www.trademarksa.org/news/mombasa-sh16bn-sugar-import-scam-unearthed) are likely not substantial enough to drive prices down either.

23 Kenya Sugar Board Data (KSB), 2011.

24 See CHISANGA ET AL. (2014).

25 Media articles report that the cost of sugar production in Kenya is more than double that of other COMESA countries; $700 (Sh59,500) per ton compared to $323 (Sh27,455) per ton. It costs $300 to produce one ton of sugar in Zimbabwe, $310 in Malawi, $340 in Swaziland and $340 in Sudan.

http://www.the-star.co.ke/news/article-130060/kenya-spends-more-produce-sugar-mp;

http://www.businessdailyafrica.com/High-costs-sour-outlook-for-local-sugar-industry/-/539546/1929486/-/r1lqf4/-/index.html

26 See http://www.pc.go.ke/index.php?option=com_fsf&view=faq&catid=3&Itemid=535.

27 Kenya Sugar Board figures show Mumias had higher market share than this in 2009 and 2012. Mumias claims a 60 percent market share on its website— but this includes imports. This suggests that when we look at the wholesale market it may be even more concentrated that local production figures suggest. FAS (2008) reported a production share of 50 percent for Mumias in 2007.

28 Kenya Sugar Board Data.

percent of local production. To some extent the high level of concentration in the market is probably driven by economies of scale–it is cheaper to produce and market sugar at large scale. There are many markets where the sugar sector is highly concentrated. Regional markets such as South Africa, Tanzanian and Zambia have fewer players than Kenya (Zambia only has one), and yet ex-factory prices in Kenya have consistently been the highest for the past decade as illustrated below in Figure 1. However, the combination of a concentrated market and a very high level of protection mean that there is little real price competition in the market.

Figure 1: Ex-factory sugar prices

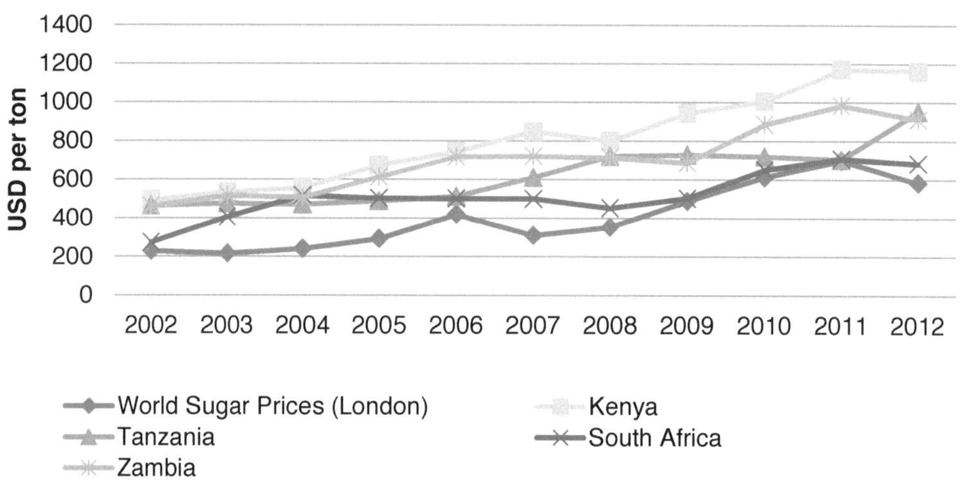

Source: Reproduced from Chisanga et al (2014)

The sugar cane growing sector and its vertical relationship with sugar millers is a key driver of Kenyan sugar production that will need attention if the sector is to be become more competitive. Out growers produce 92 percent of cane in Kenya, similar to South Africa (93 percent), but contrasting with Zambia (40 percent), where cane yields are the highest in the region.[29] As we will see in the following sections, sugar production follows cane deliveries very closely. In addition, a number of factories in Kenya have been complaining that they are unable to get sufficient cane to produce at full capacity.[30] Chisanga et al (2014) argued that the high production price of Kenyan sugar is due to a combination of low capacity utilization (too little cane, or overinvestment in capacity) and inefficient production (poor management, aging machinery). Mumias' capacity utilization in 2012 had reportedly dropped to 55 percent.[31] The fact that sugar cane production has not increased to meet demand by millers suggests that there is some kind of competitive problem in between the sectors (cane production and milling).

The public discourse surrounding the sugar industry often focuses on the "need" to protect the domestic industry against COMESA, rather than the problems in the domestic value chain[32] and how these might be addressed. Tariff and non-tariff barriers to competing imports are no panacea for the domestic

29 Chisanga et al. (2014).

30 See for example http://www.businessdailyafrica.com/Cane-shortage-exposes-Kenya-to-Comesa-rivals/-/539552/1667464/-/ybdsy8z/-/index.html.

31 Chisanga et al. (2014).

32 Id.

challenges in the sugar industry. On the contrary, it is precisely this protection against competition from more efficient producers that allows the sugar sector in Kenya to remain so unproductive. A new policy to improve the competitiveness of the sector will require, beyond trade policy reform, a careful look at the production of cane smallholders, with particular focus on the vertical relationship with sugar factories.

Overall, due to the factors discussed above, Kenyan sugar prices remain very high relative to international prices. From 2009 through to 2012, Kenyan wholesale prices were on average 149 percent above the international wholesale sugar price.[33] Compared to international wholesale prices, Kenyan wholesale prices have to account for additional costs incurred by sugar importers, including Value Added Tax ("VAT"), the Sugar Development Levy ("SDL"), international shipping, port clearing related charges and inland transportation. Taking all of these into account, we could expect the removal of all trade barriers to bring down Kenyan prices by approximately 28 percent (full calculations and explanations are available in the appendix). This is probably a lower bound estimate, since further reductions in import parity would be possible via cutting other costs associated with importing. Perhaps a more realistic example is what could be achieved by moving to the EAC-CET finished products tariff of 25 percent on sugar, and cutting some of the costs of importing, including the clearing fees. We estimate that a scenario like this might lead to a decline in sugar prices of 19 percent.[34]

2. The Sugar Crisis of 2011: Potential Explanations of Price Spikes

In 2011, retail sugar prices increased sharply—at first glance this appears to be a much more pronounced increase than that of international prices over the same period. Retail sugar prices in Kenya started increasing rapidly in June 2011, rising from an average of KSH 95/kg in the first five months in the year, up to an average of over KSH 150/kg from June 2011 through to January 2012. The price spike reached its peak in November at KSH 173/kg (a more than 80 percent increase), but had declined to under KSH 120/kg by February 2012 after which it remained stable for the remainder of the year. The increase in prices coincided with a much more moderate increase in world sugar prices. The left panel of Figure 2 shows the price evolution of retail prices in Kenya alongside international prices.[35] The two vertical markers indicate the period of the price spike—we will keep these markers on all the graphs we use for our analysis, to keep our focus on the 2011 crisis.

After adjusting international prices for the costs that would be incurred to import for the domestic retail market, the spike in prices in 2011 does not seem so unusual. The right panel of Figure 2 once again compares Kenyan retail prices to international prices, but now adjusted for the additional costs that would be added to import sugar into Kenya, and deliver it to the retail market (VAT, SDL, international shipping, port clearing related charges, inland transportation and retail margins).[36] From this adjusted curve, one can see that the difference between Kenyan sugar and the international comparison price (as shown by the

33 We use the No.11 raw sugar futures contract from the coffee, sugar and cocoa exchange for the world price for the duration of this paper. For this comparison, we convert into Kenyan shillings at the average mid-market exchange rate for the period. We use the Kenyan wholesale sugar price as reported by FAS.

34 See appendix for full calculations and assumptions.

35 We use retail prices because wholesale prices are not available over a long period. See the analysis of wholesale/retail margins over a shorter period.

36 Prices include ad valorem import tariffs of 100 percent or a specific duty of $200/MT (whichever is higher), VAT at 16 percent, sugar development levy (currently 4 percent, 7 percent prior to November 2007), the estimated costs of shipping, port charges and inland transport).

distance between the two curves) was actually relatively low compared to the long-term average.[37] Looking at the price series, it does not appear that there is a strong equilibrium relationship between them[38] —the considerable barriers to trade in Kenya keep local prices insulated from the international market (after these costs, international imports are more expensive than Kenyan prices). The international price adjusted for trade barriers forms something of a weak upper bound to Kenyan prices—when domestic prices rise above these, we can see that they typically drop back down fairly rapidly.

Figure 2: Kenyan retail and international wholesale sugar prices

At nominal levels (left panel), inclusive of import costs and other standard costs (right panel)

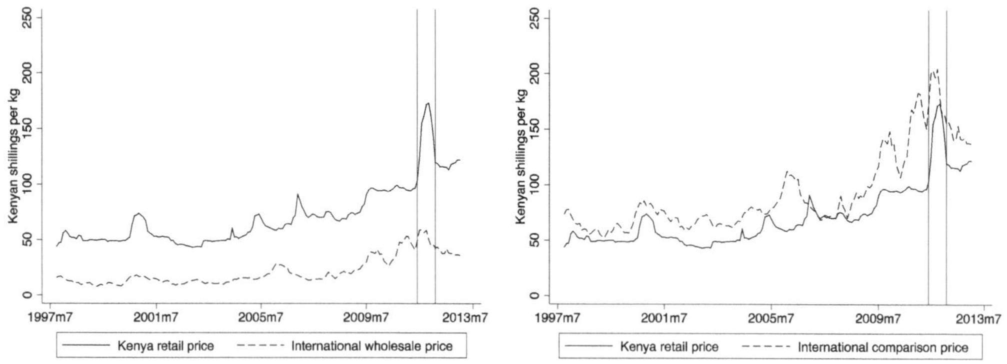

Source: No.11 Raw Sugar futures contract from the Coffee, Sugar and Cocoa Exchange, obtained from the International Monetary Fund (IMF). Kenyan retail prices from Kenyan CPI. All prices in Kenyan Shillings per kg. Adjustments in the right panel include VAT, SDL, international shipping, port clearing, inland transportion , and retails margins.

With the Kenyan market at least somewhat decoupled from the international market by tariff and non-tariff barriers, we look to the domestic supply to understand the origins of the 2011 crisis. Sugar cane deliveries, sugar production and sugar imports are all potential contributors to be assessed. We show below that the price spike in 2011 can be very substantially accounted for by a combination of a very large local production drop and lower than expected imports. High world (and COMESA) sugar prices likely played only a marginal role in the crisis.

The supply of sugar cane to factories dropped precipitously in mid-2011, with the production of sugar mirroring the change closely (see the left hand panel of Figure 3). A drop in the supply of cane to local sugar producers just after the middle of the year is a normal seasonal pattern, but the drop in 2011 was very large even for the low season. Unfortunately, data on cane deliveries is not available over a longer period. However, we do have data on sugar production reaching back to 2000 (see the right hand panel of Figure 3), and we can reasonably infer that production is substantially driven by the seasonality in cane deliveries as illustrated in the left hand panel. At its lowest point in 2011, sugar production fell to the lowest levels in a decade.

---

37 Note how the calculated border price actually rose above the Kenyan retail price a few times in the period leading up to this. It is difficult to guess what was behind this. Potentially some combination of production and COMESA imports, or changes in other costs such as transport over time.

38 An Engel-Granger test of cointegration produces a test statistic of 3.012, which is rejected at the 5 percent level, but not the 1 percent level. Inspection of the graphed residuals suggests non-constant variance over time.

Figure 3: Deliveries of sugar cane and sugar production (left panel), Sugar production only (right panel)

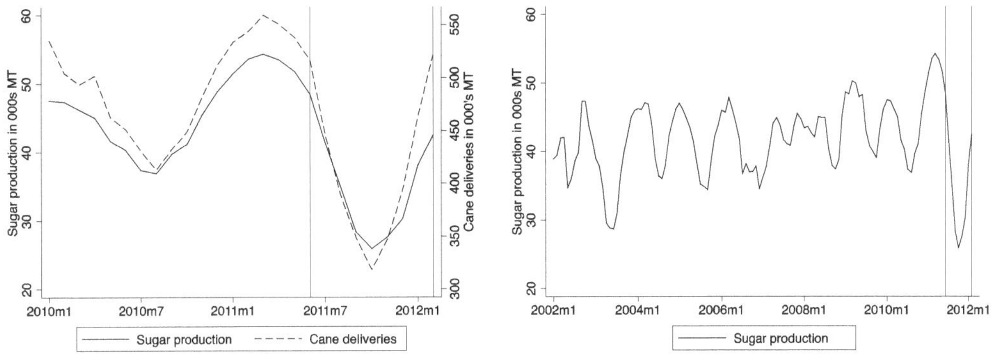

Source: KNBS, author calculations. All series have been smoothed using a four-month moving average (current month and three previous).

Imported sugar is the natural channel through which a supply side shock would typically be cushioned, but government interventions, that restricted imports from COMESA, limited the role of imports. Kenya imports sugar every year to cover the structural deficit between domestic production and consumption. In 2011, imports collapsed due to government blocking imports of COMESA sugar[39] (see the left hand panel of Figure 4), although COMESA's regional shortage and high world prices would likely have led to some decline in any case. Note that the lockout of COMESA sugar began before the drop in local sugar productionso the source of supply side easing had been cut off before the crisis even began. Imports of sugar rocketed up in early 2012, in response to reversal by the government, even as local sugar production also recovered. The easing in supply brought retail sugar prices back down, although not quite to their previous levels (something to which we will return later).

39 The Government of Kenya allowed few imports in 2011 due to a pending lawsuit regarding imports from COMESA (FAS, 2012).

Figure 4: Imports of sugar (left panel), and comparison of total supply with a naive prediction (right panel)

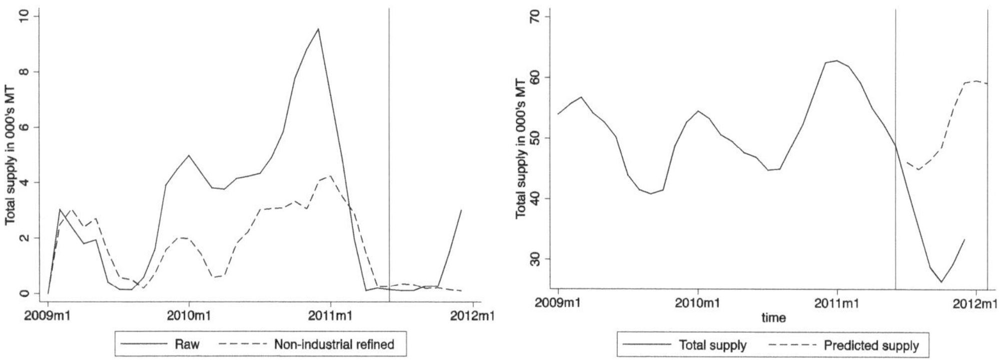

Source: Data is from Trademap and KNBS. Sugar marked as raw is brown and does not require further processing for human consumption. All series have been smoothed using a four-month moving average (current month and three previous).

When import response has not been inhibited, falls in domestic production have not had such large price effects. Contrast the situation in 2011 with the import response to the much smaller drop in production in 2010 (which from looking at Figure 3,still looks somewhat unusual for the season). The left hand panel of Figure 4[40] shows the very strong import response in 2010, primarily from COMESA countries, easing tightness in local supply over the period and resulting in stable domestic sugar prices. In 2009, there was only a slight price hike (see Figure 2) corresponding to the seasonal drop in production. The import response to tight supply in 2009 was smaller than 2010, but still much quicker than that in 2011 (see left hand panel of Figure 4), which is why the price spike was much smaller. Note that the raw imports here are primarily of brown sugar, which is sold directly to consumers as opposed to truly raw sugar that has yet to be refined at all.

The 2011 decline in overall supply was very large relative to what we would have expected from previous years. The right hand panel of Figure 4 shows the overall supply picture (local production and imports), as well as a naïve prediction of what supply would have looked like had the average seasonal and overall trends since 2009 persisted.[41] At the peak of the price surge, total supply was close to 50 percent of that which might have been expected under "'normal'" seasonal conditions. Note that looking at the price series we do not typically observe seasonal differences in prices. It is only when seasonal fluctuations in production are exceptional and/or imported supply is sufficiently disrupted (as in 2011) that we would expect to see big price changes.

The evidence available does not suggest that anti-competitive conduct within the local industry was a major cause of the sugar crisis. There are clear indications that there were real production and import shocks to supply that merited a price increase. Anecdotal reports mention that there were shortages on

40 Including only HS codes 17011190 (raw cane sugar, not jiggery) and 17019990 (refined sugar, not for industrial use). As explained earlier, raw sugar under this HS code is actually refined or partially refined brown sugar. Amounts under beet sugar are negligible and can be ignored.

41 The predicted supply is estimated from regressing the total supply (production plus imports) between January 2009 and May 2011 on monthly dummies and a time trend. This is not intended as any reasonable forecast of the counterfactual, merely an illustration of what might have occurred had previous seasonal and overall patterns continued.

the market, and both wholesalers and retailers undertook quantity rationing.[42] This suggests that retail prices could actually have increased further, to the point where the market cleared — not something that is consistent with the view that price increases were caused by collusion. In addition, those reports assert that, in August 2011, Mumias—Kenya's largest sugar company—announced a recommended retail price to curb price rises by retailers (such a move might be problematic in some contexts, as it may be a tool for anticompetitive practices, although that does not appear to be the case here). At the time, there were even stories that some sugar mills might close due to the acute lack of cane[43] —again suggesting that the production shock was genuine. Nonetheless, longer-term anticompetitive practices in the industry cannot be ruled out.

Prices spiked throughout the value chain during the crisis, driven by ex-factory prices and wholesale margins, but this does not necessarily represent anticompetitive behavior. The left hand panel of Figure 5[44] shows ex-factory, wholesale and retail sugar prices. One can see that these prices are quite tightly linked together. A large portion of the price spike in 2011 came from the ex-factory price, but there was quite a dramatic change in wholesaler and retail margins (right hand panel of Figure 5). Retail margins actually fell while wholesale margins increased sharply.[45] However, even though wholesale margins increased over the period, additional evidence would be needed to assess potential anticompetitive conduct at the wholesale level. The price change may simply reflect the need to recover fixed costs in the face of lower volumes due to the shock to cane supplies. As noted in the previous paragraph, the fact that shortages persisted suggests that these prices could have been increased even further to clear the market.

Figure 5: Factory, wholesale and retail prices (left panel), Implicit wholesale and retail margins (right panel)

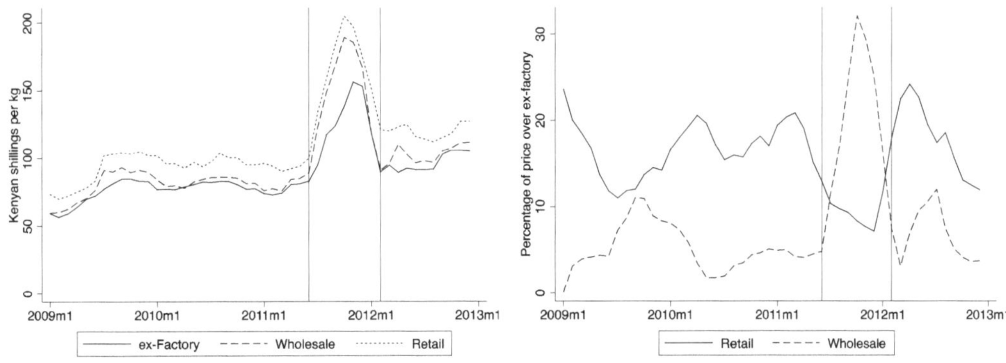

Source: Foreign Agriculture Service (FAS), reporting Kenya Sugar Board (KSB) data, author calculations. Implicit margins have been smoothed using a four-month moving average (current month and three previous).

Entry into the industry, which occurred at the end of 2011, may have created some price pressure, but given the scale of the entrants, this is unlikely to explain a significant portion of the price reduction

42 See for example: http://agritrade.cta.int/Agriculture/Commodities/Sugar/Uncertain-future-for-Kenyan-sugar-sector-and-wider-EAC-developments and FAS (2013).

43 See for example: http://allafrica.com/stories/201107290072.html.

44 Retail prices reported by FAS here are very slightly higher than the retail prices recorded under CPI. This is likely due to differences in sampling/weighting.

45 Kenya Sugar Board quarterly data available online gives a confusing picture of this period, due to what is certainly a typo in the third quarter of 2011. In these data the mean value for the third quarter of 2011 is outside of the high-low range reported for the same period.

post-crisis. The entry of additional millers in December 2011, while timed almost perfectly with the decline in prices, is unlikely to have played a large role in bringing sugar prices down. The two collectively accounted for a tiny fraction of the market[46] and would have been unable to significantly undercut the big players. On the contrary, entry could have been a response to trade protection that allows an opportunity for supernormal profits in the sector. It is much more plausible that the recovery of domestic production (through the channel of recovering cane deliveries) coupled with an influx of imports eased supply sufficiently for prices to drop.

There have been a few other sharp spikes in Kenyan sugar prices over the past decade that may be linked with similar combinations of production and import shocks as described in 2011. Figure 6 shows prices and domestic sugar production together, with vertical lines indicating the price spikes. Clearly, each price spike is associated with domestic production declining, but there are also many cases where production declines and there is no associated price spike. What we have seen in our analysis of the 2011 crisis (and the brief comparison of 2010 and 2009) suggests that the periods when the price increased are likely those where there is a reduction in imported sugar, paired with the observed drop in local production. Barriers to trade thus exacerbate local production shocks, creating high prices.

Figure 6: Domestic retail prices and production of sugar

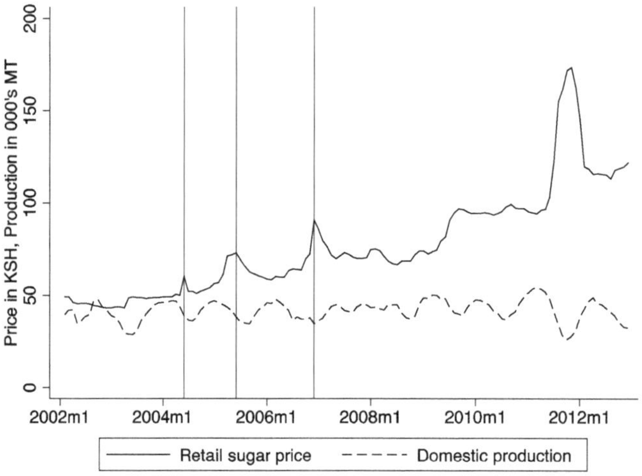

Source: Data is from KNBS, author calculations. Domestic production of sugar has been smoothed using a four-month moving average as before.

Subsequent to the sugar crisis international prices continued to fall, but after an initial period of decline, Kenyan prices rose slightly again most likely due to further local production shocks. Looking back at Figure 2, Kenyan prices did not drop off as steeply as international prices after the crisis, and indeed even began to rise slightly shortly after the crisis. While we do not have a sufficiently long period of import or cane production data to examine this, we can see from Figure 6 above that domestic production took another historically large dip from mid 2012, suggesting that further local production shocks were likely to blame for sugar prices not continuing their post-crisis decline.

46 The two collectively accounted to 5 percent of production in June-July 2012 according to the KSB. It is likely that this was even lower as they started production in December 2011.

A combination of local production shocks and barriers to trade provide a plausible explanation for the sugar price surge of 2011. In general we could summarize the drivers of sugar prices in Kenya with the following points:

» Kenya is a high-cost producer of sugar, and does not produce enough sugar to meet domestic demand (there is a structural deficit), even at current (and historical) high prices. Problems between the cane sector and the sugar manufacturing sector, extensive government involvement and uncertainty about the future may play a role in maintaining this situation.[47]

» Kenya has formidable trade barriers in place including exceptionally high tariffs (100 percent), COMESA import quotas and NTB's including a licensing regime that allows discretionary blocking of any sugar imports. These trade barriers prevent any real price competition from imports and restrict the process through which imports can ease tight supply in the context of a local production shock. This makes Kenya susceptible to price crisis.

3. Welfare Impact of High Sugar Prices: Effects on Household Income and Poverty Incidence

How much would a decline in Kenyan sugar prices, driven by a move towards a more competitive market, affect consumer welfare? To have a closer look at this question we will examine the effects on consumers of a sugar price decrease of 20 percent, rounding up the scenario discussed in section 2.1–removal of licensing, a reduction in the import tariff to 25 percent together with cutting some of the costs of imports. The decreases that would be possible in sugar prices through policy reform exceed these, but this kind of decrease represents a realistic goal in the shorter term (where sugar would be treated in the same way as other finished goods in the EAC at a tariff of 25 percent). We will show that even a 20 percent decrease in sugar prices has surprisingly large effects on incomes and the incidence of poverty in Kenya.

47 It is difficult to guess how exactly government has influenced prices. ODI (2010) reports that "government still intervenes in price setting intermittently (e.g. to hold prices down when there are sugar shortages due to a poor harvest during which the price would otherwise rise) ," but given government role in production (broadly accepted to be expensive relative to the region) it is hard to guess what prices would be under a competitive market structure.

Figure 7: Mean annual household expenditure on sugar *per adult equivalent* (left panel), Mean annual household expenditure *share* on sugar (right panel), both by income decile

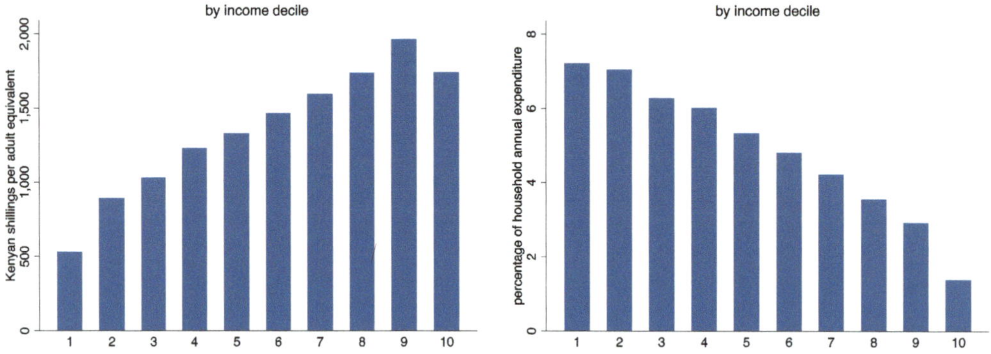

Source: KIHBS (2005/06), author calculations.

Sugar is an important good for Kenyan households, and particularly the poor. Households spend more on sugar as they become richer, but the *proportion* of their income spent on sugar falls progressively. The left hand panel of Figure 7 shows household annual per adult equivalent[48] expenditure on sugar by income decile. We can see quite clearly that higher income households consume more sugar per adult equivalent than lower income households, although this trend slows towards the richest end of the distribution. The right hand side of Figure 7 shows that the household expenditure share (the percentage of their total consumption expenditure) on sugar declines strongly with income. So as people become wealthier, they spend only a small portion of their additional income on sugar—something that makes intuitive sense.

Figure 8: Equivalent income effects, with zero or estimated elasticity (left panel), Equivalent income effects for Urban/Rural with estimated elasticity (right panel)

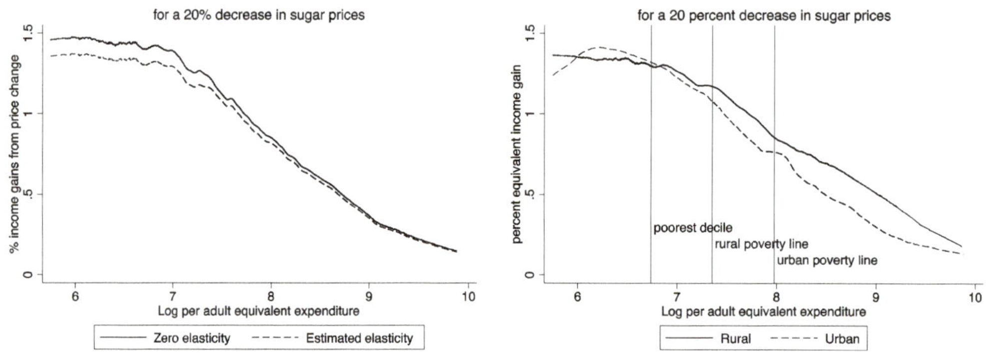

Source: KIHBS (2005/06), author calculations. Estimated elasticities used were estimated for each group of poor/non-poor and urban/rural. The estimates and description of the applied methodology is available in the appendix.

48 An adult equivalent is a measure of household size that is adjusted for children. The idea is essentially that children do not require as much as adults and so a household of an adult and two children would have a lower per adult equivalent than three (which would be the adult equivalent of a household of three adults).

In the situation where households do not change the quantity of sugar they purchase in response to a price change, poor households will evidently benefit significantly more from lower prices. A 20 percent decrease in prices will correspond into a 20 percent decrease in expenditure on sugar for all households and of course a corresponding increase in remaining disposable income. However, households do not all spend the same portion of their budgets on sugar as we have already seen. As a consequence of their higher budget shares in sugar, poor households will be more affected by the change in sugar prices. The solid line in the left hand panel of Figure 8 plots the average gains against log income[49]—this shows very clearly that poor households gain much more in relative terms from a decrease in sugar prices (and conversely that they are much harder hit in relative terms by high sugar prices).

The poor still gain substantially more from price decreases in sugar, even when we account for changes in consumption patterns in response to a price change. We would typically expect households to increase the quantities of sugar they consume in response to a decrease in prices. However, in most cases we would also typically expect that total household spend on the good would decline – households use some of their "saved" income from lower prices to purchase other goods. We can incorporate this kind of behavior into our estimates using elasticity of demand, a measure of sensitivity to price.[50] The dotted line in the left hand panel of Figure 8 incorporates estimates of the elasticity of demand for sugar in Kenya – here we can see that the positive impact of a price reduction on the poor is somewhat reduced by their price sensitivity.[51] However, the fact that poor households are still more affected (and substantially so) remains—the gain to poor households is equivalent to an increase in their overall expenditure of more than 1 percent. The right hand panel of Figure 8 plots the estimated gains (including substitution effects) separately for urban and rural households[52]—showing very similar results. We see very slightly lower impact on the urban population here—driven by both lower shares in sugar relative to income and (in the case of the urban poor) higher estimated elasticities. The vertical lines on the figure indicate the rural (left) and urban (right) poverty lines— giving a sense how the poor and non-poor are differentially affected.

Lower prices that could be achieved by removal of trade barriers and more efficient domestic production would have a significant effect on poverty. We estimate that just over 40,000 families would cross the poverty line (out of poverty) as a consequence of a 20 percent price decrease in sugar—an approximate 1.5 percent decrease in poverty for Kenya overall. We use the estimated equivalent change in real income[53] added to current household expenditure to estimate "post-reform income.'" Comparison of the post reform income with the thresholds of the rural/urban poverty lines, in Kenya, produces welfare estimates. Even though the equivalent income effects of the sugar price on households are relatively small compared to total expenditure (mean of 0.9 percent, median of 1 percent), the effects are higher on poorer house-

---

49 This plot was estimated using a (non-parametric) lowess smoother implemented using the routine developed by Cleveland (1979) in Stata. Unlike regression techniques, this method does not require us to make any assumptions about the functional form of the average sugar expenditure share by log adult equivalent expenditure. Note that we have cut off the far left hand side of the distribution where almost all households consume zero as it is easier to understand visually, and there are very few households in this position. Those households that do not consume sugar at all are at worst not affected at all by a decline in the price of sugar.

50 The price elasticity of demand is the percentage change in quantity demanded (on average) associated with a percentage change in price. If the elasticity is between -1 and 0, then for a price decrease, quantity consumed would increase, but expenditure would still fall (since the change in price would outweigh the change in quantity).

51 The welfare impact including household substitution effects is given by the compensating variation. This is estimated using a second order Taylor series expansion of the derivate of the expenditure function with respect to own-price, dropping the effect of curvature. See Porto (2010) and Mghenyi et al. (2011) for derivation. Elasticities of demand are estimated using simple log-log regressions for four groups defined by the categories or poor/non-poor and rural/urban. Estimation using the method of Deaton (1989) found these elasticities to be high, suggesting that if anything we are understating the impact here (through overstating substitution). See appendix for the estimated elasticites from both methods.

52 Again, we have truncated the plot on the left hand side to remove the bottom 1 percent of households.

53 The technical term for this is the compensating variation.

holds, many of which sit very close to the poverty line. This striking result is indicative of (a) the inelasticity of sugar demand (people do not easily change their consumption of sugar), (b) high average consumption of sugar, and (c) the vulnerability of poorer households to price changes.[54]

Lower sugar prices might affect the welfare of sugar smallholders, but even if there is complete price pass-through, the net welfare impacts are still positive. We are focusing on consumers, rather than producers in this analysis. Producers are difficult to incorporate into the analysis as we lack information about the pass-through between sugar and sugar cane prices. Chisanga et al (2014) argues that the majority of rents in the value chain lie at the level of the miller, rather than the farmer.

The fact that sugar factories in Kenya are generally operating below capacity due to cane shortage suggests that even if some sugar factories closed their doors, there would still be excess demand for cane, and as such cane prices would be unlikely to fall. Nevertheless, we can stress test our results by making two very simplistic assumptions: (a) cane prices move in lockstep with sugar prices, and (b) the elasticity of substitution of cane farmer is zero. Both of these are extreme (worst case) assumptions, but they provide us with an upper bound of the potential effects on smallholders. Under these two assumptions, cane-growing households would have median income losses of 0.7 percent of their incomes.[55] The net decrease in poverty taking this adjustment into account would be 1.05 percent. So even in the worst-case scenario for cane growers, the net effect on poverty is a substantial decline.

4. Concluding Remarks on Sugar

Sugar prices have a large impact on the welfare of Kenyan households and reforms in the sector could plausibly achieve substantial price decreases. We have demonstrated that sugar prices in Kenya are important in terms of real income and poverty. For a 20 percent decrease in sugar prices we have shown that poor households would experience gains equivalent to 1 percent of income, with a decline of poverty of 1.5 percent. While gains among wealthier households are lower, they remain significant. We estimate a reasonable import parity benchmark without trade barriers to be at least 28 percent below current Kenyan wholesale sugar prices, suggesting that a decrease of 20 percent via domestic and trade policy reform is very much achievable.

Current barriers to trade essentially isolate the Kenyan market from international competition, providing support to high prices. There is some legitimacy to complaints from sugar producers that the international sugar price is not "fair." Recent estimates suggest that the current world price is around 30 percent higher than what would occur under free international competition[56] However, the natural protection created by the costs from arrival in the port in Mombasa to market in Nairobi easily exceeds this. Current import controls and tariffs of 100 percent are excessive, especially in addition to the natural protection due to transport costs. The Kenyan market could be opened to competition by removing import controls and phasing down tariffs. We estimate that phasing down to the EAC-CET finished product rate of 25 percent, paired with reforms to ease costs of importing, could result in price reductions

54 There are a very large number of Kenyan households that have consumption levels that are very close to the poverty line (KIHBS, 2005/06). Thus small changes in income can generate large changes in poverty as measured by the national poverty line. The annual per adult equivalent poverty lines for rural and urban areas at the time of the survey were KSH 18,746 (USD 256) and KSH 34,954 (USD 477), respectively.

55 The mean is higher at 2.4 percent due to a few very large cane growers who take much larger losses.

56 See the appendix for a full review, only an excerpt of which appears here.

in sugar of 19 percent.[57] In the short term, at least dismantling NTBs that block imports from COMESA (including the quota and import permits) is likely to have a significant downward impact on sugar prices, to the benefit of consumers.

There is a need for policy reform to create a better balance between support for domestic sugar producers and the welfare costs on Kenyan households. The key question is whether Kenya can become a low cost producer of sugar. If Kenya has the capabilities to become a competitive producer of sugar, then the question is how to help the industry make this transformation without compromising consumers (and the poor in particular) through high prices. If Kenya cannot become a low cost producer of sugar, then in the long run it would be better to lower trade barriers and allow other countries to subsidize Kenyan consumption of cheap sugar. The resources used for sugar production would be better used in an industry in which Kenya is able to become competitive. This would entail an adjustment period for local producers that, if not carefully managed, would result in the failure of Kenyan businesses and a loss of employment.

At the level of the domestic industry, some work needs to be done to establish why there has not been more investment to improve productivity in the sugar industry. It could be that the delay in privatizing the industry together with uncertainty surrounding the impact of open trade with COMESA is stalling investment in the sector, but there may be other reasons. Chisanga et al (2014) argues that a variety of factors, including excessive government involvement, barriers to domestic investment, and problematic vertical relations with the cane sector, among others, are affecting sugar production in Kenya. Recent reports of sugar millers operating well below capacity support the idea that there may be some problems upstream in the cane-growing sector, or in the structure of the relationship between the two sectors.[58] Certainly, completing the progress towards open trade with COMESA should help to resolve uncertainties in the investment climate, as well as discipline domestic sugar prices. However, further work will be needed to examine other obstructions to competitiveness.

III. The Maize Sector

Maize is the most important staple crop in Kenya, particularly for the poor. Average annual household consumption at the time of the last household survey (KIHBS of 2004/5) was approximately 105 kg per adult equivalent,[59] estimated at roughly 38 percent of gross caloric intake.[60] Average annual household expenditure on maize totaled KSH 1,863 (USD 25) per adult equivalent,[61] which is roughly 10 percent of the rural poverty line. The same level of consumption in current prices would cost approximately KSH

57 This is slightly lower than the estimated distortion in the world market, but other factors such as transport costs provide some level of natural protection.

58 Given that sugar prices are so high, it seems strange that there can be a simultaneous long-term shortage of cane. Typically we would expect the prices for cane to rise, and further market entry by farmers to increase production of cane. The fact that cane shortages persist suggests there is a serious problem in the value chain between the cane growing and sugar milling sectors.

59 Estimation accounts for population weighting and removing outliers in the same method as described for sugar. FAOSTAT figures for national supply are slightly lower than these estimates, coming in at 83kg per capita in 2005. However, other academic sources (for example. Jayne et al, 2005) cite figures circa 98kg, suggesting that the FAO estimate is on the low end.

60 The average for 2005/2006 was 38 percent, very close to the average for the 2000's of 37 percent. Caloric contribution of maize has been on slow decline from the 1990's, when it averaged 41 percent. These statistics were estimated using FAOSTAT data.

61 The expenditure is that reported in the survey, including both the amount purchased and the value of that consumed from own production or stores. Converted to USD terms using the average exchange rate of 73.35KSH/USD from July 2005–June 2006.

3,913 (USD 46) per adult equivalent on average.[62] Per capita consumption of maize has declined very slightly over the past decade, reflecting the gradual rise of alternative staples in Kenyan diets, but there is still no other staple with a consumption share that approaches that of maize.[63]

Maize is consumed in a variety of forms in Kenya.[64] Green maize or dried grain is usually boiled with beans in a stew called Githeri. Milling the dry grain in local "posho" hammer mills produces a whole meal flour (or posho flour). The posho millers sell unbranded ("loose") flour produced from their own supply, or provide a "custom" milling service at a fixed rate per unit. This flour is commonly consumed in the form of a stiff (ugali) or soft (uji) porridge. Sifted flour is produced by the large industrial milling firms and sold in various retail outlets. The price of this kind of meal is generally higher— it has a lower extraction rate, higher packaging cost and longer shelf life.[65] Sifted flour is consumed in the same way as whole meal flour. An even more expensive variety of sifted flour, "fortified flour," is available at a premium price with the addition of vitamins and minerals.

Removal of subsidies during liberalization changed the relative importance of posho flour and sifted flour in the market. Sifted flour was heavily subsidized until 1993, and together with government restrictions, this resulted in large industrial millers dominating the urban market.[66] The removal of the subsidies and restrictions in 1993 resulted in a rapid transformation of the market, as posho flour quickly gained a strong foothold. Within two years, prices of both posho and sifted flour dropped substantially, to the benefit of consumers in general and the poor in particular.[67] Subsequent narrowing of the price premium of sifted flour over posho meal (reportedly due in part to a decline in the degree of refinement of sifted flour), has led to a relative fall in the consumption of posho meal, although its consumption still substantially exceeds that of sifted flour among poorer households.[68]

This section gives an overview of the maize market in Kenya, and discusses some of the factors that drive local prices. We then look at the impact that these price changes have on the welfare of Kenyan consumers.[69] We show that, maize prices are important for household welfare in Kenya (particularly that of the poor). Although household production of maize does substantially insulate many households from the effect of price changes,[70] the poorest rural and urban families are generally large net buyers and will benefit the most from lower prices. We close with a brief review of some recent actions by the Competition Authority of Kenya ("CAK") in the maize milling sector, and how these have affected prices.

---

62 The change in prices is estimated as the price change in sifted flour between the year from July 2005 to June 2006 and the most recent price available at the time (October 2012). We use the change in sifted flour to be conservative, as it was slightly lower than that for dry maize. The exchange rate used is the average of October 2012, 85.16KSH/USD.

63 FAO estimates have fallen since the time of the survey, as cited above, to 77kg in 2009. Estimates of percentage caloric intake have also fallen as noted above. Consumption of other staples, notably wheat, have risen over the same period.

64 See De Groote and Kimenju (2012).

65 ILO & UNIDO (1984).

66 Jayne and Argwings-Kodhek (1997) estimated that sifted flour had a market share exceeding 90 percent in urban areas prior to liberalization.

67 Jayne (1997).

68 Kirimi et al. (2011), De Groote and Kimenju (2012), Hoffman (2013), Jayne (1997). See next section for analysis of current consumption.

69 Mghenyi et al. (2011) produced robust estimates of the impact of large maize prices change on rural households in Kenya. Unfortunately, the sample used was not nationally representative, and comparisons with KIHBS 2004/5 suggest that the sample does differ substantially from the population. We replicate some of these results for a representative sample, to assess how maize prices affect income and poverty for Kenya as a whole.

70 See Mghenyi et al. (2011).

1. Government Interventions in the Maize Sector Have Led to Higher Prices

The Kenyan government continues to intervene extensively in the grain market, with the most reliable estimates suggesting that this has increased prices by an average of 20 percent. There was a period of "liberalization" in the grain market during which sifted flour subsidies were removed (1993) and NCPB interference declined (1995 – 2000) with a cut in central buying/selling and the removal of internal trade restrictions. However, NCPB activity rose steadily over the following decade.[71] The NCPB currently purchases around 10-20 percent of locally produced maize grain, at a fixed price, frequently above that which would exist under a competitive market.[72] Purchased grain is mostly sold on to millers, with some excess sold outside of the country. NCPB actions from 1995 – 2004 are estimated to have increased the price of maize grain by approximately 20 percent on average.[73] This benefits the small subset of farmers who are net-sellers of maize at the expense of the majority who are net-buyers.[74]

The high tariffs on maize grain probably do not have a very large effect during times of plentiful regional supply, although at times the Government has used barriers to trade to defend higher prices created by NCPB activity. Tariffs at 25-30 percent during the period 1995-2004 were estimated to increase maize prices by approximately 4 percent in Nairobi,[75] but apparently informal (illegal) imports from within the region were rampant at the time. Currently, the EAC-CET of 50 percent on maize generally means that no imports from outside of the EAC/COMESA cross the border, except during exceptional circumstances when the tariff is typically waived.[76] However, free trade with lower cost producers in the EAC/COMESA typically covers Kenya's maize deficit and disciplines prices. Regional maize prices are quite closely integrated, with maize entering Kenya tariff free from within the EAC (Uganda and Tanzania—often informally)[77] and other COMESA trade partners in the region (Zambia and Malawi). Integration with Tanzania is considerably weaker than that with Uganda, in part due to the role of export bans that have been instituted by Tanzania upon occasion.[78] Generally, Kenyan prices remain somewhat above Ugandan prices—trade costs between Kampala and Nairobi prevent a single price from holding across the region and upon occasion Kenya has even impeded regional trade to keep domestic prices artificially high.[79] Various divergences between Kampala and Nairobi wholesale prices illustrated in Figure 9 may be due in part to this.

71 d'Hotel et al (2012). Previous share of marketed maize purchased by the NCPB estimated at 50-70 percent; with the NCPB also exercising other controls on the market for maize (Jayne et al, 2008).

72 See Ariga et al. (2010), FAS (2013), d'Hotel et al. (2012).

73 Estimated by Jayne et al (2008) using a reduced form vector autoregressive model. High maize grain prices may have benefitted some of the poor who grow maize, but most farmers are net maize buyers, with the majority produced by a very small portion of (mostly larger and wealthier) producers.

74 Jayne et al. (2008).

75 Jayne et al. (2005).

76 Jayne et al. (2005), Nyoro et al. (2004), Jayne et al. (2008), Jayne and Tschirley (2009).

77 There are not tariffs applied between these nations, so informal imports are a not a problem in terms of compliance. However, it does mean that we must approach the import data with caution, since the formal doubtless underestimate total flows of trade.

78 See World Bank (2009).

79 See World Bank (2009).

Figure 9: Wholesale prices of maize in Nairobi, Kampala and International commodity markets

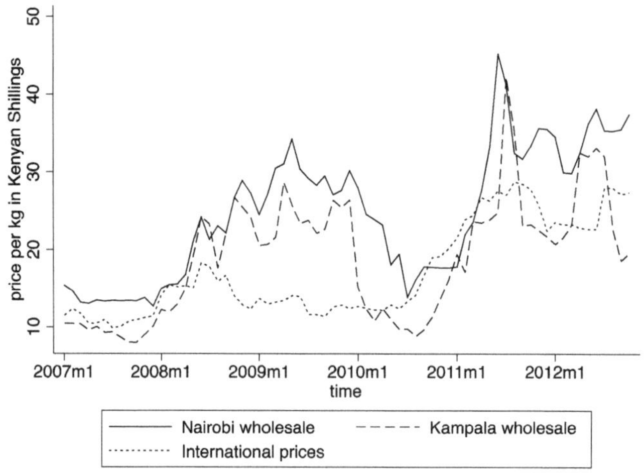

Source: Nairobi and Kampala wholesale from FAO, International price given by the US No.2 Yellow, FOB Gulf of Mexico, US price, as reported by the IMF. All prices in Kenyan shillings per kg.

During times of tight regional supply, Kenyan prices have risen substantially relative to international prices. Figure 9 shows Kenyan and Ugandan wholesale prices, as well as international prices.[80] While they mostly move together, there are some clear instances where they diverge—for example in 2009, and 2011/2012. During times of short regional supply (or when disruptions such as violence or export bans affect trade), when importers need to look beyond the region, the tariff (50 percent) has a large and significant effect, preventing imports from bringing prices down.[81] Maize grain imports have averaged about 10 percent of consumption over the last decade,[82] but annual flows have shown considerable volatility—in 2009 for example, imports (mostly from South Africa) spiked to 38 percent of local supply.[83]

The use of ad hoc changes to the import tariff policy during times of tight supply creates further problems. During times of tight supply, large millers lobby the government for a remission of the duty on grain,[84] which sometimes results in a sudden removal or reduction of the duty (prior to joining the EAC this could be done unilaterally, but now can still be done now via an agreed remission of duty). Due to the scale economies inherent in importing grain, it is typically the large millers (directly or via the NCPB) that are best positioned to access low-tariff or tariff-free grain during these periods of duty remission. This also has a side effect on competition from a posho meal perspective, as these small-scale millers are often unable to access sufficient maize grain during these times.[85] In addition, the associated

80 International price given by the US No.2 Yellow, FOB Gulf of Mexico, US price, as reported by the IMF. We are not able to adjust the maize prices appropriately for costs incurred through importing, due to lack of data, most particularly on tariffs that have varied substantially over time.

81 Ariga et al. (2010).

82 FAOSTAT data 2000 – 2009. Reports of unrecorded informal and illegal imports across borders with Uganda and Tanzania suggest that actual imports may have been much higher.

83 FAOSTAT data 2000 - 2009.

84 Kirimi et al. (2011).

85 Kirimi et al. (2011).

reduction in flour costs tends to lag the change in tariff, because of bottlenecks in transport infrastructure and trader withdrawal from the market due to unpredictable government interference.[86] This means that consumers continue to pay higher prices for longer, before the imports bring prices back down.

The ban on GMO imports of maize, and the way in which it has been varied over time, is another source of uncertainty in maize prices. The Biosafety Act of 2009 created the National Biosafety Authority and granted it broad powers for the control of Genetically Modified Organisms ("GMOs"). This includes the control of imported GMOs such as GMO maize. Since this time, the control of imported GMO maize has been erratic, with periods during which a complete ban has been in place, while others imports by millers (for the production of flour only) have been allowed. In addition, the National Biosafety Authority has not been the sole regulator, with direct intervention by the Ministry of Health, following decree from cabinet in 2012.[87] This ban has an important effect on imports, since there are only a very limited number of countries from which Kenya can source non-GMO maize. During 2009, and even throughout 2010 mostly from South Africa.[88] After South African (GMO) maize was blocked, imports dropped substantially. The GMO ban may in essence separate Kenya from other sources of maize outside of the region, even if the tariff is reduced.

Further down the value chain, the Competition Authority of Kenya ("CAK") (formerly the Monopolies and Price Commission) has taken action against potential anticompetitive pricing practices in sifted flour. CAK assessed the sector and provided pertinent recommendations based on their antitrust enforcement and advocacy powers. The removal Cereal Millers Association ("CMA") clauses that allowed for price coordination was a good move and the investigation itself may have triggered a response lowering prices of sifted maize flour. In addition, the recommendations based on the actions of the National Cereals and Produce Board ("NCPB"), aimed at reducing the heavy burden of maize grain prices on consumers, were timely. We will return to this in more detail in section 3.4.

We can summarize briefly what we know about the maize market in Kenya as follows:

» NCPB actions have increased the price of maize by 20 percent on average between 1995 and 2004, and given the continued high levels of purchasing, it is likely that they will continue to inflate prices substantially.

» Inconsistent application of trade policy and bans on GMO maize imports have played a complementary role in inflating maize prices in Kenya. During times of plentiful regional supply of maize, these are less important as other producers in the region are able to produce at competitive prices (although trade costs do erode the competitiveness of the prices). During times of tight regional supply these factors have caused prices in Kenya to rise significantly above world prices, with the short term management efforts of government creating additional complications.

» CAK has played a positive role in improving the competitive environment in the sifted flour sector, with additional pertinent recommendations relating to the activities of the NCPB in the grain sector.

---

86 Jayne and Tschirley (2009), Kirimi et al (2011).

87 See FAS (2012).

88 Trademap mirror data. Another substantial source of GMO maize was the United States.

2. Households in the Maize Sector: Consumers and Producers

Patterns of maize consumption in Kenya are complex, with differences across the income distribution both in quantity and form consumed. The left hand panel of Figure 10 illustrates the average annual expenditure on maize per adult equivalent across expenditure deciles. Maize consumption generally increases up until the 7th decile, after which it remains fairly constant. This is a common pattern for a staple—as income increases, households tend to consume more of the staple, but if incomes increases sufficiently then they begin to substitute superior alternatives. Households also make different choices between types of maize as they become wealthier. Consumption of dry grain and loose flour first increases and then decreases in total expenditure, while sifted flour increases across all deciles. This suggests that households view sifted flour as a superior substitute relative to maize grain

Figure 10: Maize consumption: Household expenditure per adult equivalent (left panel), Household expenditure *share* (right panel)

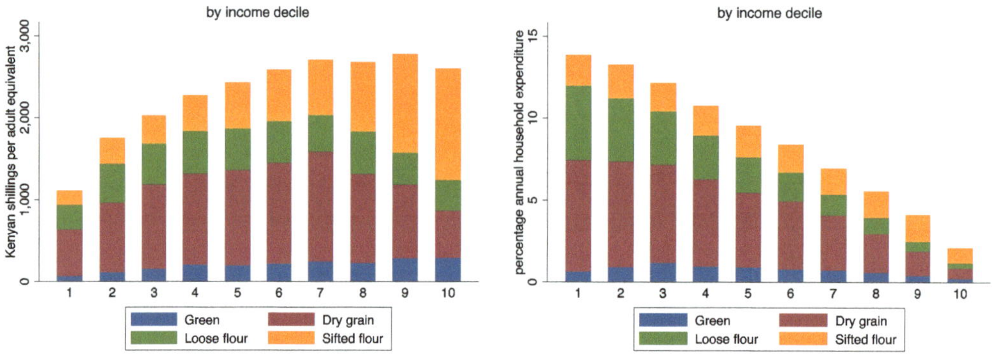

Source: KIHBS (2005/06), author calculations.

Maize consumption as a percentage of total expenditure decreases in total consumption expenditure. While households do consume more maize as their total expenditure increases, the rate of increase of the former is slower than the latter, as shown in the right hand panel of Figure 10 above. This graph illustrates that the budget share of maize declines monotonically across income decile. This makes intuitive sense: as incomes increase households spend more on maize, but they don't spend all of the additional income on maize—clearly there are also other products they wish to consume. So, wealthier households spend a much smaller portion of their total expenditure on maize. Households in the poorest decile have an expenditure share on maize that is almost seven times that of the wealthiest decile.

There are some differences between the makeup and level of urban/rural consumption of maize. The patterns of increasing overall expenditure, and decreasing expenditure shares, relative to income holds across both rural and urban households. However, on average, rural households consume substantially more maize in general and maize grain in particular, while urban households consume more sifted flour. Some part of this pattern is likely explained by differences in geographical availability of the different kinds of maize (as opposed to just prices and preferences). If we suppose that where a product is widely available we would typically observe at least some households consuming it, then we can infer that where we find no households consuming a product it is probably not widely available.

The first two columns of Table 1 show the percentage of survey clusters (small geographical areas) where each product was consumed in the week of the survey, broken down by urban/rural. Given that only 64 percent or rural (and 63 percent of urban) clusters consumed loose flour at all, we can be fairly sure that in at least some of these clusters this product was not available. The last two columns of the table show the percentage of households overall that consume each kind of maize—this, in comparison with the clusters columns, gives a sense of how household's consumption bundle of types of maize varies widely across the country. In addition to what is shown in the table, most households only consumed one (49 percent) or two (35 percent) of the four types of maize during the week of the survey.

Table 1: Geographical consumption of maize

	% clusters consuming		% household consuming	
	Rural	Urban	Rural	Urban
Green	43%	80%	14%	26%
Grain	95%	71%	66%	25%
Loose flour	64%	63%	29%	19%
Sifted flour	55%	96%	26%	63%

Source: KIHBS 2004/5, author calculations

The fact that many households grow maize for their own consumption, and for sale, must be taken into consideration for the analysis of the welfare effects. Roughly half of all Kenyan households grow maize, although only 14 percent sell any of their produce.[89] The left hand panel of Figure 11 shows mean annual sales and consumption of own-production of maize across income deciles. Notice that unlike demand, we have a strong inverse U-shape for supply—those in the middle of the distribution produce the most. Those that grow and sell are concentrated within rural areas, although there are a few urban households that grow maize.

Figure 11: Maize production: Annual value of own-production (left panel), and Annual expenditure share of own-production

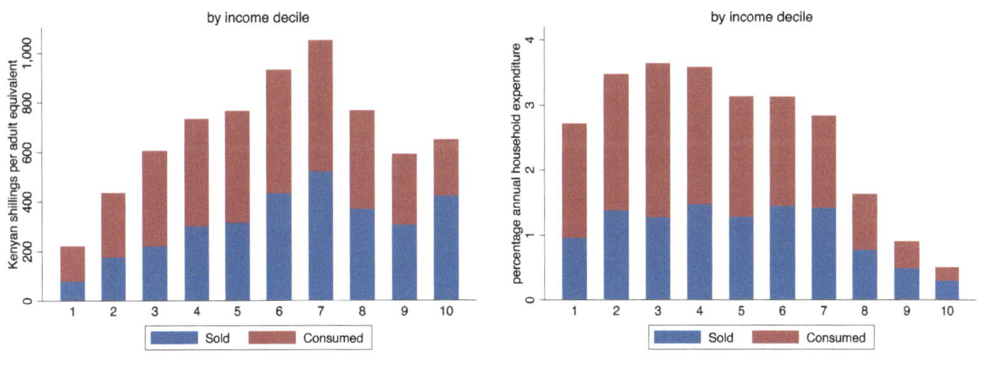

Source: KIHBS (2005/06), author calculations.

89 Estimated from the KIHBS 2005/6, as the percentage of household's with non-zero annual incomes from maize of maize, accounting for household weights.

Relative to their incomes, people across most of the lower and middle of the distribution produce a significant volume of maize. The right hand panel of Figure 11 shows the value of own-production maize consumed and sold, as a percentage of total expenditure, across expenditure deciles. Notice here how much higher the bars are in the poorer end of the distribution (as compared to the left hand panel of Figure 11)—even though these households do not produce that much maize, their production is significant relative to the size of their total consumption levels.

3. Welfare Impact of High Maize Prices: Effects on Household Income and Poverty Incidence

In this section we estimate the welfare impact that could be achieved through a 20 percent average decline in maize prices. The most recent reliable estimates of NCPB purchases show that these activities inflated maize prices by 20 percent on average over a ten-year period.[90] Using the analysis of household demand and supply of maize, we now estimate the impact of a 20 percent decrease in prices on welfare in Kenya—i.e. what could feasibly be achieved by eliminating price increases due to recent NCPB actions. Similar analysis can easily be applied to other changes in maize prices, whether relating to the short-term management of crisis, or to longer-term structural policy. We know that trade policy (tariffs) and the policy towards GMO maize have also affected prices, although at this stage we lack credible estimates as to the size of those effects beyond their complementary role along with the NCPB as mentioned above. The results in this section underline the importance of maize prices and the fact that lower prices will yield significant benefits for Kenyan consumers, and most particularly the poor. Given that we have used only the estimate of the impact of NCPB, we can consider this a lower bound of what is achievable through adjusting current policies.

We will apply the hypothetical average 20 percent price decrease to all kinds of maize (green, dry grain, loose flour and sifted flour) across all parts of Kenya. World Bank (2009) showed that maize prices across Kenya are fairly well integrated, suggesting that it is reasonable to assume constant geographical effects on average. In addition, price history suggests that the margins between different steps in the value chain are fairly constant over time. We do not have prices for green maize, but these are the smallest segment, and there is no reason to believe that prices for green maize would not move in similar patterns to those of dry grain. In the next section we show that while margins between sifted flour, loose flour and dry grain do fluctuate over time, in the longer term they are generally very stable. The only point at which they have deviated substantially from this stability was during the aftermath of the 2009 price spike, when sifted flour prices fell more slowly than grain prices.

Putting together household consumption and production from the previous section, it is clear that lower income households are on average much larger net buyers of maize relative to their incomes. To the extent that households grow their own maize, they are insulated from the effects of price increases, and may even benefit from them. So to understand total welfare impacts we work with net consumption (consumption less production). Figure 12 shows mean net purchases of maize as a percentage of expenditure, across income deciles. Only 8 percent of households are net sellers of maize, as compared to 17 percent with net purchases of zero and 75 percent with positive net purchases. From the figure we can see that those at the poorer end of the distribution are far more affected than the wealthy. The

90 See background section.

net budget share of those in the poorest decile households is estimated to be 6.5 times that of the wealthiest decile.

Figure 12: *Net* expenditure share on maize

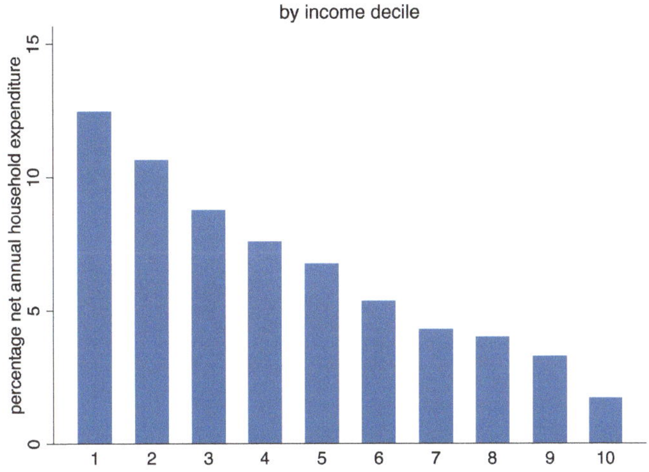

Source: KIHBS (2005/06), author calculations.

Without accounting for change in behavior, poorer households will benefit to a greater extent from the lower prices that can be gained from better-functioning markets. If we ignore behavior change for a moment, a change in the price of maize will affect households in direct proportion to their budget share on this item. The solid line in the left hand panel of Figure 13 illustrates the impact of a 20 percent decrease in maize prices across income levels—the y-axis measures the gain in income that would have equivalent effect on a household's welfare to this price cut. This figure illustrates precisely the same concept that we covered with respect to sugar.

Figure 13: Equivalent income effects of a 20 percent price decrease in maize: With zero or estimated elasticity (left panel), Rural/Urban with estimated elasticity (right panel)

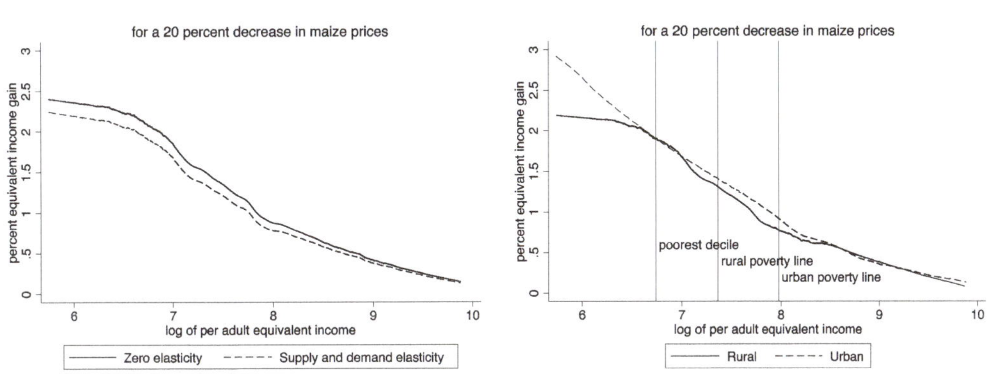

Source: KIHBS (2005/06), author calculations. Elasticities are taken from Mghenyi et al (2011). For supply this is an elasticity of 0.4. For demand the largest elasticity is used (for the sake of conservatism); -0.55 across the whole sample.

Altering current policy to reduce maize prices by 20 percent would have approximately the same effect as a real income increase of 1.2 percent on average, with much greater gains falling on the poor. When prices fall, on average we would expect people to purchase more of that product (but probably not so much that their total expenditure on the item increases). At the same time, we would usually expect an average decrease in the production of maize by some suppliers (since the profits to be earned are lower). As in the case of sugar, we can incorporate this behavior into our estimates using demand and supply elasticities.[91] The dotted line in the left hand panel of Figure 13 does exactly this – showing very slightly reduced welfare gains[92] across the distribution of expenditure.[93] Notice that below a certain level of expenditure, households experience average welfare gains equivalent to more than 2 percent of total expenditure. Compare this to the wealthier end of the distribution, where equivalent income gains are below 0.5 percent. Clearly, a decline in maize prices will substantially benefit the poor.

Separating the welfare effects of rural and urban groups, suggests that impacts *by* income level are generally very similar. The right hand panel of Figure 13 shows the estimated welfare impact curves (including elasticities)[94] separated into rural (solid line) and urban (dotted line). The only point where the two lines diverge is just below the boundary of the bottom decile of expenditure (as indicated by the solid line on the left hand side). This divergence is explained by the fact that the poor in rural areas typically grow quite a lot of maize, reducing their net purchases, as opposed to the urban poor, few of whom grow maize. This suggests that the poorest of the urban population have the most to gain from lower maize prices. However, the portion of the population in this group is small (only 0.04 percent of urban households are in the bottom expenditure decile).

Table 2: Projected changes in household poverty from a 20% decrease in maize prices

	Rural	Urban	Total
percentage of poor out of poverty	2.00%	1.72%	1.95%
percentage non-poor into poverty	0.17%	0.01%	0.12%
Net change in poverty	-1.77%	-1.69%	-1.75%
Contribution to net change	82.37%	17.63%	

Source: KNBS, author calculations

A decrease in maize prices of 20 percent would result in a significant decline in poverty[95] in both rural and urban areas. We estimate that a maize price decrease of 20 percent (through the estimated average equivalent income gains of 1.2 percent) would result in a net decline in poverty of 1.8 percent. This

91 As with sugar we use a second order Taylor series expansion to estimate the effect. The only difference here is that we include supply effects, which we ignored in the case of sugar.

92 Deaton (1989) argues that the first order impacts are good enough for the purposes of policy, since the difference made by elasticity's in most cases would be small and estimates of these difficult to produce in a defensible way. These results are consistent with this view.

93 We use elasticities from Mghenyi et al (2011). For supply this is an elasticity of 0.4. For demand we follow their largest elasticity (for the sake of conservatism) of -0.55 across the whole sample. Inspection of the size of the effect in the graphs suggests that the magnitude of assumed elasticities will not substantially change the results.

94 Extending these results with the use of elasticities for all of the different kinds of maize, that differ across rural/urban and poor/rich areas is not practical with the data available. In addition, we can be sure, from our analysis of Figure 2.6, that this would only marginally change our estimates. The fact that maize has been and continues to be by far the dominant staple in Kenya, despite the large price swings of recent years, there is no reason to suspect that elasticities would be particularly large, nor that differences.

95 When we talk of poverty here, we mean those that have household per adult equivalent expenditures below the national poverty lines.

result is consistent with other studies linking maize prices and poverty in Kenya.[96] Table 2 above shows the make-up in the net changes in poverty, including those moving from poor to non-poor and those moving from non-poor to poor across both rural and urban areas. The net poverty gains are concentrated in rural areas, with 82 percent of the net poverty gains living in rural areas. It is unfortunate that any households would be harmed by such reform, but those who gain very substantially outnumber those who lose. The number of households that move into poverty as result of the decline is roughly 10 percent of the number that move out of poverty.

4. Actions by the Competition Agency in the Maize Sector

The Monopolies and Price Commission of Kenya (now the Competition Authority of Kenya) conducted an investigation into potential collusion by large-scale millers of maize over the period 2009 – 2010. This followed spiking maize prices and recommendations of the maize sector survey report prepared by CAK in December 2008. The report highlighted anti- competitive concerns, particularly focusing on the CMA, which had clauses suggestive of price coordination in its constitution. The Monopolies and Price Commission did not determine whether a price fixing cartel was in fact being operated by the CMA, but the CMA was asked to amend its constitution to remove clauses that could facilitate price fixing. This process started in early 2010 and was concluded with a final edition forwarded by the CMA in February 2011.

Figure 14: Sifted flour, loose flour and maize grain prices (left panel), and Sifted flour margins over maize grain prices (right panel).

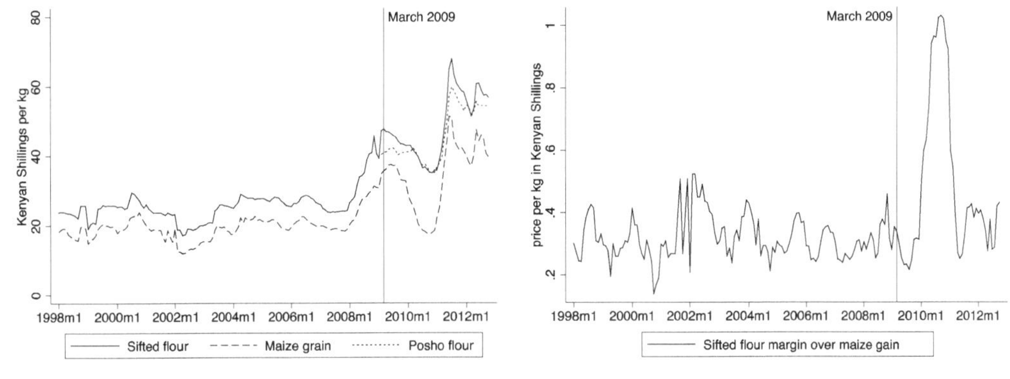

Source: KNBS, author calculations

Although no evidence was found to conclude that the CMA was operating as a cartel, a small, unexplained drop in sifted flour prices following the investigation could be indicative of a response to pressures for setting more competitive prices. Immediately after the investigation began in 2009, sifted flour prices started falling despite the fact that grain prices were still rising, as was the price of posho flour. This is illustrated in the left hand panel of Figure 14, where the vertical line indicates March 2009. Similarly, the right hand panel of Figure 14 shows the margin of sifted flour over grain prices— to the right of

96 See Jayne et al (2008) for a review. These results most look at the welfare impact of a price increase.

the vertical line (March 2009), the margins of sifted flour dropped. Over the five months following March 2009 (April – October), the average margin of sifted flour over the price of grain was only 24.6 percent as compared to the average over the previous five years of 30.9 percent.[97] It is not the fact that this margin dropped that is unusual—as is clear from the margin history, drops of this size have happened in the past—but rather the fact that this occurred during a period where grain prices were still rising. This might be an indication of collusion, and investigation by the commission prompted a change from the millers. However, there could well be other reasons that account for this change, and available evidence is certainly not sufficient to conclude that there were in fact cartel activities being carried out.

The very large increase in margins starting in late 2009 period should not necessarily be interpreted as anticompetitive. Sifted flour prices actually fell across the entire period of this margin spike. This increase in margins was caused by grain prices falling very rapidly back towards the historical average (see the left hand panel of Figure 14), while sifted flour prices fell more slowly. The slower fall of sifted flour prices may have been due to either (a) stocks of higher priced grain already purchased by millers, or (b) wariness about further grain price fluctuations given the unprecedented price shifts over the previous months. The higher margins were not maintained during the price spikes that started in early 2011, during which margins dropped once again. After the end of the unusual margin spike, margins have remained slightly higher than historical levels (the average from April 2011 through until October 2012 was 36 percent as opposed to the average prior to March 2009 of 32 percent). Further data and analysis would be required to assess whether this reflects anything other than the costs of managing risks associated with much more volatile grain prices.

Even if sifted flour prices have been inflated by a hypothetical cartel at some point, the impacts on consumers and poverty would be much lower than those associated with grain price hikes.

A decrease in sifted maize prices (only) of 5 percent (the approximate amount that margins dropped post-investigation as outlined above) would increase real income by 0.1 percent.[98] This is only 5 percent of the size of the average impact we estimated would be caused by a grain price decline of 20 percent. The much more modest size is due to the fact that the average budget share of sifted maize is just under 2 percent, as opposed to the average total budget share of all kinds of maize at approximately 7 percent. In addition, the impacts of sifted flour changes are less concentrated on the poor, since as we showed above sifted flour is a smaller portion of poor consumer budgets than other kinds of maize. This is not to say that sifted flour prices are not important—clearly they still matter for consumers—but their importance is overshadowed by the importance of maize grain prices.

The Monopolies and Price Commission of Kenya 2011 report on the maize market focused on NCPB activities and included a set of recommendations regarding its future conduct—reflecting the accurate assessment that this is the more important concern in the value chain. This shift of focus towards maize grain prices is well advised, and the potential gains from removal of barriers to competition are much larger than those to be gained in the flour market. However, continued vigilance regarding potential cartel activities (as the CAK continues to show)[99] is important, particularly the trade barriers against imported flour (EAC-CET of 50 percent on maize flour).

97 Margin calculated as the price per kg of sifted flour over the price per kg of maize grain.

98 This is estimated using the first order method (i.e. without accounting for substitution effects), as we do not have reliable estimates of own or cross price elasticities of demand for the different kinds of maize.

99 See for example in the popular media: http://www.businessdailyafrica.com/Cartels+put+on+notice+over+high+flour+oil+prices/-/539546/1643524/- /item/0/-/bb1kxmz/-/index.html.

5. Concluding Remarks on Maize

We have shown that eliminating the 20 percent average increase in maize prices caused by NCPB central buying would be equivalent to an increase in average incomes of 1.2 percent, and with an associated 1.8 percent reduction in the poverty rate. While certainly there would be some that = lose from lower prices, the number of households moving into poverty would be only 10 percent of the number moving out of poverty. The gains on average significantly outweigh the losses. In addition, the 20 percent price decrease that we have focused on is a smaller price variation than that which has actually happened over recent years. From the beginning of the price spikes in January 2008 to their peak in June 2011, maize prices in Kenya increased by 64 percent in real terms[100]—far exceeding the increases in world prices. These spikes have often been due to the barriers in place that prevent maize imports from entering the country from outside of the EAC/COMESA to ease tight supply during times of a poor regional harvest. These spikes could be significantly moderated through appropriate policy action.

Minimizing effects that the NCPB has in terms of increasing maize prices should be an important element of reform. The role of the NCPB in increasing prices needs to be addressed. This is something that has already been touched on by the Competition Authority of Kenya (former Monopolies and Price Commission). The Ernst and Young "Draft Final Report on Study of Restructuring of the National Cereals and Produce Board" released in April 2014, puts a strong emphasis on the role that the NCPB has played in increasing prices. The document notes "in Kenya government directives on prices to be applied by NCPB have distorted the functionality of markets and the Board's profitability." An important consideration of any reform should be the way in which it is expected to affect the price- altering effects of NCPB actions.

A more consistent and open trade policy will support lower maize prices through increased competition, but perhaps, more importantly, it will reduce the chances of a price crisis through a better market response in times of supply side shocks. Trade policy needs to be reformed such that times of tight regional supply do not have such a large effect on prices. Reducing the tariff rate, and committing to and communicating a consistent policy regarding how tariffs are managed in these times, will help the market to function better in these times. A consistent approach to GMO imports is a key complementary component. In the longer term, low, stable maize prices would also encourage farmers to diversify into cash crops with more growth potential (as opposed to staying in maize for subsistence).

100 Grain prices went from a national average of 20.3KES/kg to 51.21KES/kg in nominal terms over this period. However CPI rose more than 56 percent over the same period. Real prices have since fallen (both due to a reduction in nominal prices and further inflation), such that the net real increase since January 2008 is 20 percentstill a large impact on consumption baskets. Data source: KNBS.

IV. Concluding Remarks

Policy reform that could reduce maize and sugar prices is an opportunity for Kenya to improve household welfare, most particularly that of the poor. Lower prices of these foodstuffs will have the equivalent effect of increasing real incomes, with larger gains falling on the poor. As with almost all policy reform, there will be some net losers from such reforms— but those who lose are much fewer in number and wealthier on average than those who gain. As such, the proposed reforms are both welfare enhancing for Kenya and pro-poor. In addition, more competitive markets have benefits in terms of the strong incentives they create to drive productivity increases among producers.

More stable and pro-competition domestic and trade policies are recommended to increase consumer welfare. The action of the competition authority is key both to advocate for less distortive government policies and to detect anticompetitive behavior that can exacerbate the burden on the poor. Their investigations of the maize milling sector and their recommendations regarding the NCPB are both excellent examples of CAK playing precisely this role. We will not rehash the specific policy recommendations for trade policy and internal intervention here as these have been adequately dealt with in each section.

Extending this work through structural models that incorporate labor market and longer- term substitution effects would improve our understanding of food prices in Kenya. Ravallion (1990) showed that incorporating labor effects relating to high food prices in Bangladesh could result in positive effects in the longer run. There are two reasons to believe that this kind of effect is unlikely to alter the general welfare conclusions of this paper. First, these effects typically take a long time to have an impact—in the case of Ravallion (1990), positive net effects were only observed after four years. None of the price spikes of Kenyan maize price away from world prices has lasted even close to this long. Second, recent studies suggest that these labor market effects may be much smaller than previously believed.[101] Nevertheless, further structural work on these markets would enhance our understanding, and if the required data becomes available this would be an intriguing pursuit.

101 See Wodon and Zaman (2008).

Appendix

A1. Sugar Price Calculations

This appendix outlines the assumptions and calculations behind (a) the estimated import parity series for international sugar imports, and (b) the relevant benchmark to which to compare current Kenyan sugar prices.

a. Estimating Import Parity Prices

We use the international price series provided by the IMF, from the No.11 Raw Sugar futures contract from the Coffee, Sugar and Cocoa Exchange. This price is FOB the vessel of the importer at the port of origin. To adjust this price to import parity we need to make the following adjustments.

» Shipping and insurance. We use the estimated price for shipping a light 20ft container from the Pelotas Port in Brazil to Mombassa Kenya obtained from the seafreightcalculator.com (USD 2257). We divide this by an estimated container contents of 20MT. Monroy et al (2013) use 25MT in this calculations, but this is higher than the net capacity of a typical light 20ft container, so we take a slightly more conservative stance. We assume insurance costs of 1% of FOB value of the shipment. The shipping and insurance costs are added to the price of the sugar to calculate CIF.

» Import tariffs. Import tariffs are the higher of the ad valorem duty of 100% or the specific duty of $200/MT. For the period under study, the CIF price never dropped low enough for the specific duty to apply.

» VAT. VAT is applied at a rate of 16% to the value of CIF plus the import tariff.

» Sugar development levy. The sugar development levy is applied to the value of CIF. The SDL rate is currently 4%, and was 7% prior to November 2007.

» Costs associated with arrival at the port, clearing, inland transport and importer margins. Monroy et al (2013) provide an excellent breakdown of all the costs incurred from arrival of a container at the port through to completion of inland transport to Nairobi from 2005 – 2011. We remove the portions of their calculations that are variable (i.e. percentage based) to calculate an average fixed portion. The variable portion is 5% of CIF (including letters of credit and clearing fees). The fixed portion averaged 7.6 across the period. We added this directly as a fixed portion. Variation is low enough that this should not make a significant difference to our estimates and since the data are not available for the whole period, we prefer this over attempting to use specific annual estimates.

» Retail margins. International sugar does not arrive at the port in saleable form. It arrives in bulk, and must be packaged and distributed on the local market. We apply the average margin between wholesale (50kg bags) and retail sugar in the domestic market to the import parity 'wholesale price' as calculated by taking into account all of the above bullet points. The average margin is 15%. This is calculated from FAS monthly data for the period 2009 – 2012. In addition, the margin calculated using quarterly data from the KSB on the period 2003 (Q1) to 2013 (Q1) given the same average margin.[102]

Figure 15 below illustrates how the components discussed above contribute to the import parity price estimated over the period 2005 – 2011, for which we have all the data that was then used to separate the fixed and variable components for the whole period. Note that over this entire period, with exception of 2007, the import parity price remained higher than the local Kenyan price (shown by the black line). This

102 We corrected one typo in the KSB data in Q3 2011, where the mean is shown to be outside the high/low range. This was the only point where the KSB data diverged from the FAS series.

is why there have been no imports of (non-industrial) sugar into Kenya with exception of from COMESA (subject to quota and licensing), which is not subject to the tariff.

Figure 15: Components of import parity price

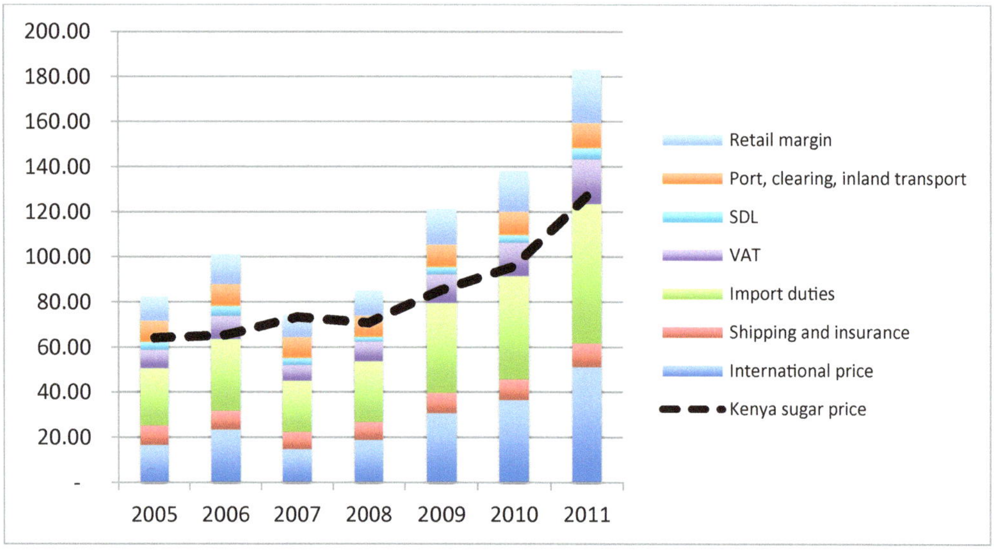

Source: KNBS, IMF, Monroy et al (2013), author calculations

Inspection of the graph shows that the import duties are easily the largest component of the import parity price—even larger than the actual international price itself. Import duties are currently so high that it completely excludes international imports. Over the period 2009 – 2012, it would have required a cut of over 50% to bring the import parity price down to the Kenyan price on average. The fact that import tariffs are so high as to insulate the local price from import parity prices except during exceptional times complicates the calculation of how much we might expect Kenyan prices to full under a more open trade regime. This is the calculation to which we now turn.

b. Estimating Benchmarks to which Kenyan Sugar Prices Can Be Compared

The relevant benchmark when considering reforming trade policy to open Kenya to international competition is that of import parity in a context of lowered trade barriers. This is the situation that is most likely to occur given removal of those barriers—a useful counterfactual against which to weigh the current situation. Certainly it would be possible to lower prices further if some of the other costs associated with importing were lowered (e.g. costs at the port, costs of inland transport), but a large percentage of these require much longer-term effort to reform. One quick win in respect of reducing these costs would be the removal of the clearing fees (2 percent).

To estimate the benchmark we focus on a comparison between wholesale sugar prices and import parity without trade barriers. We remove import duties (which also impacts on other costs, such as VAT), and retail margins. Retail margins are removed because, at least for the period 2009 – 2012 we have reliable wholesale prices, and we are more concerned with the most recent prices in term of assessing a benchmark with which to compare Kenya's current situation. Retails margins may also be affected by other things that are not directly related to sugar policy (e.g. packaging costs, internal transport costs), and for this reason it is simpler to remove them. We also know that retail prices are responsive to wholesale, so all things held equal we can expect price reductions at the wholesale level to be passed on. Figure 16 below illustrates the results, showing that in general import parity (with zero trade barriers) has been below Kenyan wholesale sugar prices. However, the margin is not that large – Kenyan wholesale prices are estimated to have exceeded this (completely open) import parity price by 39 percent on average over the period 2009 – 2012 (illustrated by the difference between the two lines on the graph). This implies that a move to completely open trade would result in an average price decline of 28 percent.[103]

Figure 16: Kenyan wholesale price compared to import parity with no trade barriers

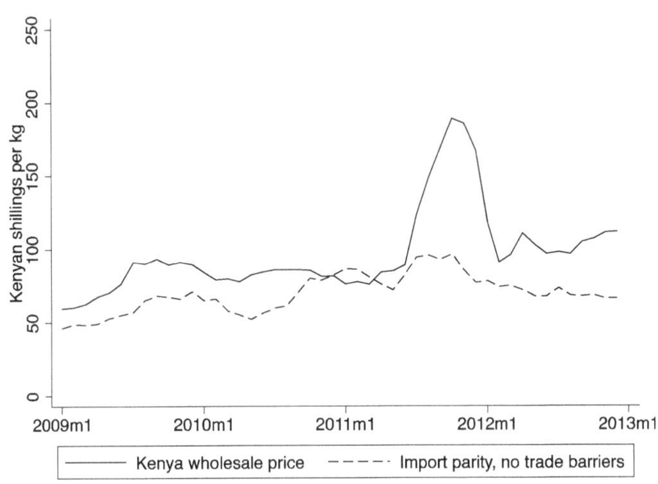

Source: KNBS, FAS, author calculations

A more realistic potential scenario for reform would be to consider reducing the EAC-CET rate on sugar to 25 percent from 100 percent (which would treat sugar on par with other finished goods[104]), remove the licensing regime and cut costs to import through removing clearing fees and simplifying procedures at the port. In this scenario, we assume that in the longer term Kenya could halve costs between arrival at the port and final destination. We estimate under these assumptions that Kenyan wholesale prices over the period 2009 – 2012 would have exceeded the import parity price by 23% on average. This implies that a move to completely open trade would result in an average price decline of 19 percent.

An alternative scenario to consider would be one in which the world sugar market was fully liberalized (leading to international sugar prices rising by approximately 30 percent—see appendix A3), and the Kenyan sugar industry become competitive in this environment. If this scenario had occurred between 2009 – 2012 then, even ignoring the costs associated with delivering the sugar fob to a vessel in mombassa, we would expect wholesale sugar prices to drop by 53%. In this situation, we would expect no international imports into Kenya, since local production would be cheaper than import parity.

103 0.39/1.39=0.28.-

104 The Broad Economic Categories (BEC) nomenclature identifies some forms of sugar as mainly intermediate goods for industry, but non-industrial refined sugar (HS code 170199) is identified as a final consumption good.

A2. Estimation of Elasticities

In general we have described the methodology we have employed in the main text, or in some cases, in footnotes. This appendix briefly presents the estimates of the elasticities of demand used for the welfare analysis. For more complete details of the estimations in this paper, the Stata do-files are available on request from the authors.

Table A1 below shows, in the first two columns, the average budget shares of sugar across the categories of rural/urban and poor/non-poor. The elasticities in the second two columns were estimated using a simple log-log regression. While simple to estimate, this suffers from numerous econometric problems. For an overview of these issues, see Deaton (1997). From the table we can see that elasticity of demand for sugar is higher (in absolute value) (a) for urban consumers relative to rural consumers, and (b) for poor consumers relative to non-poor consumers.

Table 3: Budget shares and price elasticities

	Average budget share		**Log-log elasticity**		**Deaton method elasticity**	
	poor	non-poor	poor	non-poor	Poor	Non-poor
Rural	6%	4%	-68%	-28%	-47%	5%
Urban	5%	2%	-89%	-48%	-74%	-4%

Source: Kenya Integrated Household Budget Survey (2004/05), author calculations. The equation estimated for the estimation of log-log elasticity is $\ln(Qi) \sim \ln(Pi) + ui$, where Qi is quantity of sugar purchased by household i, Pi is the price of sugar faced by household Pi, and ui is the error term. The estimation followed for the Deaton elasticities is considerably more complex and can be found in Deaton (1989).

We also estimate elasticities using the method proposed by Deaton (1989), which appropriately accounts for zero purchases, measurement error and quality shading—see the last two columns of Table A1. Note that this method has a far larger impact on the estimates of the non-poor—reducing them to very close to zero. We have not used these as our main estimates in the paper, which represents a more conservative stance, as these elasticities would result in larger welfare impacts in all cases. It would also increase the estimated effects on the poor relative to the non-poor.

A3. The International Sugar Market

The international market for sugar is one of the most distorted of all agricultural commodities.[105] The United States, EU and Japan are among the worst offenders in terms of distortionary policy—using subsidies, import quota's and tariffs among other interventions to keep their domestic market prices high, while simultaneously depressing the world market price.[106] Only a handful of countries such as Brazil, Australia and Cuba have been able to produce at this artificially depressed world price.[107] Beyond the substantial welfare costs this imposes on consumers in those countries where prices are kept artificially high, these distortions ensure that inefficient sugar producers, mostly in OECD countries, continue to produce, while much more cost efficient countries are unable to produce.[108]

105 Sandry and Vink (2008).

106 See Mitchell (2004).

107 Mitchell (2004).

108 See OECD (2007) and Elobeid and Beghin (2006).

There is a consensus within the literature that full multilateral liberalization of the market would result in a significant rise in the world price of sugar, along with significant declines in the domestic price of highly protected markets. Studies from 2006/2007 estimate the increase in world prices at 40-50 percent; very similar figures to those produced by a whole set of previous studies.[109] Such an extreme price change might be eroded over time as supply from low cost nations (e.g. Brazil) responds to the change in world market,[110] but is still likely to be significant. In addition to the price change, the adjustment to liberalization would involve a large shift in production from high-cost producers (particularly beet sugar producers in the EU and US) towards low cost producers most in less developed countries.[111]

There have been some changes to the world market in the years since these studies. Over the last decade the EU has moved steadily from being a net exporter, to being a substantial net importer. This has been driven by both expansions in preferential access via EPA (Economic Partnership Agreements) and EBA (Everything But Arms) agreements as well as by a decline in protection through the 2006 sugar reforms.[112] The United States, while maintaining its long protection of its market, continued to open market access under NAFTA (most preferential agreements such as AGOA exclude sugar). However, a study in 2010 shows that NAFTA had a much smaller effect than expected, probably due in large part to domestic prices in Mexico that actually exceeded those of the United States.[113]

Both the US and the EU were concerned that countries with which they had preferential agreements would take the opportunity to arbitrage the difference between domestic and international prices. For example, Mexico could import cheap world-price sugar and export more expensive domestically produced sugar to the United States. So far, this does not seem to have materialized in the EU and the US.[114] Kenya faces a similar concern in COMESA where countries such as Egypt have much lower import tariffs and so can access world market sugar at very low prices.

So there is some legitimacy to complaints from producers that the world price is not 'fair'—most probably the current market price is 30-40 percent higher than what would occur under free international competition. They key question as to how Kenya can best respond to this is whether Kenya can become a low cost producer of sugar. If Kenya has the potential to become a competitive producer of sugar, then the question is how to help the industry to get there without compromising consumers (and the poor in particular) though exceptionally high prices. If Kenya cannot become a low cost producer of sugar, then in the long run it would be better to lower trade barriers and allow other countries to subsidize Kenyan consumption of cheap sugar. The resources used for sugar production would be better used in an industry in which Kenya is able to become competitive. This would entail an adjustment period for local producers that, if not carefully managed, would result in the failure of Kenyan businesses and a loss of employment.

---

109 Elobeid and Beghin (2006) estimate a change in the world price of 48 percent on full liberalization. OECD (2007) estimate a change of 40 percent and 42 percent in the world prices of refined and raw sugar respectively. Michell (2004) cites a list of studies including Sheales et al (1999) at 41 percent, Wohlgenant (1999) at 43 percent and Borrel and Pierce (1999) at 38 percent.

110 Mitchell (2004) and Elobeid and Beghin (2006).

111 Elobeid and Beghin (2006), OECD (2007).

112 EU (2013).

113 Knutson et al (2010).

114 Knutson et al (2010), EU (2013).

The South African Competition Experience: A Review of Fifteen Years into a New Regime

Dennis M. Davis

dennis_davis22@hotmail.com

Judge, High Court of Cape Town
Professor, University of Cape Town

Abstract

This paper examines the experience of the South African competition authorities in implementing the ambitious competition legislation introduced in 1998 ("Competition Act"). It analyzes a series of cases decided since the entry into force of the Competition Act that have raised significant substantive questions of competition law which rarely find their way to the equivalent competition authorities in the developed world. For example, the paper describes the issues that both the Tribunal and the Appeal Court faced in the excessive pricing case ArcelorMittal. Furthermore, there's a synthesis of the Walmart merger, which raised challenging questions on the role of public interest considerations in merger analysis.

Finally, the paper examines a set of procedural issues, including the Tribunal's choice of an adversarial system and the consequent weight to be given to expert's evidence.

I. Introduction

Bill Kovacic has noted that the effectiveness of competition regulation is increasingly recognized as being affected, not only by the quality of the doctrinal and analytical foundations of the regime, but equally by the manner of its implementation.[1] It will be my argument in this paper that these two challenges should not be posed as binary opposites, but as problems which are inextricably linked to each other.

To foreshadow this argument, the problem which faces developing countries as they adopt new competition laws which to a large extent have an intellectual and jurisprudential pedigree in the developed world, and in particular the law of the United States and the European Union, is that competition law in a developing country must be implemented invariably within a context of an economy facing a transition from a government which was a central economic participant to a government which is supposed to act as a referee, albeit an active one, in a competitive process.

Understandably, legislation which is introduced in a developing country may not solely concern "pure competition matters," but could include political and social goals which are critical to this process of transformation. As Dr. Seema Gaur has said of the Competition Commission of India: "[It] is a very young competition agency [...] the sheer size of the country, the diversity of people, the culture and language, the diversity of sectors and business practices, and the country's large and disparate economy makes both enforcement and advocacy highly challenging. Further, decades of government controls have resulted in a weak competition culture in the economy, and several areas of the economy are still subject to a variety of controls. In these sectors, a truly competitive market is still to evolve. The task is further complicated due to the challenges posed by the increasingly transnational nature of business activities and India's integration into the global economy."[2]

The same description holds true of South Africa. High market concentration is a characteristic, not only of scale-dependent heavy industry, but also of many consumer products. For example, there is virtual monopoly in beer—with South African Breweries holding more than a 90 percent share in the clear beer market. Some of this high concentration is the legacy of a history of State concessions during the apartheid period; some is attributable to scale factors; and further the effect of sanctions during the 1980's resulted in a small group of conglomerates owning an increasing share of publicly quoted companies.

At the time of democracy in 1994, five investment conglomerates—all which emerged from the mining houses of the nineteenth century—accounted for 84 percent of the capitalization of the Johannesburg Stock Exchange, and Anglo American alone accounted for 43 percent.[3] At the same time as the Johannesburg Stock Exchange is regarded as the world's tenth largest, the Gini coefficient which measures income disparity remains at approximately 0.60 and therefore ranks as amongst the worst, if not the worst, in the world.

It is small wonder that in 1992, when the African National Congress ("ANC") published its Policy Guidelines for a Democratic South Africa,[4] the document contained a program of remedial action to deal

---

1 See William E. Kovacic, *Competition Law in the BRICS Countries: More than an Acronym* in Competition Law in the BRICS Countries 322 (Adrian Emch, Jose Regazzini & Vassily Rudomino eds., 2012).

2 See Dr. Seema Gaur, *Regulators Introduction, Recent Activities and Policy Priorities in India* in Competition Law in the BRICS Countries 109 (Adrian Emch, Jose Regazzini & Vassily Rudomino eds., 2012).

3 See Organisation for Economic Co-Operation and Development ("OECD"), *Competition and Policy in South Africa: An OECD Peer Review* 10 (2003), *available at* http://www.oecd.org/daf/competition/prosecutionandlawenforcement/2958714.pdf.

4 See *Ready to Govern: ANC Policy Guidelines for a Democratic South Africa* (1992), *available at* http://www.anc.org.za/show.php?id=227.

with the concentration of economy power on the grounds that this pattern may be highly detrimental to balanced economic development.

In November 1997, the Department of Trade and Industry ("DTI") responded to this policy when it published a document entitled Proposed Guidelines for Competition Policy ("Proposed Guidelines").[5] In it the DTI stated: "This set of policy guidelines fuses these different mandates, by assuring the public that on one hand competitiveness and efficiency are pursued, and on the other that this process will ensure access to many more people previously denied an equal opportunity to participate in the economy."[6]

Of particular significance was the DTI's approach to the institutional framework, which is captured in the following paragraph: "The government's view is that monopolies law should be effected by a competent, professional agency with powers to investigate and to respond rapidly and robustly to anticompetitive conduct. The decisions of the tribunal envisaged will be subject to judicial review, but it is Government's intention to take enforcement of competition law out of the hands of the criminal courts and to avoid the prospect of lengthy, complex and costly litigation. The possibility of politically-inspired intervention will also be removed by eliminating the exercise of ministerial discretion in the enforcement of competition law and by a more precise definition of both the mandate of the policy structure and its relationship to the Minister and government policy. As already elaborated, our political choices will be exercised in the mandate extended to our industrial strategists and, from there, to our competition authorities."[7] The drafters, mandated by government to draft an Act, followed this approach and the ensuing Competition Act of 1998[8] ("Competition Act") established three institutions, which were to be directly involved in the application of the law: the Competition Commission ("Commission"), the Competition Tribunal ("Tribunal") and the Competition Appeal Court ("Appeal Court"). These institutions were confronted with ambitious goals. The purpose clause in the Competition Act includes economic efficiency, but extends further in that the primary purpose "to promote and maintain competition"[9] is augmented by six particular sets of goals:

(i) to promote the efficiency, adaptability and development of the economy;

(ii) to provide consumers with competitive prices and product choices;

(iii) to promote employment and advance the social and economic welfare of South Africans;

(iv) to expand opportunities for South Africans participation in world markets and recognize the role of foreign competition in the Republic;

(v) to ensure that small and medium-sized enterprises have an equitable opportunity to participate in the economy, and

(vi) to promote a greater spread of ownership, in particular to increase the ownership stakes of historically disadvantage persons.

The motivation for these objectives is set out earlier in the Preamble to the Competition Act which characterizes the mischief that the law seeks to address as past practices flowing from apartheid which

5 See Department of Trade and Industry, Pretoria, *Proposed Guidelines for Competition Policy: A Framework for Competition, Competitiveness and Development* (1997), hereinafter "Proposed Guidelines", *available at* http://www.polity.org.za/article/proposed-guidelines-for-competition-policy-2007-03-15.

6 Id., para. 4.

7 Id., para. 8.3.1.

8 See Competition Act 89 of 1998, hereinafter "Competition Act".

9 Id. at para. 2.

led to: an excessive concentration of ownership and control, inadequate constraints upon anticompetitive trade practices, and unjust prohibitions upon full and free participation of the economy. As a result, the Preamble states that the economy "must be open to greater ownership by a greater number of South Africans,"[10] and that an efficient, competitive economic environment should be created which balances the interests of workers, owners and consumers and focuses on development which will benefit all South Africans. If most legislation of a social and economic nature represents an autobiography of a nation, these particular objectives reach deep into South Africa's history and the skewed and racist nature of development which preceded constitutional democracy, the cumulative consequences of which constituted the greatest challenge a democratic South Africa was required to solve.

Within this ambitious legislative context, this paper will focus on specific key questions relating to the law which was spawned by the Competition Act and the procedures which were adopted by the relevant competition authorities, in particular the Court of First Instance, the Tribunal.

II. The Law

1. Presumptions

As Eleanor Fox and Michal Gal have noted in an instructive article,[11] competition laws like many other legal systems are based on presumptions which are designed to make the analysis more efficient and easier to implement by the relevant authority. Accordingly, presumptions which are included in legislation should affect, inter alia: the complexity of the regime, the nature of the burdens of proof, the level of transparency, and the number of prohibitions contained in the relevant law.[12]

To some degree, the presumptions contained in the Competition Act have proved to be successful in meeting these objectives. Section 7[13] contains a set of presumptions dealing with a dominant firm, a concept which is the gateway to the prohibition against abuse of dominance, as set out in Section 8.[14] A firm is irrebuttably dominant in a market if it has at least 45 percent of that market; it is rebuttably dominant if it has at least 35 percent, but not less than 45 percent, in which case it can rebut the presumption by showing that it does not have market power or, if it has less than 35 percent of the market, the competition authority is required to show that it does have market power.[15]

This provision has worked with considerable success in that, in a significant clutch of cases, it has removed the need for the Commission, possessed of resources and few organizational economists, to prove complex questions of dominance. In key cases dealing with abuse of dominance, the defendant has generally held more than 45 percent of the relevant market share and, accordingly, this fact has obviated the need for

---

10 Id. at Preamble.

11 See Eleanor M. Fox & Michal S. Gal, *Drafting Competition Law for Developing Jurisdictions: Learning from Experience* N.Y. University Law and Economics Working Papers. No. 374, 2014.

12 Id. at18.

13 Competition Act, *supra* note 8, at para.7.

14 Id. at para. 8.

15 Market power is defined to mean the power of a firm to control prices, to exclude competition or to behave to an appreciable extent independently of its competitors, customers or suppliers.

the Commission to make a showing or for the Tribunal or, on appeal, the Appeal Court to deal with complex economic questions which would otherwise be posed in the inquiry concerning market power.

Section 4[16] of the Competition Act deals with horizontal practices which are prohibited. Section 4(1)(b) provides that an agreement between or concerted practice by, firms, or a decision by an association of firms, is prohibited if it is between parties on a horizontal relationship and if it involves any of the following restrictive horizontal practices:

(i) directly or indirectly of fixing a purchase or selling price or any other trading condition;

(ii) dividing the markets by allocating customers, suppliers, territories, or specific types of goods or services; or

(iii) collusive tendering.

On the face of it, the adoption of a *per se* prohibition covering cartel activity which was rampant in South Africa prior to the introduction of the Competition Act, and, all too sadly, continues notwithstanding considerable success on the part of the Commission, has proved to be a very wise piece of drafting. However, when the America Natural Soda Ash Corporation, a non-stock, non-profit Delaware corporation formed by five United States Soda Ash producers in the early 1980's to export their products abroad, was the subject of South African litigation, problems arose. Both the Tribunal and the Appeal Court held that once the conduct complained of was found to fall within the scope of the section, this was the end of the enquiry. Not necessarily so said the Supreme Court of Appeal, a non-specialist court which, owing to a provision in the South African Constitution, held the last word until recently in relation to competition matters.

It asked the question "when has prohibited price-fixing occurred?"[17] Referring to United States jurisprudence, the court held that the enquiry was to be approached "by 'characterizing' the conduct complained of to determine whether it constitutes that form of conduct that the courts have through case precedent labeled 'price fixing' but have not comprehensibly defined." The Supreme Court of Appeal held that where the prohibition is contained in the Competition Act, rather than developed by judicial precedent, the prohibited form of conduct must be established by construing the relevant section, Section 4(1)(b). Once the ambit of the section has been established, the enquiry moves to determine whether the conduct in issue falls within the terms of this prohibition.[18] The Supreme Court of Appeal held that this was a factual question that must be answered by recourse to relevant evidence. Accordingly, the Supreme Court of Appeal held that the Tribunal and the Appeal Court were incorrect in their understanding of the statutory per se prohibition. Evidence was required to be led before the Tribunal to establish whether the character of the conduct complained of coincided with the nature of the prohibited conduct.

The characterization approach adopted by the Supreme Court of Appeal has given rise to a measure of uncertainty as to how much and when evidence is required to be led by the Commission. Similarly, the nature of the section has given rise to problems with regards to the treatment of franchising agreements and hence has led to a level of uncertainty which was not necessarily predicted by the drafters when the Act was formulated.

Section 5(2)[19] provides that the practice of minimum resale price maintenance is prohibited. Again, questions have been raised whether resale price maintenance should not have been subjected to a rule of

---

16 Competition Act, *supra* note 8, at para. 4.

17 See *American Natural Ash Soda Corporation v. Competition Commission* 2005 (6) SA 158 (SCA) at para. 43.

18 Id., paras. 44-46.

19 Competition Act, *supra* note 8, at para.5.

reason approach, albeit that the idea was that it was better for an under resourced Commission to be able to prove the existence of a practice of resale price maintenance, without having to engage with economic evidence to prove that the practice should be prohibited. The objective was to ease the burden on both the Tribunal and the Appeal Court, which commenced with members who were not particularly experienced with competition matters and, hence, might have struggled to engage adequately with an intricate balancing exercise that would otherwise have been required if a per se prohibition had not been included in the Act.

2. Ambitious Substantive Provisions

Given the ambitious objectives which are set out in the purpose clause read together with the Preamble, the Competition Act contains provisions which place a significant burden on an under resourced Commission and thus upon the Tribunal and the Appeal Court. Take for example the following: in terms of Section 8(a), it is prohibited for a dominant firm to charge an excessive price to the detriment of consumers. This provision has given rise to two complicated cases. A completed case concerned ArcelorMittal[20] and another involves Sasol.[21] It is no coincidence that in both cases that these were massive corporations which were super dominant in their respective markets. In both cases, the defendants had commenced as state owned institutions. Understandably, Section 8(a) was included because of a concern over the practices of resource extractive industries and, in particular, the practice of import parity pricing which resulted in South Africa's mineral resources being exported in an unprocessed form and then sold back into South Africa to small and medium sized producers, at a price which did not reflect the benefits of South Africa's locational advantage or its bounty of resources.[22] The Competition Act drew directly from the European Union judgment in United Brands Company;[23] hence the challenges posed by this section are immense. The competition authorities are required to negotiate beyond the idea that the mere possession of market power is contrary to competition law and that pricing power derives from market power. As David Lewis has noted, "one important source of market power is innovation and other, pro-competitive conduct. The rents derived from the possession of market power will, in most circumstances, sooner or later attract new entrants, the more so if the dominant incumbent takes 'excessive' advantage of its privileged position."[24]

Secondly, the section required that the competition authority avoid taking on the role of a price regulator, a difficulty which was appreciated by the Competition Tribunal in the Mittal case. Finally, Section 8(a) requires the authority to devise a test of excessive pricing which is capable of general application as opposed to simply dealing with the particular dispute.

The Mittal case revealed the challenge posed by the ambition of this section. It is a difficult provision to implement sensibly for any competition authority, let alone one with the limited resources which confront developing countries such as South Africa. In Mittal, plaintiff relied on European jurisprudence and argued that the case could be resolved by a comparison between two price points followed by the evalu-

---

20 See Mittal Steel South Africa Limited, Macsteel International BV, Macsteel Holdings (Pty) Limited v. Harmony Gold Mining Company Limited, Durban Roodepoort Deep Limited (70/CAC/Apr07), *available* at http://www.comptrib.co.za/cases/appeal/retrieve_case/1049.

21 See *Sasol Oil Proprietary Limited v. Nationwide Poles CC* (49/CAC/Apr05), *available at* http://www.comptrib.co.za/cases/appeal/retrieve_case/542.

22 See, for an excellent discussion of the Mittal case, David Lewis, *Thieves at the Dinner Table: Enforcing the Competition Act: A Personal Account*, 173 (2012), *available at* http://www.idrc.ca/EN/Resources/Publications/openebooks/374-7/index.html.

23 See Case 27/76, *United Brands Company and United Brands Continental BV v. Comm'n*, E.C.R. 207 (1978).

24 Lewis, *supra* note 22, at 177.

ation on whether the difference between the two price points, being the competitive price and the actual price, represented an excessive price. Defendant contended that the authorities were required to analyze profitability and it attempted to demonstrate, on its version that it was not earning excessive profits and therefore it could not be charged with the practice of excessive prices. In turn, plaintiff contended that while a profitability analysis might well assist in informing the validity of a defense of charging a higher price in one market than in another, it failed to address the need to cross subsidize losses which it may incur in order to gain economic scale; that is, it failed to provide a conclusive finding.

The Tribunal ignored most of the evidence presented to it and found that, as Mittal was super-dominant, it was an uncontested firm in an incontestable market. The market structure and the presence of insurmountable barriers to entry accorded it an unusual degree of market power which allowed Mittal to engage in output reducing conduct by way of an exclusive distribution and market agreement, and the further imposition of a price which was the very highest it could sustain. As the Tribunal stated: "The circumstances giving rise to Mittal SA's pricing power in respect of some its domestic consumers depends on the existence of a range of factual issues that we do not encounter in the market place every day, even in those markets habituated by a long extant dominant firms [...]. The statutory definition [of excessive price] as opposed to the ordinary word 'excess' [...] requires one to find a relationship between a price and an economic value that admits of no reasonable explanation, that is, that of an explanation that does not rely upon the exercise of the degree of market power that arises from super-dominance."[25]

The Appeal Court held that a decision which ignored all of the evidence, both the plaintiff and defendant, which had run into thousands of pages of records, and found that super dominance alone was sufficient to ground the law of excessive pricing was not a finding that was in accordance with the Act and the specific nature of Section 8(a), the wording of which could not be disregarded without any attempt at interpretative engagement by the Tribunal. However, it recognized the difficulties outlined by the Tribunal and thus created a rebuttable presumption that, if a firm is super dominant, as was the case in Mittal, there was an onus placed upon the firm to justify its pricing structure. In turn, this required an engagement with the evidence that Mittal had put forward.[26] Accordingly, the matter was remitted back to the Tribunal for an evaluation of the evidence which never took place because the case was settled.

This long running saga of litigation highlights a major difficulty confronting a competition law for a developing country: on the one hand, there is a clear legitimate and justifiable concern that powerful corporations, whose powers were derived by way of previous government intervention, should not adopt pricing policies which subvert the economic ambitions of small and medium sized business in the country; however, if the requirements to prove an excessive pricing case prove to be so complex and the evidence needed to make out a case based upon the statutory wording so nuanced, questions arise as to whether this constitutes the best use of the limited resources of the competition authority in a developing country faced, as in the case of South Africa, with numerous pressing and immediate competition problems, in particular cartels.

A further legal complexity sourced in the Competition Act's ambition concerns mergers. The Competition Act provides that, notwithstanding the traditional analysis as to whether the merger is likely to substantially prevent or lessen competition, public interest grounds are important in determining the outcome of the merger. In particular, Section 12A(3) provides: "When determining whether a merger can or cannot be

---

25 See *Harmony Gold Mining Limited, Durban Roodepoort Deep Limited vs Mittal Steel South Africa Limited, Macsteel International Holdings BV* 153-154 (13/CR/Feb04), *available at* http://www.comptrib.co.za/assets/Uploads/13CRFeb04reasons.pdf.

26 *Mittal Steel South Africa Limited, Macsteel International BV, Macsteel Holdings (Pty) Limited v. Harmony Gold Mining Company Limited, Durban Roodepoort Deep Limited* (70/CAC/Apr07), *available at* http://www.comptrib.co.za/cases/appeal/retrieve_case/1049.

justified on public interest grounds, the Competition Commission or the Competition Tribunal must consider the effect that the merger will have on:

(i) a particular industrial sector or region;

(ii) employment;

(iii) the ability of small businesses, or firms controlled or owned by historically disadvantaged persons, to become competitive; and

(iv) the ability of national industries to compete in international markets."[27]

An examination of the wording of the section illustrates an immediate difficulty: is it possible that competition orthodoxy, notwithstanding a competition authority, can seamlessly incorporate these public interest issues into a core competition evaluation without doing violence to the former set of considerations? This was the challenge which confronted the competition authorities in the case of Walmart.

The problem with which the Walmart merger confronted South African competition authorities was whether a merger which does not substantially prevent or lessen competition, and indeed may cause a significant reduction in prices in the relevant market, should have conditions attached to it because the merger may impact negatively on public interest considerations as specified in the Competition Act.[28] The specific question arises as to Walmart's global purchasing powers which would divert some of the targeted company's (Massmart) procurement away from local suppliers to imports, thereby displacing local industries in the supply chain. In turn, this raises the question of the relationship between specified public interest criteria and the implications of global value chains for developing countries such as South Africa. The complex relationship between industrial policy, globalization and competition concerns are highlighted in this case. The difficulty which confronted the Competition Tribunal and the Appeal Court concerned the paucity of expert evidence which could guide adjudication, and arrive at a proper evaluation of the relationship and the weight to be given to traditional competition grounds and public interest factors, as contained in Section 12A. The union parties to this case argued for a more nuanced consumer welfare standard which they suggested was sourced in the very text of the Competition Act. While the Walmart case as presented on appeal, would not in the Court's view have been decided differently, this conceptual challenge will doubtless arise again.

---

27 Competition Act, *supra* note 8, at para. 12A(3).

28 See *Minister of Economic Development v. Competition Tribunal v. Walmart Stores Inc.*, (110/CAC/Jul11, 111/CAC/Jun 11), *available at* http://www.comptrib.co.za/assets/Uploads/Wal-Mart-and-Massmart-decision/110111CACJun11-Walmart-judgment.pdf; *Wal-Mart Stores Inc. and Massmart Holdings Limited* (73/LM/Nov10), *available at* http://www.comptrib.co.za/cases/large-merger/retrieve_case/1269.

III. Procedure

In this section, I wish to concentrate on two issues: (1) the approach adopted by the Tribunal to its hearings, and (2) the related question of the accountability of the Tribunal to the Appeal Court.

The Competition Act provides that the Chairperson and other members of the Competition Tribunal, viewed collectively, must represent a broad connection to the population of the Republic and comprise sufficient persons of legal training and experience. It further provides that every member of the Tribunal must have a qualification in economics, law, commerce, industry or public affairs.[29]

Given that the Tribunal was not required to be staffed by judges or by experienced litigators, it is not entirely surprising that the first chair David Lewis had only a background in economics and his deputy, Norman Manoim, an attorney, was possessed of limited commercial experience. However, both had participated in the drafting of the Competition Act and were the two key appointments when the Tribunal assumed office. It was thus surprising that, given this paucity of litigation experience, the Tribunal ran its proceedings in an adversarial fashion. This was not a requirement mandated by the Competition Act and, upon reflection, it may have been better, given the personnel of the Tribunal, to have adopted a more inquisitorial model for hearings. The chosen model requires the presiding officer to be experienced in the wiles of advocates who come before it, vastly experienced litigators, who then effectively run the process in a manner which is not conducive to an expeditious outcome.

In the case of mergers, hearings have generated vast records, often without a clear focus upon the major issues which require resolution and, with evidence not been sufficiently precisely presented, which would allow for a justifiable and coherent process of reasoning, at the very least by an appeal court faced with a record that, all too often, resembles a jurisprudential stream of consciousness. Merger hearings should be conducted in an inquisitorial fashion with the Tribunal determining upfront the key questions for determination and then ensuring that the hearing focuses upon the resolution of these issues.

In the case of restrictive practices and abuse of dominance cases, there are pleadings by way of the initial complaint which is lodged and affidavits which accompany the initiation of a case. Again, one would be excused for thinking that there was an absence of any pleading when the record is examined on appeal. Upon reflection, two amendments require consideration. In the first place, it may be advisable to appoint, as a presiding officer of the Tribunal, a lawyer vastly experienced in litigation; ideally a senior counsel prepared and able to take on the task to insure that the hearings are more coherently conducted. Secondly, merger hearings should be run on an inquisitorial basis to ensure both coherence and expedition of resolution.

The Act provides that the Appeal Court may consider an appeal arising from the Competition Tribunal in respect of any of its final decisions, as well as any of its interlocutory decisions that may, in terms of the Competition Act, be taken on appeal.[30] The question arises as to whether an appellate court should only have a review power, along the lines of the European Court of Justice. This suggestion is fortified by criticism which has been lodged against the Appeal Court, namely that, notwithstanding that the judges are presumed to be appointed on the basis of their commercial economic and financial background in addition to their legal qualifications, the court has failed to appreciate the nuances of competition jurisprudence. Much of this criticism has come from the Tribunal itself and its acolytes which is understandable. Judicial officers do not like to be overturned.

---

29 Competition Act, *supra* note 8, at para. 28.

30 Competition Act, *supra* note 8, at para. 37

This criticism may be generated irrespective of whether a review or appellate power is granted to an appeal court. Very often, the division between a review and an appeal power is extremely porous in that appellate bodies, confronted with cases which offend their conception of justice, stretch a review power to approximate that of an appeal. In my view, the better approach is for a court to adopt a deferential attitude to the manner in which the Tribunal evaluates evidence, in particular economic evidence, and to adopt a policy of stricter scrutiny in respect of legal questions. In turn, this will demand a more rigorous application to evidence by the Tribunal than has been the case to date. It follows that, a re-examination of the composition and hence expertise of the Tribunal is thus worthy of further consideration.

IV. Conclusion

The criticism of the Tribunal, Appeal Court and the Competition Act, notwithstanding the record of South African competition jurisprudence over the past fifteen years, reveals a significant serious attempt to engage with the considerable challenges which were posed by the Competition Act in its attempt to target the particular problems of the South African economy inherited as a result of the legacy of apartheid. To date, the body of law and enforcement has achieved demonstrable competitive outcomes for the economy and has improved the competition environment for economic activity. In summary, in the main, the authorities have met to the considerable challenges posed.

The suggestions, both substantive and procedural, in the paper are ones which should be born in mind by any developing economy that is considering a competition regime or an amendment to an existing regime. But, whatever the advice given to a developing jurisdiction, complexity cannot be excluded, for this is inherent in the nature of the economic development required by such societies. Fox and Gal capture eloquently the point which I seek to make: "Whereas developed economies with already functioning markets can afford to focus solely on efficiency, disregarding its distributive effects based on the assumptions that when markets are free and open competition itself will generally create positive distributive effects, this is not true of developing jurisdictions. There, the focus must be on the efficient inclusive development of their markets, which gives weight to distributive concerns as part of the long-term development of an economy. This is because developing jurisdictions cannot afford to disregard distributive concerns, for economics, political and social reasons. Accordingly, the mix of competition and cooperation might sometimes be different than in developed economics."[31]

31 Fox & Gal, *supra* note 11, at 44.

International Antitrust Cooperation: Expanding the Circle

Molly Askin[1]

maskin@ftc.gov

Counsel, Office of International Affairs, US Federal Trade Commission

Randolph W. Tritell[2]

rtritell@ftc.gov

Director, Office of International Affairs, US Federal Trade Commission

Abstract

International antitrust cooperation among competition agencies began as a way to minimize tensions created by the extraterritorial application of antitrust laws. It was facilitated by agreements between governments and competition agencies, as well as through multilateral organizations. Efforts to address competition issues through the World Trade Organization foundered, and many more countries adopted competition laws in the 1990s and 2000s. Cooperation expanded to promote consistent analyses and outcomes and to provide opportunities for competition agencies to work with one another on enforcement, policy, and training. Today, competition agencies in emerging and developing countries cooperate with one another and with more experienced agencies bilaterally and through multilateral organizations, including the ICN, OECD, UNCTAD, and regional organizations. The Federal Trade Commission and the Department of Justice's Antitrust Division are engaged in enforcement cooperation and policy cooperation with a large and growing number of competition agencies. Policy cooperation often includes providing

1 The views expressed are those of the author alone.

2 The views expressed are those of the author alone.

comments on draft laws and regulations, sharing experiences through technical assistance programs, and engaging in discussions regarding substantive and procedural aspects of competition law enforcement.

Cooperation among competition agencies will continue and will expand to address new challenges.

One of the most significant developments accompanying the widespread adoption of competition laws worldwide has been the growth in cooperation among antitrust enforcement agencies. Although cooperation instruments evolved out of a need to minimize frictions caused by the "extraterritorial" application of competition law, particularly by the United States, in recent years, cooperation has expanded through bilateral agreements, multilateral organizations, and a variety of informal arrangements to encompass many young competition agencies as well as those in developed countries. Today, cooperation is an important vehicle for agencies to share experience, promote sound policies, and coordinate their activities, and it continues to support compatible analysis and outcomes in cross-border investigations. This article explores the evolution and benefits of international antitrust cooperation, the US Federal Trade Commission's cooperation with an expanding circle of agencies, and opportunities and challenges in further developing cooperation.

I. The Rocky Road to International Antitrust Cooperation

Cooperation among antitrust enforcement agencies evolved after years of conflict over the cross-border application of antitrust law. Early cases in the United States interpreted the Sherman Act as not reaching conduct abroad. In *American Banana Co. v. United Fruit Co.*,[3] the Supreme Court held that "[a] conspiracy in this country to do acts in another jurisdiction does not draw to itself those acts and make them unlawful, if they are permitted by the local law." However, in the 1940s, the Supreme Court, in *US v. Aluminum Co. of America*, adopted an effects-based approach, applying the Sherman Act to conduct taking place outside the United States if it had a direct and intended effect in the United States. The Court held that "any state may impose liabilities, even upon persons not within its allegiance, for conduct outside its borders that has consequences within its borders which the state reprehends."[4]

As antitrust laws spread, other jurisdictions adopted the effects doctrine. For example, in the Wood Pulp cartel case, the European Commission ("EC") challenged the conduct of US, Canadian, Finnish, and Swedish wood pulp producers, which set prices for wood pulp sold to consumers in the European Union.[5] The US association's conduct was exempt from US antitrust laws under the Webb-Pomerene Act for its activities as an export association. On appeal before the European Court of Justice ("ECJ"), US and Canadian firms argued that condemning their conduct violated principles of international comity. The ECJ held, however, that anticompetitive conduct by parties located outside the European Union ("EU") that reached an agreement outside the EU could be liable under the Treaty Establishing the European Economic Community based on the conduct's anticompetitive effect in the Common Market.[6]

This "extraterritorial" application of antitrust law generated international tensions, particularly when the conduct challenged as illegal was lawful or even encouraged by the other country's government. These issues came to a head in the late 1970s when a US court entered default judgment against non-US firms that took part in a cartel involving uranium. A US firm alleged that companies based in Canada, South Africa, Australia, and France violated the Sherman Act by setting minimum prices and allocating sales.[7] Several foreign firms challenged jurisdiction through US-based subsidiaries and others did not answer the complaint. The US district court entered default judgments against nine companies.[8] The governments of Australia, Canada, South Africa, and the United Kingdom filed amicus curiae briefs arguing that the actions of the non-US firms were outside the court's jurisdiction under the Sherman Act.[9]

---

3 213 U.S. 347, 359 (1909).

4 *US v. Aluminum Co. of America (Alcoa)*, 148 F.2d 416 (2d Cir. 1945). *Accord, Continental Ore Co. v. Union Carbide*, 370 U.S. 690, 705 (1962); *US v. Sisal Sales Corp.*, 274 U.S. 268, 275-276 (1927).

5 Commission Decision No. 85/202/EEC of 19 December 1984, relating to a proceeding under Article 85 of the EEC Treaty (IV/29.725Wood Pulp). Article 85 of the EEC Treaty is now Article 101 of the TFEU. At the time of the case, the European Union was called the European Economic Community.

6 Joined Cases 89, 104, 114, 116, 117 and 125 to 129/85, A. Ahlstrom Osakeyhtio and others v. Commission ("Wood Pulp"), Sept 27, 1988, [1988] ECR 5193 (ECJ). See also John J. Parisi, *Cooperation Among Competition Authorities in Merger Regulation*, Cornell International Law Journal, Vol. 43, 2010, at 58, *available at* http://www.lawschool.cornell.edu/research/ILJ/upload/Parisi.pdf.

7 *In re Uranium Antitrust Litigation*, 617 F.2d 1248 (7th Cir. 1980).

8 Id.

9 Id.

While the uranium case was pending, several jurisdictions took steps to protect their citizens and businesses from the so-called extraterritorial application of US antitrust law by enacting "blocking statutes." Such statutes impose penalties for complying with discovery ordered by foreign courts but allow for certain modes of discovery under the Hague Convention on Taking Evidence Abroad in Civil or Commercial Matters. The United Kingdom's blocking statute was described as "primarily a reaction to the accumulation of attempts by the United States since the 1950s to impose its own economic and other domestic policies [...] outside its territorial jurisdiction, without regard for the trading interests of other countries."[10] Other countries including Australia, Belgium, Canada, France, South Africa, and Switzerland also adopted blocking statutes. The United Kingdom also enacted a "clawback" statute to recoup the trebled portion of damages awarded in US private antitrust litigation,[11] stating that their goal was to "reassert and reinforce the defenses of the United Kingdom against attempts by other countries to enforce their economic and commercial policies unilaterally on us" in response to "the extra-territorial application of domestic law."[12]

While the case law on extraterritorial application of US antitrust law evolved through private litigation, political tensions that developed during the Laker Airlines civil litigation led President Reagan to suspend a Department of Justice criminal antitrust investigation. In the civil case, Laker argued that predatory price-fixing among US, Belgian, British, Dutch, and German airlines forced Laker out of business. After the civil suit was filed, British Airways sought and won an injunction in a UK court that established that certain foreign firms were not liable for damage suffered by Laker and prevented Laker from pursuing antitrust claims in the US.[13] A blocking order was also issued under the UK blocking statute. In response, the US judge issued temporary restraining orders preventing other non-US defendants from seeking injunctions that interfered with jurisdiction of the US courts.[14]

Shortly thereafter, the World Trade Organization ("WTO") began discussing competition issues in the Uruguay Round of negotiations, and discussions continued into the 2000s. The WTO established a Working Group on the Interaction between Trade and Competition Policy at the 1996 WTO Ministerial Conference in Singapore. The working group issued reports analyzing the relationship between trade and competition law and between WTO members' competition laws and enforcement mechanisms. The group also identified options for creating a multilateral framework for competition policy that could address the challenges presented by extraterritorial application of antitrust laws.[15]

The European Union, supported by many members, sought to introduce competition rules, including cooperation provisions, into the WTO during the Doha Round, which began in 2001. The United States questioned the benefit of WTO competition rules, including mandatory cooperation provisions, particularly if they would be subject to dispute settlement. Many developing countries, some of which did not have a competition law or were concerned about taking on new obligations, opposed WTO competition disciplines. In 2004, the WTO General Council removed competition law from the agenda for the Doha Round of meetings, stating that competition policy "will not form part of the Work Program set out in that

---

10 Press Release, *U.K. Dep't of Trade and Indus., Protection of Interests Bill* (Oct. 31, 1979).

11 Protection of Trading of Interest Act at Sec. 6 (1980).

12 Mr. John Nott, Secretary of State for Trade, 973 Parl. Deb., H.C. (5th ser.), Vol. 1533, 4:43pm (1979), *available at* http://hansard.millbank-systems.com/commons/1979/nov/15/protection-of-trading-interests-bill.

13 British Airways, (1984) 1 Q.B. at 169-203 (judgment by Sir John Donaldson M.R.). The House of Lords ultimately overturned the injunction, *British Airways Board v. Laker Airways Ltd.*, (1984) 3 W.L.R. 413.

14 See *Laker Airways Ltd. v. Sabena, Belgian World Airlines; KLM Royal Dutch Airlines*, 731 F. 2d 909 (D.D.C. 1984); *Laker Airways Ltd. v. Pan American World Airways*, 559 F. Supp. 1124 (D.D.C. 1983).

15 WTO, *Documents of the Working Group on the Interaction between Trade and Competition Policy*, *available at* http://www.wto.org/english/tratop_e/comp_e/wgtcp_docs_e.htm.

Declaration and therefore no work towards negotiations on any of these issues will take place."[16] The WTO competition working group has since disbanded.

Cooperation provisions are an increasingly common feature of bilateral and plurilateral trade agreements. However, as discussed below, most practical cooperation mechanisms have evolved through bilateral contacts and soft law initiatives in multilateral competition bodies.

II. The Development of International Antitrust Cooperation

Even as efforts to establish multilateral competition rules foundered in the 1990s and 2000s, many nations adopted competition laws and established competition agencies. Increased levels of enforcement by a multiplicity of competition agencies generated a need for mechanisms to minimize conflicts and for agencies to work together on enforcement, policy, and training. To meet this need, cooperation evolved to include work with counterpart competition agencies on individual cases ("enforcement cooperation") and policy cooperation. Policy cooperation occurs through bilateral and multilateral relationships and can include competition agencies providing input on proposed laws, regulations, and agency guidance, sharing information and experience, and developing competition policy norms through multilateral organizations. Competition agencies, including the Federal Trade Commission ("FTC"), have found that cooperation helps avoid conflicts in enforcement outcomes, increases predictability, and enables more efficient use of limited agency resources.

1. Early Examples of Enforcement Cooperation

The adoption and increased enforcement of competition laws by trading partners led to the first instances of enforcement cooperation by the Federal Trade Commission and Department of Justice's Antitrust Division (together, "US Agencies"). Cooperation in merger reviews was more common than in other types of investigations because agencies often had similar review timelines and had a shared interest in compatible analysis and remedies. Merging parties supported and encouraged cooperation to facilitate efficient reviews and non-conflicting outcomes, and sometimes agreed to waive the confidentiality of information they submitted to reviewing agencies, which allowed the cooperating agencies to cooperate more closely.

An early example of US-EU merger cooperation was the 1994 Shell/Montedison transaction. The discussions between FTC and the EC's Directorate-General for Competition ("DG COMP") staff included how the differences in the applicable US and EU member states' contract and intellectual property laws affected the analysis of competitive effects and how remedies could be structured to ensure they were compatible.[17] During that year, the FTC and DG COMP also cooperated in the investigations of several mergers of pharmaceutical firms while the Department of Justice's Antitrust Division ("DOJ") cooperated with DG

16 WTO, *Doha Work Programme—Decision Adopted by the General Council on 1 August 2004*, WT/L/579 (Aug. 2, 2004) at 3, *available at* http://www.wto.org/english/tratop_e/dda_e/ddadraft_31jul04_e.pdf.

17 Robert Pitofsky, Chairman, US Fed. Trade Comm'n, Remarks Before the Fordham Corporate Law Institute 22nd Annual Conference on International Antitrust Law and Policy: International Antitrust–An FTC Perspective, (Oct. 26, 1995), *available at* http://www.ftc.gov/public-statements/1995/10/international-antritrust-ftc-perspective.

COMP in merger investigations including WorldCom/MCI and MCI WorldCom/Sprint.[18] During the 1990s, parties became more comfortable granting confidentiality waivers ("waivers") to facilitate enforcement cooperation. As cooperation and providing waivers became more common, FTC and DG COMP staff engaged in enforcement cooperation, comparing legal and economic theories, holding joint meetings with merging parties, and collaborating on remedies.

The DOJ also cooperated on cross-border cartel investigations, often invoking bilateral Mutual Legal Assistance Agreements ("MLATs") to facilitate information sharing.[19] For example, in the late 1990s and early 2000s, antitrust agencies in Australia, Brazil, Canada, the EU, Japan, Mexico, New Zealand, Switzerland, and the US cooperated in the investigation of a global cartel involving certain vitamins.[20]

As cross-border mergers also involved emerging and developing countries that had enacted competition laws, additional opportunities for enforcement cooperation emerged. For example, in 1998, antitrust enforcement agencies in Australia, Zambia, and Zimbabwe consulted regarding their review of the Coca-Cola/Schweppes merger.[21] The following year, Zambian and Zimbabwean agencies discussed aspects of the merger between Rothams of Pall Mall and British American Tobacco.[22]

a. Cooperation through Multilateral Organizations

As enforcement cooperation became more common throughout the 1990s, the US Agencies continued to work with other competition agencies through multilateral organizations to develop competition policy and promote convergence. The concept of convergence, which involves more closely aligning substantive policies, is different from cooperation, but the two activities are closely linked. Taken together, cooperation and convergence increase the likelihood of consistent outcomes.

The US Agencies have sought to promote cooperation and convergence through various multilateral competition organizations such as the Organization for Economic Cooperation and Development ("OECD"), International Competition Network ("ICN"), the United Nations Conference on Trade and Development ("UNCTAD"), and regional competition bodies. Beginning in the 1960s, the OECD,[23] through its Competition Committee,[24] and UNCTAD[25] facilitated dialogue and collaboration among agencies from developed and developing countries on issues related to competition law, policy, and enforcement cooperation.

---

18 See Bruno Zanettin, Cooperation Between Antitrust Agencies at the International Level, 2002, at 105, citing Commission Report to the Council and the European Parliament on the Application of the EC-US Agreement, 1 January 2000 to 31 December 2000, at 6.

19 See Charles S. Stark, Chief, Foreign Commerce Section, Antitrust Div., US Dep't of Justice, Improving Bilateral Antitrust Cooperation, Remarks at the Conference on Competition Policy in the Global Trading System: Perspectives from Japan, the United States, and the European Union 4 (June 23, 2000), *available at* http://www.justice.gov/atr/public/speeches/5075.pdf.

20 See John M. Connor, *The Great Global Vitamins Conspiracies: 1985-1999*, at 108, *available at* http://ssrn.com/abstract=885968.

21 UNCTAD at p. 18.

22 Id.

23 The OECD consists of thirty-four economically developed countries: Australia, Austria, Belgium, Canada, Chile, Czech Republic, Denmark, Estonia, Finland, France, Germany, Greece, Hungary, Iceland, Ireland, Israel, Italy, Japan, Korea, Luxembourg, Mexico, Netherlands, New Zealand, Norway, Poland, Portugal, Slovak Republic, Slovenia, Spain, Sweden, Switzerland, Turkey, United Kingdom, and the United States. Numerous non-members participate: Brazil, Bulgaria, Chinese Taipei, Colombia, Egypt, India, Indonesia, Latvia, Lithuania, Malta, Peru, Romania, Russian Federation, South Africa, Ukraine. It aims to promote sound economic policies and economic growth.

24 The Competition Committee has held over 100 meetings since its founding in 1961 and provides a forum for senior representatives of members' competition agencies to exchange ideas and discuss policies of mutual interest, conduct peer reviews, and develop best practice recommendations. See Remarks of Angel Gurría, OECD Secretary-General, 100th Meeting of the Competition Committee, Paris, 20 February 2008, http://www.oecd.org/competition/competitionbringsprosperity.htm.

25 UNCTAD was established in 1964 as a forum to address trade, investment and development issues. UNCTAD's mandate is to "promote international trade; formulate principles and policies on international trade and related problems of economic development; and initiate actions for the negotiations and adoption of multilateral legal instruments in the field of trade." UNCTAD has convened an "International Group of Experts" on competition law that meets annually and develops competition policy statements, best practices and peer reviews of competition

In the 1990s, discussions among several competition agencies focused on how they could work together and promote sound competition policy and convergence. These discussions led to the creation of the ICN, which was formed in 2001 "to facilitate effective international cooperation to the benefit of member agencies."[26] The ICN and other multilateral organizations continue to support cooperation and convergence; their work in the last twenty years is discussed in sections III and IV.

b. Memorialization of Cooperation

Beginning in the 1970s, some antitrust agencies entered into bilateral and multilateral written agreements on cooperation. For the US Agencies, written agreements are not a prerequisite for enforcement cooperation but they provide a useful framework for enforcement cooperation and have served as catalysts for increased engagement. Antitrust agencies in some jurisdictions require written agreements in order to engage in case cooperation. Cooperation agreements typically provide for notification of enforcement matters that implicate the other agency's interests, investigative assistance through sharing non-confidential information, traditional and positive comity, and consultation to address disputes. The US has entered into government-level agreements that are legally binding, though they do not contain an enforcement mechanism or supersede domestic law, and also into agency-level Memoranda of Understanding. With one exception mentioned below, they do not allow for the sharing of confidential information without waivers from the parties.

2. Bilateral Agreements

The US entered into its first antitrust cooperation agreements in response to tensions over "extraterritoriality." Agreements with Germany in 1976, Australia in 1982, and Canada in 1984, reflect the mutual desire to reduce and manage conflicts. As more countries embraced competition law and adopted their own effects tests, the objectives and content of the agreements evolved to primarily facilitate and enhance inter-agency engagement on investigations and policy. This is reflected in the spate of agreements into which the US entered in the late 1990s. There are now ten bilateral antitrust cooperation agreements between the US and foreign governments as well as three agency level Memoranda of Understanding.[27] While cooperation agreements originally focused on developed countries with established competition agencies, in recent years they have increasingly involved countries with newer agencies such as those in Brazil, Chile, China (MOU), Colombia, India (MOU), and Russia (MOU).

In 1995, the US Congress enacted the International Antitrust Enforcement Assistance Act ("IAEAA"), which authorizes the US Agencies to enter into mutual assistance agreements that, under specified conditions, allow the agencies to share confidential investigative information in their files and to use their information gathering powers to obtain evidence to share with the foreign counterpart competition agency. The IAEAA specifies safeguards governing the exchange of confidential information. Although the statute

agencies. See United Nations Conference on Trade and Dev. (UNCTAD), *UNCTAD: A Brief Historical Overview*, UNCTAD/GDS/2006/1, at 10, http://www.unctad.org/en/docs/gds20061_en.pdf.

26 International Competition Network, "History," http://www.internationalcompetitionnetwork.org/about/history.aspx.

27 All agreements and arrangements are available at http://www.ftc.gov/policy/international/international-cooperation-agreements. The US Agencies also entered into enhanced positive comity agreements, which include a presumption of deference to the other jurisdiction's enforcement under certain conditions, with the EC and Canada but they have never been invoked.

was greeted with hopes and, by some, fears of widespread sharing of confidential information, the United States has been able to enter into only one such agreement, with Australia.[28]

In addition to the many bilateral agreements involving developed countries, emerging and developing countries have entered into cooperation arrangements. For example, Romania and Bulgaria have entered into an agreement,[29] Zambia and Zimbabwe have a Joint Protocol on the exchange of information in competition cases,[30] and agencies in Peru and Colombia entered a cooperation agreement that "allows for the exchange of confidential information and requires both agencies to maintain confidentiality of the information shared between them and to use it only for purposes of competition law enforcement."[31] Turkey "has entered into eight MOUs signed on the basis of mutual consent, willingness and determination of the parties," with the aim of "encourage[ing] cooperation through the exchange of non-confidential information and meetings."[32] As of 2011, Brazil had entered into "bilateral agreements with seven foreign agencies [...] and five of them have explicit provisions on cooperation and avoidance of conflicts in order to minimize any potentially adverse effects of one country's competition law enforcement on other countries' interests in the enforcement of its respective competition laws."[33]

Some emerging and developing countries' competition laws also directly address aspects of cooperation. For example, competition laws in Botswana and Zambia contain provisions regarding bilateral agreements that give effect to positive comity requests by other states.[34]

3. Multilateral Agreements

Multilateral agreements and arrangements also enable international antitrust enforcement cooperation. While non-binding, the Recommendation of the OECD Council concerning International Co-operation on Competition Investigations and Proceedings is an important informal cooperation instrument.[35] It includes provisions on the exchange of confidential information, enhanced cooperation, notifications of antitrust investigations and coordination among antitrust agencies concurrently investigating the same transaction or conduct. Non-OECD members can associate themselves with and use the recommendations.

---

28 US-Australia Mutual Antitrust Enforcement Assistance Agreement, http://www.ftc.gov/policy/cooperation-agreements/usaaustralia-mutual-antitrust-enforcement-assistance-agreement.

29 Id., OECD, *Improving International Co-operation in Cartel Investigation*, ,DAF/COMP/GF/(2012)16, *available at* http://www.oecd.org/daf/competition/ImprovingInternationalCooperationInCartelInvestigations2012.pdf.

30 UNCTAD, *Review of the Experience Gained so far in Enforcement Cooperation, Including at The Regional Level*, TD/B/C.I/CLP/10 (2011) 7, http://unctad.org/en/Docs/ciclpd10_en.pdf.

31 Id., at 6.

32 Id.

33 OECD, *Cross-Border Merger Control: Challenges for Developing and Emerging Economies*, DAF/COMP/GF(2011)13, at 108, *available at* http://www.oecd.org/daf/competition/mergers/50114086.pdf.

34 Sections 77(1) and (2) of the Botswana Competition Act No. 17 of 2009 and sections 65(1) and (2) of the Zambia Competition and Consumer Protection Act No. 24 of 2010.

35 *Recommendation of the OECD Council concerning International Co-operation on Competition Investigations and Proceedings*, as approved by Council on 16 September 2014, [C(2014)108], *available at* http://www.oecd.org/daf/competition/2014-rec-internat-coop-competition.pdf. The original recommendation was adopted in 1967.

The ICN has a voluntary Framework for Merger Review Cooperation, which is open to all ICN member agencies.[36] Regional organizations, including the European Competition Network ("ECN") and Asian Pacific Economic Cooperation ("APEC") also support and facilitate enforcement cooperation.[37]

4. Trade Agreements

Many trade agreements, including approximately half of the free trade agreements the United States has signed[38], include a chapter on competition policy. Such chapters typically include provisions that parties will cooperate in competition enforcement and policy, maintain a competition law and an enforcement agency, and consult to resolve disagreements. Importantly, these provisions are not subject to dispute settlement.

The first free trade agreement with a competition chapter into which the United States entered was NAFTA, which took effect on January 1, 1994. While its primary focus is to reduce tariffs and eliminate trade barriers among the signatory states,[39] it also promotes fair competition and cooperation among competition agencies.[40] Specifically, the signatories promise to "adopt or maintain measures to proscribe anti-competitive business conduct," "shall consult" regarding competition law and enforcement, and agree that their respective competition law enforcement agencies will cooperate.[41] To facilitate cooperation and harmonization of competition laws, NAFTA created a Working Group on Trade and Competition, although the group has been inactive since producing its initial report.[42] The United States-Chile Free Trade Agreement calls for the parties "to cooperate in the area of competition policy;" the United States-Colombia Trade Promotion Agreement contains an identical provision.[43] For the US Agencies, competition chapters of free trade agreements have not played a meaningful role in cooperation on cases or policy, particularly in relation to antitrust-specific cooperation agreements.

Other countries have entered free trade agreements providing for cooperation on competition matters, including the EU in its free trade agreements with Canada and South Korea and in the Euro-Mediterranean Association Agreements.[44] Japan has included competition chapters in bilateral economic partnership agreements with Singapore, Mexico, Malaysia, the Philippines, Chile, Thailand, Indonesia, Vietnam, and Switzerland.[45]

---

36 ICN, *Framework for Merger Review Cooperation* (2012), http://www.internationalcompetitionnetwork.org/uploads/library/doc803.pdf.

37 See, e.g., Commission Notice on cooperation within the Network of Competition Authorities, Official Journal C101, 27/04/2004, p. 0043-0053, *available at* http://eur-lex.europa.eu/LexUriServ/LexUriServ.do?uri=CELEX:52004XC0427%2802%29:EN:HTML; APEC Competition Law and Policy Group, Survey on Information Exchange on Competition in APEC Region–Phase 1, November 2012, *available at* http://publications.apec.org/publication-detail.php?pub_id=1343.

38 For example, the North American Free Trade Agreement ("NAFTA") and bilateral agreements with Australia, Chile, Colombia, Korea, Peru and Singapore. A complete list of the United States' trade agreements are *available at* http://www.state.gov/e/eb/tpp/bta/fta/fta/index.htm.

39 NAFTA, Art. 102, http://www.nafta-sec-alena.org/en/view.aspx.

40 Id.

41 Article 1501(1) and (2).

42 Article 1504; see Interim Report of the NAFTA 1504 Working Group to the NAFTA Commission, *available at* http://www.international.gc.ca/trade-agreements-accords-commerciaux/agr-acc/nafta-alena/report9.aspx?lang=en&view=d.

43 Agreement at Chapter 16.

44 http://www.ustr.gov/trade-agreements/free-trade-agreements.

45 OECD, *Cross-Border Merger Control: Challenges for Developing and Emerging Economies*, DAF/COMP/GF(2011)13, p. 164, *available at* http://www.oecd.org/daf/competition/mergers/50114086.pdf.

Many jurisdictions are also party to regional free trade and common market agreements that include provisions addressing competition issues. For example, the agreement establishing Mercosur "includes the general guidelines for cooperation between the MERCOSUR's institutions and national competition agencies"[46] and, in 2006, Mercosur's Member States signed an Agreement for Cooperation between Competition Agencies for Regional Merger Review, which provides "cooperation mechanisms between national competition agencies on merger review matters."[47] Southern African Development Community ("SADC") members adopted an agreement that contains competition enforcement cooperation commitments.[48] Member states of the Association of Southeast Asian Nations ("ASEAN")[49] cooperate to "enhance and expedite" competition policies in each country.[50] ASEAN encourages international cooperation to help member states' regulatory bodies create consistent and harmonized competition laws and policies.[51] Other regional organizations with agreements that address competition cooperation include the Andean Community, CARICOM, COMESA, SACU, SIECA, and WAEMU.[52]

III. Cooperation Continues to Expand

While arrangements and agreements that address international antitrust cooperation are increasingly common, they are not a prerequisite for either policy or enforcement cooperation. The FTC frequently cooperates with competition agencies without written agreements and welcomes cooperation with competition agencies around the world.

1. Enforcement Cooperation

Enforcement cooperation comprises a range of activities and can be based on different types of information. A considerable amount of useful cooperation can take place based on publicly available information that does not require sharing information provided by parties to an investigation. Cooperation can be more fruitful when it is based on what the US Agencies call "agency confidential" information, which consists of information that the agencies are not statutorily prohibited from disclosing but normally treat as non-public,[53] such as the staff's analysis of the relevant product and geographic markets, the competitive effects of the transaction or conduct, the timing of the investigation, and potential remedies.

---

46 OECD, *Cross-Border Merger Control: Challenges for Developing and Emerging Economies*, DAF/COMP/GF(2011)13, p. 108, *available at* http://www.oecd.org/daf/competition/mergers/50114086.pdf.

47 OECD, *Cross-Border Merger Control: Challenges for Developing and Emerging Economies*, DAF/COMP/GF(2011)13, p. 109, *available at* http://www.oecd.org/daf/competition/mergers/50114086.pdf.

48 Article 1(g), SADC *Declaration on Regional Cooperation in Competition and Consumer Policies* (Members will "pursue case specific cooperation to the extent consistent with each member's laws, regulations, and important common interests in preventing hardcore cartels, abuse of dominance, anticompetitive mergers and unilateral conduct.")

49 Indonesia, Malaysia, Philippines, Singapore, Thailand, Brunei Darussalam, Myanmar, Cambodia, Lao PDR (Laos), and Viet Nam. Member states are listed at http://www.asean.org/18619.htm.

50 ASEAN, *Regional Guidelines on Competition Policy*, 2010, *available at* http://www.asean.org/archive/publications/ASEANRegionalGudelinesonCompetitionPolicy.pdf.

51 Id., at 43.

52 See LACF, *Report on Competition Provisions in Regional Trade Agreements* (2008), *available at* http://www.oecd.org/competition/latinamerica/2013-latin-american-competition-forum.htm.

53 See United States, *Discussion on How to Define Confidential Information*, October 2013, http://www.ftc.gov/sites/default/files/attachments/us-submissions-oecd-other-international-competition-fora/1310us-confidentialinfo.pdf.

Enforcement cooperation may also occur among agencies after parties or third parties have chosen to waive confidentiality protections that allow agencies to discuss and share the party's or third party's confidential information. In merger investigations currently conducted by the US Agencies, parties routinely waive statutory confidentiality protections to facilitate enforcement cooperation. Waivers have been less common in conduct investigations, in part because the parties do not have the same incentive to conclude the investigation as they do in merger cases and because conduct investigations are less frequently cross-border. However, parties are now granting waivers in these cases more frequently.

The US Agencies have found that waivers can make investigations more efficient and facilitate more consistent analysis and remedies by agencies investigating the same matter. To facilitate understanding and use of confidentiality waivers, the US Agencies released a model waiver of confidentiality for use in civil matters involving non-US competition authorities and an FAQ about waivers.[54] Many competition agencies around the world also use confidentiality waivers, although they are used more commonly by agencies with mature competition regimes. The ICN created a model waiver of confidentiality accompanying its report on Waivers of Confidentiality in Merger Investigations.[55]

Case examples illustrate the increasing frequency and depth of cooperation with both more experienced and with newer competition agencies. For example, during its investigation of the proposed merger transaction between Western Digital and Hitachi Global Storage Technologies, the FTC cooperated with agencies in ten jurisdictions – Australia, Canada, China, Japan, Korea, Mexico, New Zealand, Singapore, Turkey, and the European Union.[56] The merging parties provided waivers of confidentiality on a jurisdiction-by-jurisdiction basis. The cooperation covered a range of topics, including timing, market definition, theories of harm, and remedies. Bilateral discussions with some agencies also covered coordinating remedies to address competitive concerns in multiple jurisdictions. Not all of the investigating agencies required remedies.[57]

During its review of Thermo Fisher Scientific's acquisition of Life Technologies in 2013 and 2014, the FTC cooperated with nine non-US antitrust agencies, including newer agencies, on the analysis and divestitures. Cooperation discussions included market definition, theories of harm, and analysis of competitive effects. The FTC coordinated its consideration of remedies with many of the agencies, including with DG COMP such that both agencies approved the same divestiture buyer on the same day.[58] Other recent matters in which the FTC has cooperated closely with counterpart competition agencies included the investigations of unilateral conduct by Motorola Mobility LLC and Google.

DOJ also has also cooperated with newer agencies in both merger reviews and in cartel matters. For example, in the Unilever/Alberto Culver transaction, DOJ cooperated with agencies in Mexico, South

---

54 http://www.ftc.gov/policy/international/international-competition/international-waivers-confidentiality-ftc-antitrust.

55 http://www.internationalcompetitionnetwork.org/uploads/library/doc330.pdf.

56 FTC Action Preserves Competition in the Market for Desktop Hard Disk Drives Used in Personal Computers, March 5, 2012, *available at* http://www.ftc.gov/news-events/press-releases/2012/03/ftc-action-preserves-competition-market-desktop-hard-disk.

57 Remedies were required by the FTC, the European Commission, China's Ministry of Commerce, the Japanese Fair Trading Commission, and the Korean Fair Trade Commission.

58 Press Release, FTC, FTC Puts Conditions on Thermo Fisher Scientific Inc.'s Proposed Acquisition of Life Technologies Corporation (January 31, 2014), *available at* http://www.ftc.gov/news-events/press-releases/2014/01/ftc-puts-conditions-thermo-fisher-scientific-incs-proposed; Press Release, EC, Mergers: Commission approves General Electric as purchaser of Thermo Fisher's divestment businesses, 31 January 201[4], *available at* http://europa.eu/rapid/press-release_IP-14-97_en.htm?locale=en.

Africa, and the United Kingdom.[59] DOJ cooperated with Brazil's competition agency on a cartel investigation involving commercial compressors used in devices such as water coolers and vending machines.[60]

Agencies around the world have been engaging in more frequent and deeper enforcement cooperation. A recent example is in the acquisition of Pfizer's Infant Nutrition business by Nestlé, which included assets in many emerging and developing markets. The transaction was reviewed by several younger competition agencies. Competition agencies in Chile, Colombia, Mexico, Pakistan, and South Africa cooperated during their reviews of the transaction, and discussions included defining relevant markets, identifying theories of harm, and coordinating remedies.[61]

2. Bilateral Policy Cooperation with Newer Agencies

FTC officials routinely share their experience with officials of foreign governments involved in developing competition laws, regulations, guidelines, enforcement institutions, and practices. The FTC encourages the development of legal frameworks and competition enforcement based on sound principles and internationally-recognized good practices. Once the agencies are operating, the FTC's bilateral policy cooperation includes informal and formal consultations, experience sharing and technical assistance. The FTC and counterpart competition agencies consult on a variety of topics, including effective legal instruments, use of economic tools, experiences in analyzing specific industries and sectors, agency effectiveness, and competition advocacy to other parts of government.

For example, bilateral policy cooperation between the US Agencies and China began as the Antimonopoly Law was being conceived and drafted, and the US Agencies worked with India on drafts of its revised competition law and implementing guidelines. Once the laws took effect, the US Agencies worked closely with the Chinese and Indian agencies on the substantive and procedural implementation of their laws. The US Agencies later entered into Memoranda of Understanding memorializing the cooperative relationship. FTC and DOJ officials have engaged in extensive technical cooperation with the Chinese and Indian agencies participated in high-level meetings to exchange experience and views and cooperated on enforcement matters under parallel review.

The FTC's relationship with the Competition Commission of South Africa ("CCSA") evolved as the CCSA gained experience in competition law enforcement. In the early 2000s, FTC, as well as DOJ, staff served as resident advisors and led many training workshops for CCSA staff.[62] A decade later, the FTC, DOJ, and CCSA are jointly leading regional training workshops for competition agencies in Botswana, Malawi, Mauritius, Namibia, Seychelles, Swaziland, and Zambia. In these workshops, CCSA staff present

59 Press Release, DOJ, Justice Department Requires Divestitures in Unilever's Acquisition of Alberto-Culver Company (May 6, 2011), *available at* http://www.justice.gov/opa/pr/justice-department-requires-divestitures-unilevers-acquisition-alberto-culver-company.

60 Press Release, US Dep't of Justice, Panasonic Corp. and Whirlpool Corp. Subsidiary Agree to Plead Guilty for Role in Price-Fixing Conspiracy Involving Refrigerant Compressors (Sept. 30, 2010), *available at* http://www.justice.gov/atr/public/press_releases/2010/262783.htm; Press Release, Conselho Administrativo de Defesa Economica (Sept. 30, 2009), *available at* http://www.cade.gov.br/Default.aspx?9caf7e8b65ba51d227142a065c.

61 See ICN MWG Teleseminar, *Cooperation in Mergers: assessment & remedies*, January 2014, presentation slides *available at* http://www.internationalcompetitionnetwork.org/uploads/library/doc940.pdf.

62 See US Federal Trade Commission's and Department of Justice's Experience With Technical Assistance For The Effective Application of Competition Laws, (Feb. 2008), at 7, *available at* http://www.ftc.gov/sites/default/files/attachments/international-assistance-program/ftcdojtechnicalassist.pdf.

and share their experiences along with DOJ and FTC staff.[63] Staff from competition agencies in Egypt, Kenya, and Zimbabwe have attended these workshops, in addition to staff from COMESA's Competition Commission. The trainings have led to many informal bilateral requests from workshop participants, and the FTC continues to deepen bilateral relations with the participants' competition agencies.

In our own hemisphere, the FTC and the Mexican competition agency led the formation of the Inter-American Competition Alliance,[64] which holds teleseminars (in Spanish) with officials from competition agencies throughout North, Central, and South America. Each member agency proposes and selects topics to present. The programs focus on practical enforcement issues, often through presentations of cases. This experience sharing has increased the contacts among agencies. The relationships fostered by the Alliance support enforcement cooperation in the Americas.

3. Multilateral Cooperation and the Role of Newer Agencies

As introduced in section II above, several international organizations support and further policy cooperation among competition agencies. The ICN, OECD, UNCTAD, and regional organizations such as APEC and the African Competition Forum provide valuable fora to deepen competition policy cooperation among developed and developing countries.

The ICN's membership continues to expand from its sixteen founding members in 2001 to agencies in one hundred and nineteen jurisdictions today.[65] Most members are from emerging and developing countries. The ICN is a consensus-driven organization in which all members are welcome to participate in and lead working groups or individual projects. The ICN is an important vehicle for policy cooperation. Its projects focus on practical aspects of enforcement cooperation that address the needs of young agencies. It has undertaken many projects that advance cooperation among its members, including model waivers to facilitate cooperation in cartel and in merger matters, a joint ICN-OECD survey on enforcement cooperation, a framework for merger cooperation, a report on cooperation in cartel matters, and cooperation provisions in recommended practices on merger notification and procedures.[66] In addition, the ICN's Advocacy and Implementation Network ("AIN")[67] and Advocacy & Implementation Network Support Program ("AISUP")[68] specifically offer support and opportunities for experience sharing between newer and experienced member agencies.

Newer agencies and agencies from emerging and developing countries are increasingly involved at the working group level. For example, during 2013 and 2014, newer agencies participated in teleseminars conducted by the Merger Working Group on International Cooperation and on welcoming calls for newer

---

63 See, e.g., Press Release, Malawi Competition and Fair Trading Commission, *Regional Workshop on Merger Analysis* (Dec. 2013), *available at* http://www.cftc.mw/index.php/2013-12-16-09-56-37/news/25-regional-workshop-on-merger-analysis.

64 See, e.g., Press Release, Malawi Competition and Fair Trading Commission, *Regional Workshop on Merger Analysis* (Dec. 2013), *available at* http://www.cftc.mw/index.php/2013-12-16-09-56-37/news/25-regional-workshop-on-merger-analysis.

65 ICN Membership Directory, http://www.internationalcompetitionnetwork.org/members/member-directory.aspx.

66 For a complete list of ICN's cooperation-related work, see http://internationalcompetitionnetwork.org/about/cooperationwork.aspx.

67 See ICN, *Advocacy and Implementation*, *available at* http://www.internationalcompetitionnetwork.org/about/steering-group/advocacy-implementation.aspx.

68 See ICN, AISUP, http://www.internationalcompetitionnetwork.org/about/steering-group/advocacy-implementation/aisup.aspx.

members held in English, French, and Spanish,[69] and participate in creating and using training modules as part of the ICN's Training on Demand Project.[70] Newer agencies also serve in leadership roles, including on the Steering Group and as working group co-chairs.[71]

The OECD's Competition Committee of the includes members from developed economies and many non-member observers from competition agencies in emerging and developing countries.[72] It includes working parties that focus on competition issues in regulated sectors and on international cooperation and enforcement. Newer agencies contribute to the OECD's policy reports and have additional interactions through the Latin American Competition Forum and the Global Forum. During the annual Global Forum on Competition, OECD members and a large group of non-members discuss competition issues relevant to emerging and developing countries and newer agencies. The Global Forum has held policy roundtables focused on issues of concern for newer competition agencies, including cooperation.[73] Any competition agency can request a peer review through the OECD, and many newer agencies have participated in the peer review process.[74]

The United Nations Conference on Trade and Development, which includes 194 members, also focuses on competition law in developing countries.[75] UNCTAD's Competition Law and Policy group has developed principles on aspects of competition law enforcement.[76] It also conducts training and capacity building to assist newer agencies[77] and conducts voluntary peer reviews.[78]

IV. Prospects for and Challenges of Future Cooperation

The benefits of both enforcement and policy cooperation continue to expand. In just two decades, since cooperation began to address the issues created by the extraterritorial application of antitrust law, much has been achieved. Today, competition agencies at all experience levels find that cooperating with counterpart agencies benefits the development of their agencies and their enforcement programs, and cooperation remains a priority.[79]

---

69 See ICN Merger Working Group, "What's new?," http://www.internationalcompetitionnetwork.org/working-groups/current/merger.aspx.

70 Training on Demand modules are *available at* http://www.internationalcompetitionnetwork.org/about/steering-group/outreach/icncurriculum.aspx.

71 The Steering Group currently includes agencies from Barbados, Brazil, Russia, South Africa, and Turkey. India co-chairs the Merger Working Group and Colombia and Brazil co-chair Cartel Working Group sub-groups.

72 OECD Competition Committee members are listed at http://www.oecd.org/competition/bycountry/.

73 OECD, *Cross-Border Merger Control: Challenges for Developing and Emerging Economies*, DAF/COMP/GF(2011)13, *available at* http://www.oecd.org/daf/competition/mergers/50114086.pdf.

74 OECD, *Country Reviews of Competition Policy Frameworks*, *available at* http://www.oecd.org/regreform/sectors/countryreviewsofcompetitionpolicyframeworks.htm.

75 UNCTAD Membership, *available at* http://unctad.org/en/Pages/About%20UNCTAD/UNCTADs-Membership.aspx.

76 United Nations Set of Multilaterally Agreed Equitable Principles and Rules for the Control of Restrictive Business Practices, TD/RBP/CONF/10/Rev.2 (2000), *available at* http://unctad.org/en/docs/tdrbpconf10r2.en.pdf.

77 UNCTAD, *Technical Cooperation in the Area of Competition Law and Policy*, *available at* http://unctad.org/en/Pages/DITC/CompetitionLaw/Technical-Cooperation-in-the-Area-of-Competition-Law-and-Policy.aspx.

78 UNCTAD, *Voluntary Peer Review of Competition Law and Policy*, *available at* http://unctad.org/en/Pages/DITC/CompetitionLaw/Voluntary-Peer-Review-of-Competition-Law-and-Policy.aspx.

79 In 2013, 84% of respondents to the ICN-OECD Cooperation Questionnaire indicated that international co-operation is a policy priority. ICN-OECD Survey Report at 36, *available at* http://www.oecd.org/competition/InternEnforcementCooperation2013.pdf.

For the FTC, cooperation, including with agencies in emerging and developing countries, is not a luxury but a necessity. It advances the objectives of convergence toward sound policy and ensuring compatible outcomes of investigations subject to multi-jurisdictional review. Competition agencies in emerging and developing countries have found "that exchanges with other agencies are very beneficial, and that experience-sharing helps them to develop strategies to approach cases and strengthen enforcement even at the national level."[80] The expansion of the number of competition laws and agencies, their scope of work, and continued globalization make it likely that opportunities to cooperate will continue to grow, and that agencies will continue to develop tools to facilitate and deepen cooperation.

It seems likely that increasing cooperation on competition policy and enforcement will continue to support convergence toward sound competition rules and enforcement. Since the ICN was created, many agencies that have adopted competition laws, regulations, and guidelines have consulted and followed the ICN Recommendations. For example, Brazil, Turkey, India, and many other jurisdictions have adopted merger review practices that conform more closely with the ICN's Recommended Practices on Merger Notification and Review Procedures,[81] which has contributed to streamlining filings in multi-jurisdictional transactions. In the area of merger analysis, agencies such as those in Korea, Finland, Germany, Singapore, and Chile have moved to a competitive effects-based analysis consistent with the ICN's Recommended Practices for Merger Analysis.[82] ICN recommendations on the Assessment of Dominance and Substantial Market Power Analysis, Competition Assessment, State Created Monopolies and Predatory Pricing have also facilitated greater international convergence toward good practices.[83] Newer as well as more experienced agencies have also used recommendations and other work product of the OECD and UNCTAD to shape their rules and guide their enforcement.[84]

Work in the ICN, OECD, and UNCTAD and at regional organizations continues to address aspects of enforcement cooperation, and the forum each organization provides for policy cooperation is ever-present. The ICN's Merger Working Group is focused on enforcement cooperation, and based on its experience-sharing work last year is drafting guidance on merger enforcement cooperation. The UNCTAD meeting in 2015 addressed merger enforcement cooperation.[85] Also in 2015, the OECD Competition Committee members discussed the types of provisions typically included in antitrust cooperation agreements.[86] In addition, the OECD's recently revised Recommendation on cooperation in competition enforcement

---

80 Id., at 11 (among respondents from non-OECD countries).

81 See Ron Knox, *Brazil raises merger thresholds under new antitrust law*, May 30, 2012, *available at* http://www.globalcompetitionreview.com/news/article/31896/brazil-raises-merger-thresholdsnew-antitrust-law/; [India's] Competition Act, 2002, as amended, Competition (Amendment) Act, 2007, para. 2 (y), *available at* http://www.cci.gov.in/index.php?option=com_content&task=view&id=18; Nicholas Hirst and Cihan Tutluoglu, *Turkey's merger control system to benefit from higher thresholds and streamlined test–lawyers* Financial Times, Jan. 9, 2013, *available at* http://www.ft.com/cms/s/2/9f2e3cca-5a74-11e2-a02e-00144feab49a.html#ixzz2Na3NuSkc.

82 See Korea Fair Trade Commission, *Guidelines for the combination of enterprises review*, December 28, 2011, *available at* http://eng.ftc.go.kr/files/static/Legal_Authority/Guidelines%20for%20the%20combination%20of%20enterprises%20Review_mar%2014%202012.pdf; Finnish Competition Authority, *Guidelines on Merger Control*, January 2011, *available at* http://www.kilpailuvirasto.fi/tiedostot/Suuntaviivat-1-2011-Yrityskauppavalvonta-EN.pdf; Bundeskartellamt, *Guidance on Substantive Merger Control*, March 29, 2012, *available at* http://www.bundeskartellamt.de/wEnglisch/download/pdf/Merkblaetter/2012-03-29_Guidance_final_neu.pdf (increased focus on economics; agency will take into account all relevant factors in its analysis); Competition Commission of Singapore, *CCS Guidelines on the Substantive Assessment of Mergers*, effective July 1, 2012, *available at* http://www.ccs.gov.sg/content/dam/ccs/PDFs/Publications/AnnexA_Revised%20Merger%20Guidelines%20for%20publication%20_3_.pdf; [Chile] Fiscalía Nacional Económica, *Guía para el Análisis de Operaciones de Concentración*, October 2012, *available in Spanish at* http://www.fne.gob.cl/wp-content/uploads/2012/10/Guia-Fusiones.pdf.

83 All ICN Recommended Practices are *available at* http://www.internationalcompetitionnetwork.org/library.aspx?search=&group=0&type=3&workshop=0.

84 See, e.g., Interview with Felipe Irarrázabal, Chile's National Economic Prosecutor, The Antitrust Source, June 2013, at 5, *available at* http://www.americanbar.org/content/dam/aba/publishing/antitrust_source/jun13_irarrazabal_intrvw.authcheckdam.pdf.

85 UNCTAD Press Release, Seventh United Nations Conference to Review All Aspects of the Set of Multilaterally Agreed Equitable Principles and Rules for the Control of Restrictive Business Practices, *available at* http://unctad.org/en/Pages/MeetingDetails.aspx?meetingid=609.

86 OECD, *Competition Issues under Discussion*, *available at* http://www.oecd.org/daf/competition/workinprogress.htm.

encourages "information gateways" that could encourage broader and deeper cooperation, including toward increased sharing of confidential information in enforcement matters.

As cooperation continues to expand and to deepen, there will be new challenges. As with past challenges, these can be overcome through discussions and interactions facilitated by a combination of multilateral and bilateral relationships.

One challenge is the variety of national laws that typically restrict sharing confidential information. Confidential information is often necessary to most effectively assist other agencies in analyzing cases and designing appropriate remedies. Confidentiality waivers have been particularly valuable in facilitating sharing confidential information, but this takes place primarily among agencies from developed countries in merger investigations. Concerns about agencies' ability to protect parties' confidential information also limit the amount of cooperation that parties are willing to authorize. Although some countries have entered into agreements that allow their competition agencies to share confidential information and some agencies, such as those in Canada and the UK, have statutory authority to do so unilaterally, legal instruments to facilitate broader sharing of confidential information had only a limited effect in overcoming these barriers. For example, the US legislation authorizing agreements that can enable such sharing was enacted in 1995 with the expectation that the United States would conclude agreements to implement it. However, for reasons such as concerns about onward sharing of information and reluctance or inability to share information for use in criminal prosecutions, as mentioned previously, only one such agreement has been concluded and that has been used extremely rarely.

Although cooperation can take place among agencies that operate with different laws, legal systems, and policies, it works best among agencies with similar frameworks. Thus, to the extent that competition agencies deviate from a consumer welfare-based model to enforcement that appears to consider industrial and other policies, the prospects for enforcement cooperation decrease. Finally, it can take time for newer agencies to feel comfortable cooperating with other agencies, particularly those they don't know well. Over time, it is likely that their confidence will grow and, through participation in multilateral bodies they will become more familiar with their counterparts and be more comfortable cooperating on cases.

The Federal Trade Commission has devoted substantial resources to furthering cooperation with its counterparts around the world. These efforts have yielded substantial benefits in promoting procedural and substantive convergence and in reaching sound and compatible results in cross-border matters. The FTC looks forward to increasing our cooperation with the expanding circle of international partners, to the benefit of all of our agencies and the consumers we serve.

International Cooperation on Competition Matters: An Emerging Enforcer's Perspective

Kiran Nandinee Meetarbhan

jaynyam@yahoo.co.in

Former Executive Director, Competition Commission of Mauritius

Abstract

Young emerging competition agencies are resource-constrained, lack the relevant personnel trained in competition law and policy and at times, the jurisdictional limitations in their legal regimes, create significant impediments in detecting and enforcing competition laws against cross-border competition problems affecting national markets. Additionally, building working relationships with advanced competition peers often requires a proven track-record of successful enforcement, especially within the realm of anti-cartel enforcement, in order to show credibility and earn the trust and respect of their developed peers. The legal limitations arising out of disparate competition regimes compounded by the severity of confidentiality and data protection requirements in some statutes further accentuate the challenges that lie in the way of effective agency-to-agency cooperation, through information sharing, in favor of developing agencies. The signing of formal bilateral cooperation instruments equally suffers from several deficiencies. Creating opportunities for South-South cooperation, enforcement and pooling of resources for capacity building in competition policy could viably provide the first step towards effective international cooperation in competition law enforcement.

I. Introduction

The Competition Act 2007 ("CA 2007")[1] has gone a long way in entrusting the Competition Commission of Mauritius ("CCM") with such powers and functions as to enable it to effectively discharge its functions. Although the CA 2007 extends the reach of our enforcement powers beyond national borders, the applicability and effective application of such powers within the realm of international antitrust investigations (relating to conduct/practices having an effect in or within Mauritius) remains yet to be tested. As of this date, the CCM has not had the opportunity of experimenting with the extraterritorial scope of the Act. Given the global pervasiveness of business transactions, it is only a matter of time before the CCM is called upon to enforce its competition legislation transnationally. At the same time, however, there is no denying that investigating restrictive business practices having an international scope naturally poses important challenges which can be resolved if effective cooperation is willfully encouraged between competition agencies—irrespective of their level of enforcement experience.

The objectives of international cooperation need not serve merely as a means to coordinate parallel investigations, but most assuredly as the avenue for improving enforcement action based on case-oriented peer-to-peer-learning from the enforcement experience of others. Viewed from an emerging agency's position, the reasons for encouraging horizontal collaboration are all the more compelling: the CCM is not a self-funded institution and relies solely on government funding for its enforcement, advocacy, capacity building and administrative requirements/expenses. Scarce human resources and limited access to expert training in contemporary issues of competition enforcement plague most young agencies. The CCM operates with an all-inclusive team of twelve junior and senior investigative officers qualified in law and/or economics, headed by one Chief Economist (as supervising officer for the economists' team) and one Legal Executive (for the legal team). Over its five years of enforcement, the CCM has been called upon to confront a high caseload of enquiries and investigations, forcing it to grapple with complex, economic theories assessing the effects of harm perpetrated in technically challenging, technology-driven, niche markets, without a comparable incremental increase in human capacity or the required specialized knowledge and expertise to comprehensively understand and assess the peculiar competition dynamics of complex markets.

In several of the cases, informal assistance has been sought from DG COMP, OECD, Competition Commission South Africa ("CCSA") and other agencies.

Mauritius (like many developing economies) is a small net-food importing economy, with heavy reliance on imports mostly from advanced, industrialized countries. Restrictive business practices stemming from the territories of mighty trading partners might well be imported into its vulnerable economy, to the detriment of the latter's consumer welfare. Whenever a developed country is investigating potential restrictive business practices on the part of those enterprises which have operations in developing countries, it is therefore a sine qua non that developed countries assist, to the best of their abilities, developing countries in the detection of such conduct by providing relevant and first-hand information, which may, for the purposes of meeting the procedural requirements, amount to reasonable grounds for launching an investigation within the younger agency's national market(s).

In today's globalized world, combating competition law infringements with an international dimension is increasingly becoming the enforcement norm, and one which does not lighten the enforcement burden

1 Competition Act 2007 *available at* http://www.ccm.mu/English/Documents/Legislations/Competition%20Act%202007_Amended_050213.pdf.

of developing competition agencies. Sharper vigilance of the competition dynamics in national and transnational net-importing markets, however difficult, remains of the essence. While competition authorities in developed economies are more likely to establish a dedicated unit specialized in market-watching and intelligence information gathering, authorities in developing countries lack both the resources and expertise to effectively carry out such intelligence gathering within national borders and, even less so, within the international forum. Increased cooperation on this front will certainly go a long way in aiding younger agencies to enhance and perfect their enforcement capacities while building coordinated working relationships among different agencies.

The most strategic solution to countering the enforcement lacunae certainly rests in investing in specialized training in investigative and enforcement skills for the benefit of our case handlers and upgrading their knowledge of competition law and economics. Such investment, while crucial for enhancing the quality of enforcement action, adds to the financial burden of the agencies in developing countries. Informal horizontal cooperation between competition agencies can actually serve to increase the expertise of an agency's personnel, hence creating new possibilities for boosting national competition control and advocacy. At the same time, cooperation ensures that the agency knows the latest trends of international competition law and economics when implementing national competition policy.

A key element of informal cooperation, however, is building working relationships based on trust. Since informal cooperation does not rely on explicit rules protecting the confidentiality of exchanged information, this kind of informal cooperation can only work if the assisting agency trusts the requesting agency to use the information properly. The exchange of non-confidential information and general views on a case might be sufficient in and of itself in many cases. Without discarding important legal differences inherent in the legislative frameworks of cooperating jurisdictions, a newly-established competition agency has much to learn from and be inspired by case theories and theories of competitive harm, as well as the body of legal and economic analysis, developed in well-advanced jurisdictions. This could fill in the gaps created by the lack of practical experience, promoting consistent case outcomes where relevant and applicable, thus allowing for the desired legal certainty in relation to what firms can and cannot do across the globe.

The key to maximizing the benefits and effectiveness of such informal cooperation mechanisms is to encourage informal contacts at an early stage of a case and include regular consultation among agencies on matters such as timing of the investigation, the theory of harm, and potential remedies, especially in cases of abuse of dominance/unilateral conduct and merger reviews.

In addition to informal cooperation mechanisms, advanced competition agencies and, more recently, emerging antitrust enforcers are increasingly turning towards different legal basis for formal cooperation, including bilateral/plurilateral cooperation agreements, fully fledged international treaties, and memoranda of understanding, among others. These agreements, if effectively used, provide a valuable tool within a competition agency's arsenal of enforcement and advocacy instruments. Whereas some non-binding Formal Cooperation Agreements ("FCAs") merely aim to formalize existing working relationships and are drafted on the basis of best endeavors, other FCAs allow more or less intense forms of cooperation between signatories. For example, they may facilitate the sharing of confidential information by including provisions for confidentiality waivers.

Among the powers vested in the Competition Commission is the authority to co-operate with other foreign competition agencies assigned with functions similar to those of the Commission,[2] without any further

2 Id., at para. 6(d).

provision specifying the modalities of such cooperation. In October 2012, the CCM concluded its first MoU with the French Autorité de la Concurrence[3] (a long-established competition agency) while the existing MoU with the Fair Trading Commission of Seychelles (a relatively new competition agency) was signed in July 2013.[4] These MoUs aim to foster closer cooperation between the signatories without creating legally binding obligations for either of them. While mandating the exchange of investigative experiences, the MoUs only vaguely mention the issue of sharing case-specific, confidential information as a means of cooperation, which the signatories "'may" consider while respecting the requirements of each party's laws.

Already limited in time to a period of five years subject to consensual renewal, limited use has been made of these bilateral MoUs in the course of the CCM's enforcement activities. This brings to the fore the issues and challenges arising out of bilateral cooperation agreements between agencies, especially those at disparate levels of enforcement in the competition arena.

II. Formal Cooperation on Antitrust Matters: Issues and Challenges

In addition to resource constraints, several other factors add to the burden of competition agencies when seeking formal cooperation on case-specific antitrust investigations. These include: legal limitations arising out of differences between legal systems regarding the treatment of anticompetitive conduct; national divergences in procedural rules; the reach of, and response to, discovery mechanisms; the administrative burden of communication and coordination and (mutual) lack of experience; and the lack of interest in cooperating closely with younger agencies, among others.

In their joint 2013 Survey on International Enforcement Cooperation,[5] the Secretariat report of the OECD in collaboration with the ICN raised concerns that, apart from regional cooperation, frequent or regular experience in international cooperation appears to be concentrated among a few more experienced agencies.

Even where cooperation is extended by a foreign agency, any information exchanged has to pass the test of being receivable and admissible as per the requesting agency's evidentiary rules. Concerns may arise where, for instance, information exchanged would have been treated as legally privileged at the receiving end. Were the CCM to be the receiving jurisdiction, the integrity of its investigation could run the risk of being compromised on the ground of procedural abuse, given that the CA 2007 guarantees the protection of legally privileged information.[6] The absence of well defined, agreed ground-rules for the exchange of information can hinder much-needed co-operation of this type, without which developing agencies like the CCM will always lag behind in walking the transnational enforcement pathway.

3 MoU between Mauritius and France, October 2012 *available at* http://www.ccm.mu/English/Documents/Legislations/MoU_Autorite%20de%20la%20Concurrence.pdf.

4 MoU between Mauritius and Seychelles, July 2013 *available at* http://www.ccm.mu/English/Documents/MOU/mou_FTC_Seychelles.pdf.

5 OECD/ICN, Secretariat Report on the OECD/ICN Survey on International Enforcement Co-operation, 2013 *available at* http://www.oecd.org/competition/InternEnforcementCooperation2013.pdf.

6 See *supra* note 1, at para. 54.

III. What Developing Countries Need: A Robust Legal Framework for Effective Cooperation

It is often seen that bringing a developed country to the negotiating table is often a herculean task for weaker, developing countries—much lesser in economic might. The developing agency has to accept whatever terms (or the least that) the developed country member is willing to offer, and account must be taken of the normally robust confidentiality and data protection requirements in place within the national regime of the stronger signatory. In most instances, the advanced competition agency would have been cautious in safeguarding its national interests when drafting the bilateral cooperation agreement provisions. In such instances, developing countries neither have the political clout to bargain for better cooperation nor to enforce the already existing (mostly non-binding) cooperation agreement. As such, there is an overarching need for developed/advanced competition agencies to adopt a more strategic approach towards international agreements and to tailor the instrument to the real needs of the relationship and to facts such as the size and importance of the other signatory country's economy, the intensity of the trade and investment relationship with the country concerned, and the degree of maturity of its competition regime.

1. Normative Confidentiality Tempered by Confidentiality Waivers

One of the most important limitations to international cooperation relates to the legal limitation within the assisting jurisdiction's competition regime, more specifically: the legal protection afforded to confidential information which constrains the ability of competition agencies to share and exchange information and other evidence obtained during an investigation. Most national competition laws do not permit the sharing of confidential information absent the consent of the party having submitted that information.[7]

Differences in legal definitions and scope of confidentiality, privacy and legal privilege, can and actually do affect an agency's ability to share certain information and equally limits its willingness to cooperate. Similarly, differences in data protection systems may complicate the exchange of information with third countries wherein, for example, transfer of personal data may become lawful only when there is adequate personal data protection in the requesting jurisdiction. The inclusion of confidentiality waivers (which apply in specific circumstances, for example, as regards information submitted by a cartel member as part of its leniency application) in cooperation agreements allows agencies to exchange confidential information about the case, especially in transnational merger reviews, quickly and at an early stage, thus facilitating coordination in an investigation. It also helps to avoid using official channels in formal cooperation procedures, thereby avoiding consequent delays, which such procedures could have entailed.

---

7 See *supra* note 1, at para. 70(iv). The Mauritian Competition Act 2007 poses a general prohibition as regards the sharing of confidential information. As a general principle, the Commissioners, the Executive Director and the Commission's staff are under the obligation to protect the confidentiality of any information given to it in confidence or obtained further to the Executive Director's investigative powers. Disclosure of any information relating to any particular business or the affairs of an individual and obtained under or by virtue of the Act, is only permitted so long as the disclosure is made inter alia: for the purpose of responding to a request made by a foreign or multinational competition authority for the production of information in circumstances where Mauritius is a party to an international agreement providing for the production or exchange of such information.

2. Administrative Assistance in the Course of an Investigation

Multinational companies, though investing significantly in developing country economies, rarely base their headquarters therein. Given the lack of financial and human resources and the demands of confidentiality, developing country agencies can at least expect reinforced cooperation on the part of their fellow advanced enforcers when the developing agency has launched an antitrust investigation into conduct of enterprises that have their headquarters based in the developed country. A request for investigatory assistance to an agency that might be better placed to obtain evidence in its own territory could enhance enforcement by the requesting agency, and also contribute to effective transnational enforcement. Developed countries may assist in the service of documents and gathering of evidence, whether through oral examination of a person or through lawful request or seizure of documents, relevant to investigations being carried out in developing countries.

IV. Concluding Remarks

The world is getting ever smaller. Technological development is shrinking our world: we can communicate with each other by videoconferencing, as well as by phone, and by emails across many time zones. This is also true for businesses and should equally be true for antitrust agencies. It is the shrinking world—the globalization of markets and businesses—that necessitates the strides that have been made, and that will continue to be made, in bringing antitrust and competition agencies around the globe together. Those same forces that are allowing businesses to go global are globalizing antitrust agencies as well.

Against the backdrop of our multipolar world of antitrust enforcement, cooperation among the national competition authorities within our region is crucial to counter the asymmetric development of competition law regimes in neighboring countries. In spite of all the efforts of developing countries to develop resource capacities, emerging markets will face resource constraints. Developing countries cannot be expected to have the wide range of expertise required, and this is where the South-South or regional cooperation is of prime importance. The capacity that an individual country may not have on its own may be available collectively at regional level. Developing countries or small states within a particular region often have a lot in common in terms of legal systems, educational institutions, etc. By pooling their resources and developing specialist centers, where each country can specialize in one aspect, the region collectively will have the skills. Then one agency in a given country will be able to call upon the specialist country to assist in an investigation where that particular knowledge is required.

Whether for enforcement or adjudication, collective action would help to reduce otherwise inadequate capacities. Obviously, a regional cooperation mechanism would contemplate that each competition authority remains sovereign. However, creating opportunities for cooperative enforcement and pooling of resources for capacity building in competition policy within our region (South-South cooperation) is the first step towards international cooperation in competition law enforcement. To what extent cooperation is and should be a step towards convergence is an issue for another day. Suffice it to say that convergence with the legal formulations of the highly developed economies is not always the most fitting route for small developing economies.

Antitrust in Emerging Economies

Blanca Rodriguez-Galindo

Blanca.Rodriguez-Galindo@ec.europa.eu

Head, International Relations Unit,
Directorate General for Competition, European Commission

Abstract

The aim of the external action of competition agencies is to promote convergence, effective enforcement and a level playing field for companies worldwide. Promoting competition culture internationally is an essential part of European Union competition policy. After giving an overview of the changes in the landscape of the antitrust world in the last 20 years, this paper describes the cooperation activities in which the European Commission and its Directorate General of Competition is engaged. The paper focuses in the relationship with competition authorities of emerging economies, developing countries or simply some of the new comers to the antitrust world. It describes the different cooperation activities with the BRICS countries (Brazil, Russia, India, China and South Africa) but also Eastern and Central European Countries. As explained in the paper the relationships with these new competition authorities is evolving from cooperation in drafting legislation and capacity building to cooperation on cases.

I. Introduction

The rise of emerging economies is one of the historical events of our time. As a natural development, the establishment of new competition regimes and agencies accompanies the appearance of new major players in the global economy. We have seen a dramatic increase in the number of competition regimes around the world since the early 1990s.

Jurisdictions with a competition law and competition authority.[1]

Jurisdictions with a Competition Law and Competition Authority*

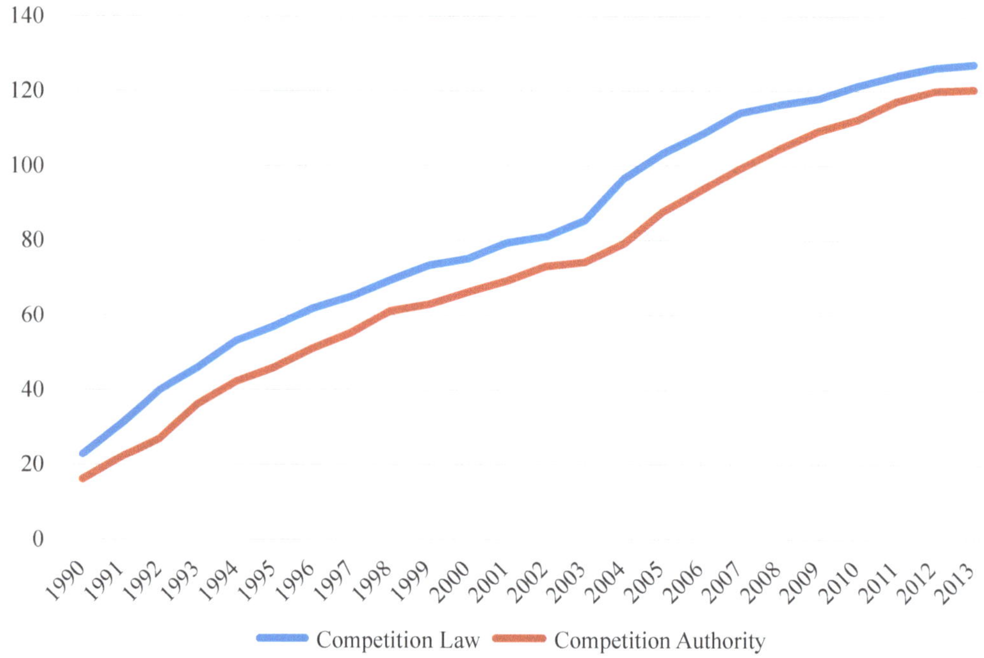

If by 1990 competition law's global coverage represented less than 25 percent of the world's population, by 2013 it had already covered 85 percent. That increase is also well illustrated by the fact that when the International Competition Network ("ICN") was created its membership was constituted by 15 competition authorities, while today there are 132 authorities, representing 118 jurisdictions. A large number of those come from developing countries or emerging economies. The prominent role played by those new competition authorities leads to new forms of cooperation among enforcers and increases the need to foster convergence. This paper describes the cooperation activities in which the European Commission ("Commission") (and its Directorate General of Competition ("DG COMP"))[2] is engaged with some of the competition authorities of emerging economies, developing countries or simply some of the new comers to the antitrust world. A particular focus will be put on some of the BRICS countries (section II), but also on the cooperation with Central and Eastern European countries who are candidates seeking

---

1 See Organisation for Economic Co-operation and Development ("OECD"), *New approaches to Economic Challenges ("NAEC"). Implications of Globalisation for Competition policy*, Seminar on Project C6,, 24 March, 2014, (DAF/COMP(2014)4/REV1), at 5 *available at* http://www.slideshare.net/OECD_NAEC/naec-seminar-on-project-c6-24-march-comp

2 When describing specific cooperation programs or actions, this paper will refer indistinctively to European Commission or DG COMP as the competition agency.

European Union ("EU") membership (section II), with which cooperation takes the form of an almost harmonization of competition laws.

Also, much can be done for emerging economies and developing countries through the various international/multilateral organizations which deal with competition issues (section IV). Finally, the EU perceives competition policy to be a key element in its trade negotiations, in particular with emerging economies; therefore, section V of this paper will briefly address the competition provisions in free trade agreements. In its conclusion (section VI), the paper contains some data illustrating the current trends of multijurisdictional enforcement.

II. Bilateral Cooperation with Emerging Economies and BRICS

The first step in cooperating with developing countries consists mostly of time spent on capacity building assistance to help them put in place their legislation and organize their competition authorities. This will progressively develop into case cooperation, once the competition authorities start their enforcement activities.

BRICS countries (Brazil, Russia, India, China and South Africa) now rank among the largest ten national economies in the world, and South Africa is in the top thirty. Therefore, the cooperation activities of the European Commission have been particularly focused on some of these countries. The Commission has signed administrative agreements, a Memorandum of Understanding ("MoU") or similar with all of them except South Africa. This establishes a sound framework for cooperation and is the basis for continued dialogue on competition policy, and the sharing of non-confidential information. The absence of an administrative arrangement with South Africa is not an obstacle for good cooperation between the two jurisdictions, as the focus is already on both cartel and mergers cases and the occasional exchange of experience on policy matters. The work that the Commission has done with BRICS is illustrated below, by using the examples of China, India and Brazil.

1. China

a. The Framework for the EU-China Competition Policy Dialogue and Cooperation

The European Commission started cooperating with the Chinese authorities on competition matters in 2003, when they were in the early stages of drafting the current Chinese Antimonopoly Law ("AML"), adopted in 2007.[3]

3 Antimonopoly Law of the People's Republic of China, August 30, 2007, and effective August 2008, *available at* http://english.mofcom.gov.cn/aarticle/policyrelease/announcement/200712/20071205277972.html.

In 2004, DG COMP signed Terms of Reference ("ToR") for a structured dialogue on competition with the Ministry of Commerce of the People's Republic of China ("MOFCOM").[4] That dialogue has led to good relations with the Chinese competition authorities through frequent contact with staff and a successful technical cooperation program. The ToR predates the adoption of the AML in 2007 and the setting up of the Chinese competition enforcement structure in 2008. According to the structure set up, MOFCOM became the merger review authority, while the State Administration of Industry and Commerce ("SAIC") and the National Development and Reform Commission ("NDRC") shared antitrust enforcement. In 2012, DG COMP signed a MoU with NDRC and SAIC to strengthen cooperation with these two agencies in the area of antitrust.[5] The new MoU provides a framework for discussions on policy matters, enforcement cooperation and technical assistance in the area of antitrust and unilateral conduct. The ToR remains the main basis for DG COMP cooperation with MOFCOM on mergers.

b. Technical Cooperation (Capacity Building and Sharing Experiences)

DG COMP has undertaken technical cooperation with China since 2004 in the competition field under the framework of the EU-China Trade Project ("EUCTP"),[6] a major EU-China trade related technical assistance project supporting the Chinese government's trade reform and sustainable development agenda, which includes the promotion of competition policy as one of its main components.

The first phase of this project (EUCTP I, 2004-2009) mainly concentrated on supporting China in drafting the AML through: frequent seminars and workshops, drawing extensively on the EU experience; translation into Mandarin of all the relevant EU legislation and studies about specific antitrust and merger issues which took into account Chinese particularities. All this resulted in a clear EU fingerprint on AML's substantive provisions, as frequently acknowledged by the Chinese Antimonopoly Authorities themselves. In its second phase, EUCTP II continues to be a good advocacy tool in promoting the adoption and implementation by China of competition rules and practices that are more in line with generally accepted international standards.

The EU-China Competition Week organized through EUCTP is an example of continuing co-operation between China and Europe in this area. Twice or three times a year, a week of seminars, workshops and conferences are held in Beijing, or in the capital of one of the provinces, for Chinese enforcement officials and policy-makers of the three Chinese Antimonopoly Authorities both at the central and provincial level.

The workshop programs include a broad range of substantial and procedural issues, including investigative techniques, procedural fairness and transparency, definition of dominance, negotiation of remedies in the context of merger review, but also dedicated sessions on antitrust enforcement in particular sectors like car manufacturing, insurance and, lately, State aid control policy (control of subsides).[7]

As the level of experience of the Chinese authorities increases, their demands and needs for technical cooperation are becoming more sophisticated. As a result, Competition Week programs involve more and more experienced case handlers and managers both from DG COMP and the national competition

---

4 Terms of Reference of the EU-China Competition Policy Dialogue of May 6, 2004, *available at* http://ec.europa.eu/competition/international/bilateral/china_tor_en.pdf.

5 Memorandum of Understanding on Cooperation in the Area of Antimonopoly Law between DG Competition and the NDRC and SAIC, 20 September 2012, *available at* http://ec.europa.eu/competition/international/bilateral/mou_china_en.pdf.

6 See further details on the EU-Chine Trade Project at http://www.euchinacomp.org/index.php.

7 See program of the most recent competition week *available at* http://www.euchinacomp.org/index.php/competition-weeks.

authorities of the EU Member States which are part of the European Competition Network ("ECN"). It is a specific feature of the technical cooperation organized by DG COMP, particularly relevant in the case of China, but also present in the programs with other BRICS and developing countries that experts from this network of 28 competition authorities which apply common rules participate in this form of cooperation as they have different experiences which can be mutually enriching.[8]

Other than the Competition Weeks, DG COMP has organized study trips to the EU for officials of the Chinese Antimonopoly Authorities. In order to ensure a sufficient response for the high demand of these trips, DG COMP has recently replaced these visits with an EU Competition Summer School which is organized in the College of Europe in Bruges once a year. The Summer School provides some thirty Chinese officials with a two-week in-depth study of EU competition law. Over time, DG COMP has also organized a limited number of internships for Chinese officials within EU national competition authorities and DG COMP itself. Such internships place a heavy demand on the allocation of resources but they have proven to be a good investment as these officials continue to be "EU ambassadors" within their authorities when they return and remain good points of contact.

c. Enforcement Cooperation

DG COMP has developed case cooperation with MOFCOM in merger review for a number of years, and contact is established whenever there are cases being reviewed in both jurisdictions in parallel. The cooperation is under development and is expanding and improving, as each side gets better acquainted with the other. DG COMP's objective is—other than rendering its own enforcement more efficient and effective—to prevent conflicting outcomes of the cases under review and to seek the acceptance by both jurisdictions of remedies that are interoperable. Of the 800 mergers that MOFCOM has reviewed since the entering into force of the Chinese AML in 2008, there has been cooperation with DG COMP in around 15 cases. If we look at the figures of the last two years, 2012-2013, cooperation between DG COMP and MOFCOM has taken place in at least 7 mergers, which represent 15 percent of all the multijurisdictional mergers that DG COMP has reviewed over this period. However, this cooperation is far less developed in the field of cartels (no cases at the moment), and antitrust in general (1 case), as the number of cases with an international dimension dealt with by SAIC and NDRC is also lower.[9]

2. India

a. The Framework for the EU-India Competition Policy Dialogue and Cooperation

DG COMP has been cooperating with the Competition Commission of India ("CCI") since 2007, when the Indian Competition Act of 2002 was amended and the CCI became fully operational.[10]

8 See an overview of the ECN *available at* http://ec.europa.eu/competition/ecn/index_en.html.

9 See graphs of enforcement cooperation in section VI at the end of this paper.

10 See The Competition Act, 2002, as amended by the Competition (Amendment) Act, 2007, *available at* http://www.cci.gov.in/images/media/competition_act/act2002.pdf?phpMyAdmin=QuqXb-8V2yTtoq617iR6-k2VA8d.

In 2009, the CCI and DG COMP reached an informal agreement on the conclusion of a Memorandum of Understanding ("MoU") on cooperation, which was finally signed at the margins of the BRICS conference in November 2013.[11]

The MoU, which is inspired by the MoUs with the Brazilian, Chinese and Russian competition authorities, creates a solid framework for the development of administrative cooperation between the CCI and DG COMP. It will be the basis for a continued dialogue on competition policy, as well as for sharing non-confidential information. It will promote cooperation among the parties and increase understanding and awareness of forthcoming approaches—in the areas of competition policy, legislation, and its application—ultimately to the benefit of EU undertakings active in India and Indian undertakings active in the EU. Cooperation is subject to the parties' respective laws, in particular those protecting confidential information. The MoU foresees that when the parties meet, they will discuss developments of mutual interest, exchange information on economic sectors of common interest, and exchange views on competition issues.

The MoU, moreover, provides a useful framework for technical cooperation between DG COMP and the CCI, which is expected to continue to build up its enforcement capacity over the next years.

b. Technical Cooperation (Capacity Building and Sharing Experiences)

Technical cooperation activities between DG COMP and the CCI started on an *ad hoc* basis in 2009 with a number of CCI officials visiting DG COMP. Later on a limited number of workshops were organized in India. However, in conjunction with the start of the negotiation of the EU-India Free Trade Agreement, the EU and India entered into the EU-India Capacity-building Initiative for Trade Development ("CITD") which was signed in December 2011.[12] As a result, funding was made available for technical cooperation in the area of competition policy from 2013, for a period of five years. Like in the case of China, competition is considered to be an important component of trade policy and, consequently, it receives a share of the funding provided for the trade cooperation program with India.

The CITD allows DG COMP to support the CCI with the aim of improving the CCI's capacity in terms of investigation, reporting and enforcement functions. The project is designed to achieve a number of results that have been adapted and tailored to the specific circumstances of the CCI:

1) The establishment of a Knowledge Management System as a centralized system for the collection and storage of data which will be a central point for information regarding investigations. The system will also allow for access to case law, guidelines, academic articles and other secondary sources.

2) The facilitation of specialized workshops on issues pertaining to competition law and competition economics. The workshops focus on the application of the key provisions of the Competition Act of India, drawing on the good practices of the EU and its Member States and covering anti-competitive conduct and economics analysis with regards to, among other areas, competition law enforcement.

Also, like in the case of China, experts from the ECN competition authorities of the Member States take part in these activities, alongside DG COMP enforcers, providing a broader range of experiences to the CCI officials.

---

11 See Memorandum of Understanding between DG Competition and the CCI, November 21, 2013, *available at* http://ec.europa.eu/competition/ecn/index_en.html.

12 See further details on the CITD at http://citd-standards.com/index.html.

Since the beginning of the CITD, two workshops have been organized covering very practical issues such as: the way to conduct a *prima facie* investigation; drafting of decisions in conduct cases; drafting of decisions in combination cases (mergers); advocacy through website and press releases; and also substantial issues like margin squeezes and predatory pricing.

c. Enforcement Cooperation

Cooperation on cases between the European Commission and the Indian CCI started slowly. In this respect, it has to be taken into account that although the Competition Act was enacted more than a decade ago, the provisions of this Act against anticompetitive agreements and an abuse of dominance only entered into force on 20 May, 2009, and the provisions dealing with combinations only on 1 June, 2011. In addition, at least until the first quarter of 2014, the CCI had not been engaged in any "Phase 2" investigation involving a combination notification. Typically, cooperation between enforcers in the process of review of mergers does not occur for mergers cleared on first phase and/or without remedies. However, with time, as CCI builds up experience in merger review, practical enforcement cooperation with DG COMP will develop. In fact, DG COMP and CCI have already started cooperating in the field of antitrust in at least one case.[13]

3. Brazil

a. The Framework for the EU-Brazil Competition Policy Dialogue and Cooperation

In 2009, the European Commission signed a Memorandum of Understanding with the then three Competition Authorities of Brazil (CADE, Council for Economic Defense, SDE, Secretariat of Economic Law of the Ministry of Justice, and SEAE, Secretariat of Economic Monitoring of the Ministry of Finance).[14] Since then, and as a result of the new Brazilian competition law which entered into force in 2012, the three authorities have merged into one—the new CADE and cooperation with the EU continues on the basis of the same framework.[15]

b. Technical Cooperation/Capacity Building and Sharing Experiences

The European Commission engaged in cooperation with Brazil when the competition regime of this country had already been in place for a while. Consequently, cooperation has focused, since the beginning, more on enforcement than on capacity building. Nevertheless, in the last two years (May 2013 and May 2014) DG COMP and CADE have organized a joint workshop on "Competition Enforcement and International Cooperation" sponsored by the EU-Brazil sectorial dialogues. Each time, the emphasis has been on discussing tools and techniques for international cooperation in the field of merger and cartel cases. One of the char-

---

13 See graphs of enforcement cooperation in section 6 at the end of this paper.

14 See Memorandum of Understanding on Cooperation Between DG Competition and CADE, SDE and SEAE, 8 October, 2009, *available* at http://ec.europa.eu/competition/international/bilateral/brazil_mou_en.pdf.

15 See Law No. 12529, 30 November, 2011, *available at* http://www.cade.gov.br/upload/LAW%20N%C2%BA%2012529%202011%20%28English%20version%20from%2018%2005%202012%29.pdf.

acteristics of these workshops—like similar events taking place in China or India—is the participation of experts and officials from the national competition authorities of ECN who contribute, alongside DG COMP, towards spreading their experiences on the enforcement of the European Union antitrust rules.

c. Enforcement Cooperation

DG COMP and CADE cooperation on cases is rather active and amounts to an average of 3 percent of all DG COMP's international cooperation. This cooperation was mostly focused on cross-border merger cases (cooperation with Brazil amounting to 6 percent of all DG COMP's international cooperation in the field of mergers between 2010 and 2011, and 4 percent between 2012 and 2013). As for cartels, cooperation amounted to 4 percent between 2010 and 2011 (with no reported cooperation on cartels for the period 2012 and 2013).[16]

CADE and DG COMP also have regular telephone contact, between teams, to discuss not only cases but also more general issues such as theories of harm, policy approaches and experiences about certain markets and sectors. This regular contact contributes greatly to ensuring convergent outcomes and the application of consistent remedies.

III. The Specific Case of Acceding Countries

We commonly refer to acceding or candidate countries as those countries that have applied for membership to the European Union. The experience of countries that have become members of the European Union in the last ten years, mainly Central and Eastern European member states, is particularly interesting when discussing antitrust policies in emerging economies. The economies of those countries underwent major economic changes, transforming themselves from State controlled economies to market economies in a relatively short time. The adoption and implementation of an antitrust framework was a key element of this process, and was even imposed as a condition for the accession to the European Union.

At the very beginning of the process of accession of those countries in 1993, during the so called Copenhagen European Council, the then Member States of the European Union agreed that the candidate countries had to meet and implement the following basic standards before acceding to the European Union: (1) establish stable institutions that guarantee democracy, the rule of law, human rights and respect for and protection of minorities (the Political Criteria); (2) introduce the existence of a functioning market economy and the capacity to cope with market forces and competition within the European Union (the Economic Criteria); (3) adopt and implement the entire body of European Union law (the *acquis communautaire*); and (4) adhere to the aims of political, economic and monetary union. In 1995, the Madrid European Council further clarified that a candidate country must also be able to put the European Union rules and procedures into effect.

In the application of those principles, as regard competition policy, the European Union consistently took the view that candidate countries can be considered to be ready for accession only if their companies and

16 See graphs of enforcement cooperation in section 6 at the end of this paper.

public authorities have become accustomed to a competition discipline similar to that of the European Union, well before the date of accession. The aim was both to protect the internal market of the European Union, and to ensure that the economic actors in the candidate countries will be able to withstand the competitive pressures resulting from the full and direct application of the competition *acquis* upon accession.

Before starting the process of accession negotiations, the European Union signed international treaties with these countries (The Europe Agreements, Association Agreements and Stabilization and Association Agreements)[17] which provided the legal framework for the process as they included *inter alia* provisions requiring that anticompetitive practices would be assessed in conformity with the European Union law and that the parties shall ensure that an operationally independent public body entrusted with the powers necessary to implement antitrust rules will be in place. This paved the way for the establishment of independent competition enforcers in these countries.

The Commission laid down, in 2001, specific necessary conditions that would allow for the closure of the accession negotiations in the field of competition. Three elements had to be in place: 1) the necessary legislative framework with respect to antitrust and State aid; 2) proof of an adequate administrative capacity; and 3) a credible enforcement record of the antitrust and State aid *acquis*. These conditions were implemented in a very strict way, and in particular the enforcement record was scrutinized with intensity before the European Commission accepted to close the negotiations on the particular competition chapter for any of those countries. A similar approach continues to be implemented in the current accession negotiations with Western Balkan Countries like Montenegro and Serbia.

As the conditions imposed on candidate countries are strict, they have to be accompanied by capacity building actions on behalf of the European Union. In addition to the regular tools like workshops, seminars and trainings, one very specific and particularly innovative scheme used by the European Union in respect of the candidate countries is the so called "Twinning programs". Twinning projects are built around European Union policy objectives. From an antitrust perspective it involves establishing a sound competition policy in the country at stake which is agreed between the public authorities of the beneficiary country and the Member States of the European Union.[18] They include a broad variety of activities, implemented by experts from Member States, leading to the achievement of mandatory results. A Resident Twinning Advisor ("RTA") is the backbone of a twinning project. The RTA coordinates the project and is seconded from the lead Member State to the beneficiary administration (i.e., the competition authority) for a minimum of twelve months. The work plan of a Twinning project usually also incorporates expert missions, training events and awareness raising visits. This matching between officials of the competition authorities of European Union Member States and the competition authorities of the candidate States has proved particularly successful in terms of capacity building.

---

17 See, among others, Europe Agreement establishing an association between the European Communities and their Member States, of the one part, and the Republic of Bulgaria, of the other part, OJ L 358, 31.12.1994; Europe Agreement establishing an association between the European Communities and their Member States, of the one part, and the Czech Republic, of the other part, OJ L 360, 31.12.1994; Europe Agreement establishing an association between the European Communities and their Member States, of the one part, and the Republic of Estonia, of the other part, OJ L 68, 9.3.1998; Europe Agreement establishing an association between the European Communities and their Member States, of the one part, and the Republic of Latvia, of the other part, OJ L 26, 2.2.1998; Europe Agreement establishing an association between the European Communities and their Member States, of the one part and the Republic of Lithuania, of the other part, OJ L 51, 20.2.1998; Europe Agreement establishing an association between the European Communities and their Member States, of the one part, and the Republic of Hungary, of the other part, OJ L 347, 31.12.1993; Europe Agreement establishing an association between the European Communities and their Member States, of the one part, and the Republic of Poland, of the other part, OJ L 348, 31.12.1993; Europe Agreement establishing an association between the European Communities and their Member States, of the one part, and Romania, of the other part, OJ L 357, 31.12.1994; Europe Agreement establishing an association between the European Communities and their Member States, of the one part, and the Republic of Slovakia, of the other part, OJ L 359, 31.12.1994; Europe Agreement establishing an association between the European Communities and their Member States, of the one part, and the Republic of Slovenia, of the other part, OJ L 51, 26.2.1999. The full text of the Europe Agreements with the candidate countries is *available at* http://www.consilium.europa.eu/cms3_Applications/applications/Accords/searchparty.asp?lang=EN&cmsid=297.

18 See further details regarding Twinning *available at* http://ec.europa.eu/enlargement/tenders/twinning/index_en.htm.

IV. Competition in Trade Agreements with Emerging Economies and Developing Countries

In its 2006 Global Europe Communication,[19] the Commission announced its intention to negotiate a new generation of ambitious bilateral agreements with the European Union's most important trading partners. In order to prevent the positive changes induced by trade liberalization from being jeopardized by private anticompetitive practices, or state induced distortions, and to create a genuine level playing field for companies investing anywhere, these agreements would have to include a strong competition dimension (i.e., antitrust, mergers and subsidies). This approach was confirmed in the 2010 Communication on Trade, Growth and World Affairs.[20] Since then, the European Union has engaged in the negotiation of some 36 trade agreements[21] with its main trading partners, industrialized countries, but also BRICS and some developing countries including, Mercosur (of which Brazil is part), Vietnam, Singapore, Ukraine and a number of others.

While the agreements differ in scope ranging from classical Free Trade Agreements to Investment Agreements and Depth and Comprehensive Free Trade Agreements ("DCFT"),[22] they share a number of common features as regards a possible competition chapter which should include: acknowledgement of the importance of free and undistorted competition; obligation to adopt and maintain comprehensive competition laws covering anticompetitive agreements, anticompetitive unilateral conduct and control of concentrations (mergers); obligation to apply antitrust and mergers rules in a transparent and non-discriminatory manner, and respect of rights of defense; provision on application of competition rules to state owned enterprises; provision calling on the parties to cooperate in their enforcement activities and provisions on technical assistance (where appropriate, in particular in the case of emerging economies). In addition, those agreements should also contain provisions on subsidies, but this goes beyond the scope of this paper.

For those jurisdictions which already have a comprehensive competition regime and already cooperate with the European Union in these matters, those competition chapters will provide a legal framework to continue and consolidate the relationship. For those who do not yet have a competition regime or are in the early stages of implementing one, the provisions of those trade agreements will help the internal advocacy.

---

19 See http://trade.ec.europa.eu/doclib/docs/2006/october/tradoc_130376.pdf.

20 See http://trade.ec.europa.eu/doclib/docs/2010/november/tradoc_146955.pdf.

21 See http://trade.ec.europa.eu/doclib/docs/2012/november/tradoc_150129.pdf (not updated).

22 Countries signing a DCFT gain special access to the internal market of the EU, but in exchange they have also to adopt specific pieces of EU legislation in, among other areas, trade, consumer protection, and environmental regulation. Examples of this are Moldova, Armenia, Georgia and the Ukraine.

V. Cooperation with Emerging Economies and Developing Countries through Multilateral Organizations

Like for most competition agencies whose core activity is enforcement, the resources of the European Commission dedicated to international cooperation are scarce and do not allow for individual attention for all those countries. Therefore, the role played by different international organizations active in the competition field is extremely valuable in order to reach out to as many of the new competition comers as possible.

Therefore, DG COMP is involved in the work of United Nations Conference on Trade and Development ("UNCTAD"), by its regular an active participation in activities like the peer reviews of competition policies of various countries, conducted by this organization (recently Namibia, Seychelles and Philippines), and discussion and round tables about issues like informal international cooperation (of special importance for upcoming agencies) and the links between competition and consumer welfare.

The work done in this field by the Organization for Economic Co-operation and Development ("OECD") deserves particular mention. DG COMP also takes part in the work of the OECD. The Global Forum on competition organized once a year by OECD, with the participation of agencies of emerging economies alongside OECD members, gives both the opportunity to interact with agencies with different development backgrounds and to address issues which are of particular importance to developing countries, like links between competition and corruption, competition and poverty or more specifically the vertical chain of supply of pharmaceuticals. The peer reviews of competition regimes undertaken by the OECD, and the recommendations issued as a follow up to these peer reviews are also a very useful tool for relatively new agencies in the way of consolidation (recent examples are Romania and Colombia). In addition, many of the product and outputs of the OECD competition Committee, while not specifically targeted at emerging economies, are nevertheless of special use to them like, for example, the different tools on ex ante assessment of competition agency activities or the new OECD Recommendation on International Cooperation. The OECD also organizes outreach activities with a special focus on upcoming agencies in its regional centers of Seoul and Budapest, where DG COMP tries to ensure regular participation.

Last but not least, is the International Competition Network ("ICN") to which DG COMP is a founding and very active member. Most of the Competition agencies of emerging economies are part of ICN and their involvement in the work of the network gives them a great opportunity to learn from the experiences of other more mature competition agencies. In addition, the ICN is focusing increased efforts on reaching out to those agencies by first of all making its work product more readily available to them (i.e., through templates, work product catalogue and the ICN training on demand, also known as the curriculum project). Each ICN working group includes the issue of ICN product implementation and outreach to newer agencies in their work plan.

Many of the ICN products have a particular relevance for new competition agencies. Just to mention a few in which DG COMP is directly involved, the Merger Working Group, co-chaired by DG COMP, has set up a specific feature for assisting newer agencies called "Outreach." Under this project, teleconferences are organized focusing on the "original fundamentals" of the ICN Recommended Practices and they are also given in different languages (English, Spanish and French) and at different time-zone friendly times. DG COMP has also organized a panel on Outreach during the merger workshop in Delhi hosted in India by the CCI between the 1st and 2nd of December, 2014. The Merger Working Group has also embarked on a project called "International Merger Enforcement Cooperation" which addresses all the issues involved in cooperation between agencies in the field of mergers. This will not only build upon the existing Recommended Practices on international cooperation, but will also expand and develop them, particularly keeping in mind the fact that merger control is more globally widespread and involves emerging economies.

DG COMP also values the activities of the World Bank aimed at competition agencies of emerging economies. It takes part in the conferences organized by the World Bank, prior to the ICN annual conference with a special focus on younger agencies.

VI. The Way Forward

Competition policy has gone global, as shown by the graphs below. The data is taken from an internal survey conducted by the European Commission, covering cases dealt with between 2012 and 2013, a majority of the DG COMP cases involved international cooperation.[23]

The trend is for multijurisdictional cases involving mergers which are reviewed by three competition authorities or more, global cartels which are investigated, as an average, by three or four jurisdictions at the same time. The agencies involved in the review of these cases are not only those from developed countries/regions like the EU, US, Canada, Japan and Korea, but more and more agencies from developing countries. Against this background, it is very important for enforcers both to maintain the effectiveness of their enforcement activities and to avoid excessive costs for the parties in a case which could result from inconsistent outcomes like divergent remedies. To achieve this, it is essential to continue to foster convergence of competition rules and coordinate enforcement actions. Cooperation has moved on from how it was fifteen-twenty years ago among mature competition authorities, and now also involves the new authorities from emerging and developing countries which are playing a very meaningful role in today's antitrust enforcement world.

23 These graphs are the result of an internal survey of DG COMP on cases finalized during the period 2012 and 2013. Cooperation is broadly defined, including informal cooperation.

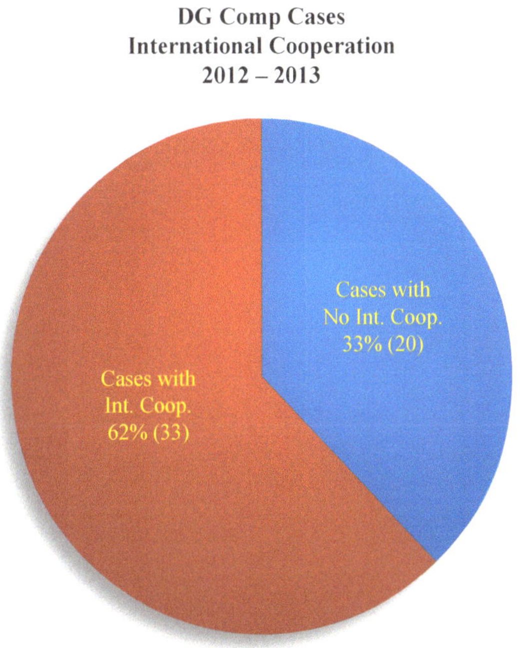
DG Comp Cases
International Cooperation
2012 – 2013
Cases with
No Int. Coop.
33% (20)
Cases with
Int. Coop.
62% (33)

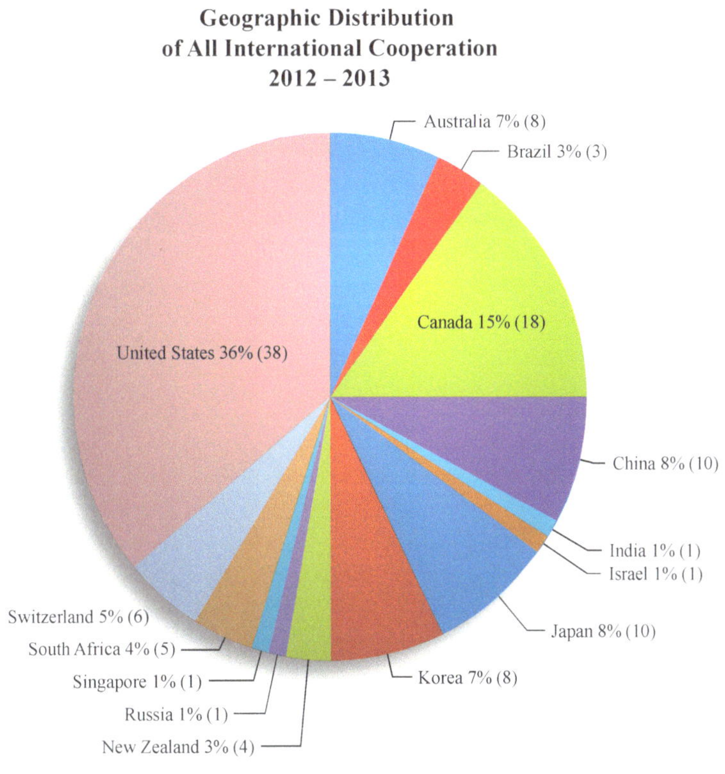
Geographic Distribution
of All International Cooperation
2012 – 2013
Australia 7% (8)
Brazil 3% (3)
Canada 15% (18)
United States 36% (38)
China 8% (10)
India 1% (1)
Israel 1% (1)
Japan 8% (10)
Korea 7% (8)
Switzerland 5% (6)
South Africa 4% (5)
Singapore 1% (1)
Russia 1% (1)
New Zealand 3% (4)

Geographic Distribution of All International Cooperation Mergers 2012 – 2013

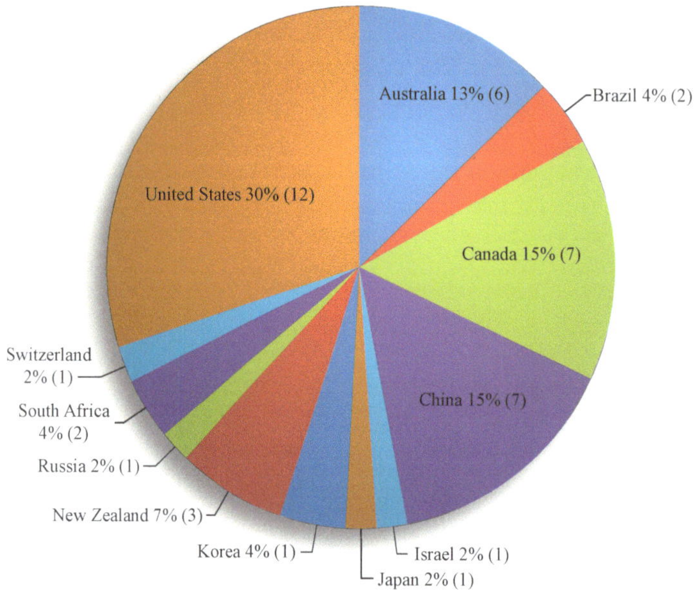

Geographic Distribution of All International Cooperation Cartels 2012 – 2013

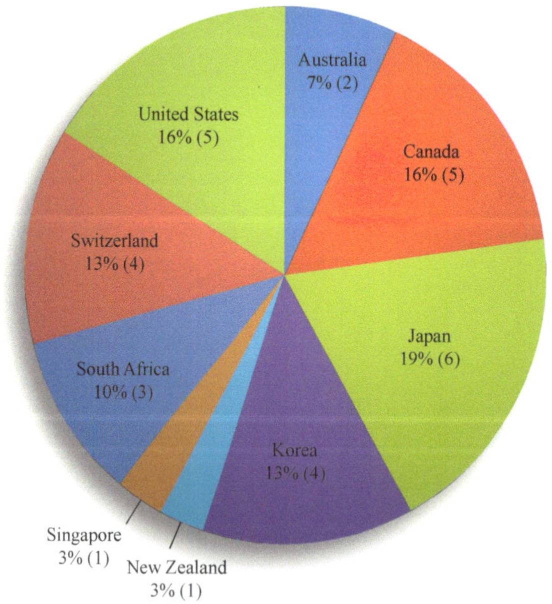

Antitrust in Emerging and Developing Countries
Geographic Distribution of International Cooperation in Antitrust
2012 – 2013

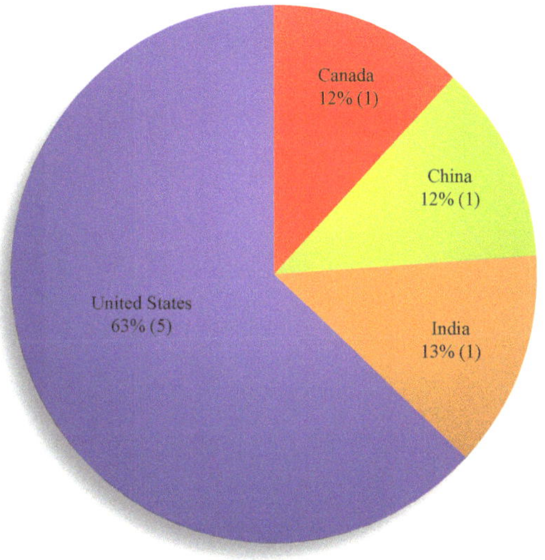

Editors' Bios

Eleanor M. Fox is the Walter J. Derenberg Professor of Trade Regulation at New York University School of Law. Before joining the faculty of New York University School of Law, Prof. Fox was a partner at the New York law firm Simpson Thacher & Bartlett. She has served as a member of the International Competition Policy Advisory Committee to the Attorney General of the US Department of Justice (1997 to 2000) (President Clinton) and as a Commissioner on President Carter's National Commission for the Review of Antitrust Laws and Procedures (1978 to 1979). She has advised numerous younger antitrust jurisdictions, including South Africa, Egypt, Tanzania, Gambia, Indonesia, Russia, Poland and Hungary, and the common market COMESA. Fox received an honorary doctorate degree from the University of Paris-Dauphine in 2009. She was awarded an inaugural Lifetime Achievement award in 2011 by the Global Competition Review for "substantial, lasting and transformational impact on competition policy." Her books include "The Design of Competition Law Institutions: Global Norms, Local Choices," with Michael Trebilcock (Oxford 2013), "US Antitrust Law in Comparative Context, cases and materials" (3rd ed. West/Reuters 2012), and books on EU law and on developing countries and competition. Her recent papers include "Imagine: Pro-Poor(er) Competition Law" (OECD and UNCTAD, both 2013), and, with Deborah Healey, "When the State Harms Competition—The Role for Competition Law," forthcoming in the Antitrust Law Journal.

Harry First is the Charles L. Denison Professor of Law at New York University School of Law and Co-Director of the law school's Competition, Innovation, and Information Law Program. From 1999-2001 he served as Chief of the Antitrust Bureau of the Office of the Attorney General of the State of New York. Prof. First is the co-author of the casebook "Free Enterprise and Economic Organization: Antitrust" (7th Ed. 2014), as well as a casebook on regulated industries. He was twice a Fulbright Research Fellow in Japan and taught antitrust as an adjunct professor at the University of Tokyo. Professor First's most recent scholarly work has focused on various aspects of antitrust enforcement and theory. These include: "The Microsoft Antitrust Cases: Competition Policy for the Twenty-first Century (with Andrew I. Gavil) (MIT Press, forthcoming 2014); and "Your Money and Your Life: The Export of US Antitrust Remedies" in Global Competition Law and Economics (Stanford Univ. Press, 2013). Prof. First is a contributing editor of the Antitrust Law Journal, foreign antitrust editor of the Antitrust Bulletin, a member of the executive committee of the Antitrust Section of the New York State Bar Association, and a member of the advisory board and a Senior Fellow of the American Antitrust Institute.

Nicolas Charbit, PhD, LLM, was admitted to the Paris Bar in 1994. He had been practicing from 1994 to 2005 in the field of competition law with strong emphasis on cartels and network industries. Nicolas wrote for French and international legal journals and taught these subjects at university and business schools. He has published several books and papers on EC and French competition law. He has completed a PhD thesis at Paris Sorbonne University on antitrust law and the public sector. He is the founding partner of the Institute of Competition Law and has been the Editor of Concurrences Review since 2004.

Elisa Ramundo graduated cum laude from the University of Bologna Law School (2002). Elisa holds a Master Degree in European Studies at European College of Parma (2004) and an LLM at the University of Chicago Law School (2010). Over the years, Elisa has gained professional experience in European, US, and International antitrust law. She worked at the US FTC (Washington, DC) as an international antitrust consultant, and in a tier-one Italian law firm as an associate in the competition practice (Rome/ Milan). She also served as a legal intern at the European Commission (Brussels). Elisa is currently the Managing Editor of Concurrences Review and is based in New York City.

Contributors' Bios

Jonathan Argent is a consultant to the Competition Policy Cluster of the World Bank Group in Eastern and Southern Africa. He has also consulted extensively in Rwanda on topics in transport and trade policy, first for the International Growth Centre and later independently. He holds honours degrees in Economics and Finance from the University of Cape Town and a Masters in Economics from University College London.

Molly Askin is Counsel for International Antitrust at the US Federal Trade Commission's Office of International Affairs. Ms. Askin works with the International Competition Network (ICN) and coordinates the FTC's participation in the ICN's advocacy working group and Inter-American Competition Alliance. Ms. Askin is responsible for bilateral cooperation and case coordination with countries in Western Europe and Northern Africa and works on technical assistance programs. Ms. Askin started her antitrust career in private practice at Howrey LLP and Baker Botts L.L.P. working on US and foreign merger, conduct, and cartel matters. She has worked for the US Senate Committee on the Judiciary and at the Delegation of the European Union to the United States of America. She holds a J.D. from Cornell University Law School with a specialization in Public Law and is admitted to practice in the State of New York and the District of Columbia. She also holds a Master of International Public Affairs from the La Follette School of Public Affairs at the University of Wisconsin-Madison, where she specialized in Transatlantic Relations and Policy Analysis. Ms. Askin also studied EU and comparative law at the Université Paris 1 Panthéon-Sorbonne.

Tania Begazo is Economist and Competition Specialist at the World Bank Group's Trade and Competitiveness Global Practice. She leads advisory on competition policy in Sub-Saharan Africa, and has contributed to the design and delivery of technical assistance on competition policy in more than fifteen emerging and developing economies. Technical assistance covers implementation of competition law frameworks including anti-cartel policy, merger control and concurrency frameworks with sector regulators, reform of anticompetitive regulations in sectors such as agriculture, energy and telecommunications, and knowledge and analytical products for competition advocacy. Previously, Ms. Gomez worked for the International Telecommunications Union, APOYO Consultoria, and the Peruvian telecommunications regulator (OSIPTEL). She advised on the design and implementation of economic regulation, economic analysis of antitrust cases, and regulatory aspects for public-private partnerships. Ms. Gomez holds a Master Degree in Public Administration in International Development from Harvard University.

Dennis M. Davis is a judge at the High Court of Cape Town, South Africa. He is also judge president of the Competition Appeal Court of Cape Town, a honorary professor of commercial law at the University of Cape Town, and a visiting professor at the Watson Institute for International Studies, among other institutions. During the negotiations for South Africa's new constitution, Mr. Davis acted as a technical legal advisor both on electoral law to the Convention for a Democratic South Africa (CODESA) and on federalism to the Constitutional Assembly. His recent research has focused on competition and administrative law, constitutional law, human rights and litigation, and socio economic rights. Davis holds an MPhil from the University of Cambridge and a BCom LLB from the University of Cape Town. He is the author and co-author of several books, including "Income Tax Cases and Materials" (1995), as well as numerous journal articles. Mr. Davis is the former host of Future Imperfect and current host of Judge for Yourself, both of which are South African television programs that debate current political and socioeconomic issues in the country.

Frank Fine has been practicing EU competition law in Brussels since 1986. He is currently Head of International Antitrust at DeHeng Law Offices, a major Chinese law firm, and the Director of EC Competition Law Advocates. Mr. Fine is the Executive Director of the China Institute of International Antitrust and Investment, formed in March 2012 under the auspices of the China University of Law and Political Science, where he serves as visiting professor. He is the author of several books on EU competition law: "The EC Competition Law on Technology Licensing" (Sweet and Maxwell) and "Mergers and Joint Ventures in Europe: The Law and Policy of the EEC." He is currently the General Editor of the LexisNexis three-volume loose-leaf treatise, "European Competition Laws." Mr. Fine obtained his law degree from Loyola Law School and he subsequently obtained an LLM (with honors) and PhD in EC Competition Law from the University of Cambridge in England. He is currently a Fellow of the American Bar Foundation and has served as vice chair of the Cartel and Criminal Practice, International and Intellectual Property Committees of the ABA Section of Antitrust Law, and was a member of the Section's Civil Redress Task Force and Publications Advisory Board.

André M. Gilberto is a partner at Chaves, Gelman, Machado, Gilberto e Barboza, and head of the Antitrust and Public Law Practices, based in the São Paulo office. He has extensive experience on antitrust, trade, public and regulatory matters. André has been providing consultancy and representation to several Brazilian and foreign companies before several government agencies in virtually all matters encompassing public law and contracts with the government. Before joining CGM, Mr. Gilberto was a partner for many years in his own firm and Campos Mello Advogados. Recent editions of Chambers Latin America recognized André as a leading individual both in Public Law and in Antitrust, being described by clients as "an expert who is clear, objective and always available," a "brilliant risk taker who uses his daring to his advantage in the most challenging of situations," "an assertive, objective and sharp lawyer who really knows his subject" and a lawyer who "takes a pro-business approach and provide proactive, tailored client service." Mr. Gilberto holds a LLM in Public Law from Universidade de São Paulo (2009).

Geeta Gouri former Member of the Competition Commission of India, is an economist with fifteen years of experience working as a Regulatory Economist, serving as Member (Economics) at the Commission for five years and prior to that as Director (Tariffs) at the Andhra Pradesh Electricity Regulatory Commission. This unique experience gives her the privilege of being perhaps the only economist in India to be associated with the premiering of the two commissions which ushered competition and markets reforms in the economy. Dr. Gouri has published extensively and delivered lectures on a wide range of subjects; "Pricing for Welfare; Petroleum Products in India"; "Privatization and Public Enterprise: The Asia-Pacific Experience" (edited); "Towards Equity: New Economic Policy and Equity" (edited).

Yong Huang is Professor of Law and the Director of Competition Law Center at University of International Business and Economics (UIBE), and he now serves as the Deputy Head of the Experts Advisory Committee of the Anti-Monopoly Commission (AMC) under the People's Republic of China State Council. Prof. Huang played a key role in drafting and shaping China's Anti-Monopoly Law (AML) through the process of making guidelines, regulations and interpretations of AML with the National Development and Reform Commission (NDRC), the Ministry of Commerce (MOFCOM), the State Administration for Industry and Commerce (SAIC), and the Supreme People's Court. He is a member of Advisory Committee of General Administration of Quality Supervision, Inspection and Quarantine of the People's Republic of China (AQSIQ). He has published many peer reviewed articles and several books on antitrust law and antitrust enforcement in China. In addition, Prof. Huang is a delegate in the Beijing Municipal People's Congress, sitting in the Congress' Financial and Economic Committee.

R. Shyam Khemani is Special Advisor Competition Policy at SKP. Before joining SKP, Mr. Khemani was a Principal Economist with the Washington, DC, based firm MiCRA (Microeconomic Consulting and Research Associates), specializing in providing applied economic analysis, litigation support and economic research services on complex competition and regulatory matters. Until recently, he was Advisor on Competition Policy in the Financial & Private Sector Development Vice-Presidency of the World Bank. He has advised governments and business in over two dozen industrial and developing countries. During 2000-2002 he served as Director at the Law & Economics Consulting Group (LECG), Paris. Previously he worked with the Canadian Competition Bureau where he was Chief Economist and Director of Economics & International Affairs. He has appeared as an expert before parliamentary committees and regulatory institutions. He also served as an Advisor to the Chairman, Raghavan committee in regards to drafting India's new competition law. He is a member of the Advisory Board of the Bureau of National Affair's Antitrust and Trade Regulation Report, co-Director of the International Bar Association's Global Forum on Competition, and serves on various working groups of ABA, ICN, the International Chambers of Commerce, and CUTS-an NGO based in India. He has served on the Faculty of Business Administration and Commerce at the University of British Columbia, among others. Mr. Khemani has published extensively in various journals (e.g., Journal of Industrial Economics, International Journal of Industrial Organization, Antitrust Bulletin, Applied Economics, Policy Options, etc.), and co-edited books on competition policy. He holds a PhD from the London School of Economics, U.K., and an MA from McGill University, Montreal, Canada.

R. Ian McEwin is an Australian lawyer with a PhD in Economics specialized in ASEAN competition law and economics. He is also a Fellow of the Australian Institute of Company Directors. He has been an expert witness in major competition law cases in Australia and New Zealand and was foundation Director of the Centre for Law and Economics in the Law Faculty at the Australian National University in Canberra. In 2002 the Singapore Ministry of Trade & Industry recruited him to help with the drafting of the Singapore competition law and the setting up of the Singapore Competition Commission. He then became the Commission's first Chief Economist. Following that he became a visiting Professor of Law at the National University of Singapore and then at Chulalongkorn University in Bangkok. He is Member of the Editorial Board of the Australian Business Law Review and a Co-Editor of Competition Policy International Journal, Boston. He was recently appointed to the Foundation Board of Advisors of the Global Antitrust Institute at the George Mason University School of Law, Washington, DC. He is currently writing a book "Competition Law in Southeast Asia for Cambridge University Press. Mr. McEwin holds a PhD in Economics and an LLB degree (First Class Honours) from Australian National University.

Kiran Nandinee Meetarbhan is the former Executive Director of the Competition Commission of Mauritius. She has been the Deputy Executive Director and Chief Legal Adviser of the Commission since its inception. Mrs. Meetarbhan has extensive experience in Competition Law and Policy. She is recognized as an expert in competition law and Policy for small states, by the Small State Network for Economic Development (SSNED). She also has more than 13 years of regulatory experience in financial services, specializing in global business, international taxation and investment funds. Following her Bar Qualifications in 1995, Mrs. Meetarbhan joined the then offshore regulator, MOBAA in 1996, where she headed the legal and business development department. In 2001, following the setting up of the Financial Services Commission, she continued her career as Executive-Legal until 2003 when she was appointed as Head of Surveillance for Insurance and Pensions. In 2007, after having spent one year at the State Law Office, she was appointed Adviser at the Ministry of Finance and Economic Development until 2009. Mrs. Meetarbhan has also been a part-time lecturer in Law and Finance, for several years. Mrs. Meetarbhan has been a member of several committees at national and regional levels including the National WTO committee on Financial Services, the Regional Integration and Facilitation Forum, the Committee on Money Laundering, the CISNA (an association of Insurance and Securities Regulators of SADC). In 2013, Mrs. Meetarbhan was awarded Africa Women Leadership Award. Through this award, Mrs. Meetarbhan is recognized as an "outstanding woman professional who has the vision, flair, acumen and professionalism to demonstrate excellent leadership and management skills in an organization, making changes and achieving results." Mrs. Meetarbhan is a Barrister at Law and holds a Master in Business Administration.

Alessandro Octaviani is a Tenured Professor of Economic Law and Political Economy at the University of São Paulo Law School (USP) (2010 - Present) and Professor of Political and Economic Law in the Graduate Program at Mackenzie Presbyterian University (2010 - Present). In both universities aims to contribute to multidisciplinary studies of Brazil, mobilizing legal and social theory, such as has been done in the research group Law and Underdevelopment: the furtadian challenge (coordinated by Prof. Octaviani since 2010). His background includes a Bachelor of Laws at USP Law School (1994 to 1999), a Master's Degree in Political Science from USP (2001 to 2005) and a PhD in Economic and Financial Law from USP (2005 to 2008). Prof. Octaviani was also Consultant for Getúlio Vargas Foundation Projects in the area of Technological Innovation (2009 to 2010), and has served as Commissioner of the Brazilian antitrust authority (Conselho Administrativo de Defesa Econômica—CADE) (2011 to 2014). Prof. Octaviani main research interests are in the fields of Economic Law and development political economy, in which he has published several articles and two books on Economic Law: "Essays, Opinions and Votes on Economic Law," São Paulo: Singular, 2014; and "Genetic resources and development: the Furtadian and Gramscian challenges," São Paulo: Saraiva, 2013. Currently, Prof. Alessandro is a visiting research fellow at King's College Brazil Institute (2014 to 2015).

Blanca Rodriguez Galindo is currently Head of Unit for International Relations in the Directorate General of Competition (DG Competition) of the European Commission. She has represented the Commission in numerous conferences and international seminars and has written and lectured on legal topics including antitrust and State Aid. Blanca started her professional career in DG Competition as an antitrust enforcer and prior to her current job, worked in other departments of the European Commission. She was a member of its Legal Service for 7 years and represented the European Commission in litigation cases before the European Court of Justice. She was also advisor on Competition and Legal matters to President Jacques Santer (1995 to 1999) and to Commissioner Mario Monti on State Aid matters (2000 to 2001). She was in charge of International Relations in DG Competition (2002 to 2007). Among other tasks during this period she advised the authorities of the People's Republic of China in the process of adoption of the Chinese Antimonopoly Law and negotiated bilateral cooperation agreements with countries such as Canada and Korea. More recently she was in charge of Control of State Aid to banks and other credit institutions and in charge of the revision of the Commission guidelines for regional aid. Blanca graduated in Law from the University of Barcelona (Spain) and has a Diploma of Advanced European Studies from the College of Europe, Bruges (Belgium). She was Emil Noel Fellow at Harvard Law School (2001 to 2002).

Mariana Tavares de Araujo is a senior partner at Levy & Salomão Advogados, where she practices in the areas of Antitrust, Regulation & Infrastructure, and Product Liability. Prior to joining Levy & Salomão Advogados, Ms. Araujo worked with the Brazilian government for nine years, four of which she served as head of the government agency in charge of antitrust enforcement and consumer protection policy. Ms. Araujo worked with international antitrust authorities throughout the world and served in leadership positions in key international competition organizations, such as chairing with the United States Department of Justice the cartels sub-group of the International Competition Network (ICN) (2004 to 2007). She also represented the Brazilian government in meetings of the OECD's Committee on Competition and of the United Nations Conference on Trade and Development (UNCTAD). Ms. Araujo provides counseling in competition-related matters for the World Bank and served as a non-governmental advisor to the ICN. She is a member of the IBA and of the ABA Section of Antitrust Law. She currently co-chairs the IBA Working Group on International Cartels and is a member of the ABA International Cartel Task Force. She is also a Law Professor at the Graduate Program of Fundação Getúlio Vargas-RJ. Global Competition Review named her on its list of the "Top 100 Women in Antitrust" and Latin Lawyer included her among the "Inspiring Women in the Legal Profession." Who's Who Legal, Chambers Latin America and Legal 500 listed her among the world's leading competition lawyers and she has been nominated by the members of the Latin American Corporate Counsel Association (LACCA) for inclusion in its list "LACCA Approved" (2013, 2014, and 2015).

Randolph W. Tritell is the Director of the Federal Trade Commission's Office of International Affairs. He is responsible for coordinating the FTC's international antitrust, consumer protection, and technical assistance policies and the FTC's involvement in cases that raise international issues. He represents the FTC in multilateral fora including the ICN, in which he serves on the Steering Group, and the OECD Competition Committee. Mr. Tritell is also responsible for the FTC's negotiation and implementation of bilateral international cooperation agreements and competition and consumer protection provisions of US free trade agreements. Prior to joining the FTC in 1998, Mr. Tritell was a partner with the New York-based law firm of Weil, Gotshal & Manges LLP. Following six years in the firm's New York office, in 1992 he opened the firm's Brussels office where he practiced European Community and international competition law. Mr. Tritell began his career at the FTC serving as a staff attorney in the Bureau of Consumer Protection (1978-81), Assistant to the Bureau of Consumer Protection Director, Timothy Muris (1981 to 1983), Attorney Advisor to Commissioner Terry Calvani (1983 to 1985), and Executive Assistant to the Chairman (1985 to 1986). Mr. Tritell obtained his law degree in 1977 from the University of Pennsylvania Law School, where he was an Editor of the Law Review. He is a 1974 Phi Beta Kappa graduate of the State University of New York at Stony Brook. Mr. Tritell is active in the ABA's Section of Antitrust Law, in which he co-chairs the International Task Force. He is a frequent lecturer and author on international antitrust issues.

Elizabeth Xiao-Ru Wang is a principal in the Competition Practice at Charles River Associates, Boston. She has provided economic analyses and has been involved in casework in a variety of industries. Ms. Wang has submitted reports to antitrust government agencies in US and in China and has published and spoken on various topics. Dr. Wang has submitted reports and presented economic analysis before MOFCOM, and advised clients on merger reviews, antitrust investigation and private litigation in China. Ms. Wang has worked with clients in Asia, North America, and Europe. She holds a PhD in economics from the University of Chicago, and a BA in economics from Peking University in China. She is a native Chinese speaker and is fluent in English. Ms. Wang is an active member of the American Bar Association (ABA). She is a Co-Chair of the China Committee and a Vice Chair of the International Antitrust Committee of the ABA's International Law Section. Ms. Wang won the ABA International Law Section award of 2014 Outstanding Collaboration between Committees.

INSTITUTE of
Competition Law
Antitrust databases and resources

The Institute of Competition Law

The Institute of Competition Law is a publishing company, founded in 2004 by Dr. Nicolas Charbit, based in Paris and New-York. The Institute cultivates scholarship and discussion about antitrust issues though publications and conferences. Each publication and event is supervised by editorial boards and scientific or steering committees to ensure independence, objectivity, and academic rigor. Thanks to this management, the Institute has become one of the few think tanks in Europe to have significant influence on antitrust policies.

AIM

The Institute focuses government, business and academic attention on a broad range of subjects which concern competition laws, regulations and related economics.

BOARDS

To maintain its unique focus, the Institute relies upon highly distinguished editors, all leading experts in national or international antitrust: Bill Kovacic, Mario Monti, Eleanor Fox, Barry Hawk, Laurence Idot, Fred Jenny, etc.

AUTHORS

3,800 authors, from 55 jurisdictions.

PARTNERS

- Universities: University College London, King's College London, Queen Mary University, Paris Sorbonne Panthéon-Assas, etc.
- Law firms: Allen & Overy, Cleary Gottlieb Steen & Hamilton, DLA Piper, Hogan Lovells, Jones Day, Norton Rose Fulbright, Skadden Arps, White & Case, etc.

EVENTS

More than 250 events since 2004 in Brussels, London, New York, Paris, Singapour and Washington, DC.

ONLINE VERSION

Concurrences website provides all articles published since its inception.

PUBLICATIONS

The Institute publishes Concurrences Journal, a print and online quarterly peer-reviewed journal dedicated to EU and national competitions laws. e-Competitions is a bi-monthly antitrust news bulletin covering 55 countries. The e-Competitions database contains over 12,000 case summaries from 2,600 authors.

www.ingramcontent.com/pod-product-compliance
Ingram Content Group UK Ltd.
Pitfield, Milton Keynes, MK11 3LW, UK
UKHW061541051026
15625UKWH00011B/561